DEATH AN.

Psychoanalytic Ideas and Applications Series

IPA Publications Committee
Gennaro Saragnano (Rome), Chair and General Editor; Leticia Glocer Fiorini (Buenos Aires), Consultant; Samuel Arbiser (Buenos Aires); Paulo Cesar Sandler (São Paulo); Christian Seulin (Lyon); Mary Kay O'Neil (Montreal); Gail S. Reed (New York); Catalina Bronstein (London); Rhoda Bawdekar (London), Ex-officio as Publications Officer; Paul Crake (London), IPA Executive Director (ex-officio)

DEATH AND IDENTITY
Being and the
Psycho-Sexual Drama

Michel de M'Uzan

Translated by
Andrew Weller

KARNAC

First published in 2013 by
Karnac Books Ltd
118 Finchley Road
London NW3 5HT

British Library Cataloguing in Publication Data

A C.I.P. for this book is available from the British Library

ISBN-13: 978-1-78049-146-2

Typeset by V Publishing Solutions Pvt Ltd., Chennai, India

Printed in Great Britain

www.karnacbooks.com

CONTENTS

PSYCHOANALYTIC IDEAS AND APPLICATIONS SERIES

IPA Publications Committee

The Publications Committee of the International Psychoanalytical Association continues, with this volume, the series "Psychoanalytic Ideas and Applications".

The aim of this series is to focus on the scientific production of significant authors whose works are outstanding contributions to the development of the psychoanalytic field and to set out relevant ideas and themes, generated during the history of psychoanalysis, that deserve to be known and discussed by present psychoanalysts.

The relationship between psychoanalytic ideas and their applications has to be put forward from the perspective of theory, clinical practice, technique, and research so as to maintain their validity for contemporary psychoanalysis.

The Publications Committee's objective is to share these ideas with the psychoanalytic community and with professionals in other related disciplines, in order to expand their knowledge and generate a productive interchange between the text and the reader.

"Death and Identity" puts together twelve of Michel de M'Uzan's most valid, original and widely appreciated writings, which cover the essence of his theoretical and clinical thinking from 1969 up to today. The theory of psychosomatics and the *psyche-soma*, the mentalization process, the development of identity, the fundamental role of life forces, the creative experience with terminal patients and with borderline mental organizations, the concepts of *chimera* and the *double*, as well as many other fertile and original ones: all these issues are delineated in these pages written by a great French psychoanalyst who has always been able, at the same time, to think in an independent and original way and to maintain stable and vital the Freudian foundations of his research.

Anglo-American readers will now benefit from this English version of de M'Uzan's fundamental contribution to the development of psychoanalysis. Special thanks are therefore due to Andrew Weller for his careful and accurate translation from French, and to everyone else who has contributed to make this book possible. As the Chair of the Publications Committee of the International Psychoanalytical Association, I feel honoured to enrich the "Psychoanalytic Ideas and Applications" series with this volume which will no doubt encounter the favour of psychoanalysts worldwide.

Gennaro Saragnano
Series Editor
Chair, IPA Publications Committee

TRANSLATOR'S ACKNOWLEDGEMENTS

I would like to thank Michel de M'Uzan and Murielle Gagnebin for their encouragement and help in finalizing this translation. A warm thank you, too, to Monique Zerbib who has kindly given a lot of her time assisting me with this task.

Andrew Weller
Paris, September 23, 2012

PREFACE

A few years ago, my mother who was dying of cancer had clearly expressed the wish to die in her home. Unfortunately, her medical condition was such that she needed frequent interventions to alleviate the discomfort due to her abdominal carcinoma. She therefore had to be transported ever more frequently to the hospital and back. As she grew weaker and weaker with the progression of her illness, the day came when she could not bear the fatigue of transportation any more; it then became impossible to keep her both at home *and* comfortable enough. My brother and I therefore had to conduct difficult negotiations with our mother who would not hear of remaining in the hospital while acknowledging that she could not stay in her familiar surroundings either. We were at a loss about how to solve the dilemma without imposing a unilateral decision on our mother. But our anguish and guilt was soon relieved by a solution that our mother had found all by herself. At one point, and to our utter amazement, she indeed calmly declared: "All right, you can take me to the hospital, because—you know what?—*it isn't me, but an other that will be going while I stay quietly at home.*"

Let me be clear that the woman who had uttered these words was perfectly sane and in touch with reality in every aspect of the dramatic situation she was courageously facing. Yet her statement at first created some embarrassment. But soon after I was reassured as I recalled what I had learned from Michel de M'Uzan about his experience of doing analytic work with patients in terminal conditions. What my brother and I were indeed suddenly witnessing was the welcome emergence of the *double* that de M'Uzan described in some of his patients and about which he elaborated a theory regarding the development of identity. In de M'Uzan's view, indeed, the *double* is not a pathological entity, although it can be put to that use; the *double* is the inevitable consequence of a fundamental split occurring in the early phase of psychic development, when identity is formed. A division in the service of psychical differentiation, this primal split is, as I understand it, what makes it possible, among other things, for "I" to refer to "me" or to "myself". The grammatical division that is required between the subject of the sentence and the "me" or "myself" of which the sentence is about rests on its unconscious psychological equivalent. It implies that identity, which we normally tend to consider as a unitary feeling, rests, paradoxically, on a divide from which results a capacity for adjustment to various situations.

The anecdote should already give the reader a hint as to what makes de M'Uzan's thought so valuable and unique. His theory always stems from wide and varied clinical experience and from a thoroughly conducted psychoanalytic practice where de M'Uzan patiently exerts close attention even to the minute movements occurring in the analysis. Conversely, the phenomena he describes are included within a theoretical frame both faithful to Freudian psychoanalysis and yet utterly original.

With the *double*, the *paraphrenic twin*, the *spectrum of identities*, the *chimera*, *paradoxical thinking*, the *same* and the *identical*, the *economic scandal*, the *vital-identital* programme, the *work of dying*, and other original contributions by de M'Uzan, you are entering the world of an analyst that harmoniously conjugates a refined description of the single analytic session with an encompassing view of the mind, or, more to the point, of the *psyche-soma*. Reading de M'Uzan offers a fresh outlook on clinical work and a refreshing perspective on the possibilities of psychoanalysis in various domains. Indeed, Michel de M'Uzan is a psychoanalyst who throughout his long career of more than fifty years has been able to build creatively on Freud's discoveries in many important domains: in psychoanalysis proper, of course, but also in psychosomatics, in his work with terminally ill patients, and in the field of artistic creation (see Gagnebin, 1996 and Gagnebin & Milly, 2012).

The two main threads running through these apparently very different domains could be deemed *the question of identity* and *the economic point of view*. The latter, inherited from Freudian metapsychology, takes into account the role of the quantity of energy in the psyche-soma, and if its reference to "energy" sounds unfashionable nowadays, make no mistake: de M'Uzan is well aware that biological energy is produced in the intracellular bodies known as mitochondria. He nevertheless makes use of the idea of a quantity and of its vicissitudes in what I see as the most consistent and comprehensive theory of psychosomatic development. For while psychosomatics was one of the fields where de M'Uzan creatively applied psychoanalysis, it obviously influenced in return his general conception of human development. His reference to quantity is therefore not merely metaphoric: de M'Uzan speaks from experience about the vicissitudes of the quantity of excitation as it is—or fails to be—recruited in the service of mental elaboration. For well before "mentalisation" (psychical elaboration) became the popular concept it is today, it was coined by the "Paris School of Psychosomatics" of which de M'Uzan was a founder and a most prominent exponent.

Concomitant with his psychosomatic experience, there is another characteristic of de M'Uzan's stance that is also noticeable in the example above. It is what I would call his reliance on the life forces. As I hinted, my mother's utterance could have been met in many quarters as the expression of a disturbed mind, whereas de M'Uzan taught me to see how a seemingly irrational event actually, and elegantly, solved an otherwise insoluble dilemma. It takes clinical and, as it were, theoretical courage to put forward the idea that such an expression of a split is actually a healthy response. In his work with terminally ill patients, de M'Uzan displayed the same courage when he clearly indicated that the aim of his work was not to help the patient *die* but to help him *live* as fully as possible what remained to be lived. As Jacques André (2008) aptly remarks, *the work of dying* described by de M'Uzan (Chapter Three of this book) is not a work of mourning. Quite the contrary. Instead of inciting the patient to gradually disconnect himself from the world and from his objects, and therefore to leave life before life has really come to an end, de M'Uzan's conception of "the work of dying" rather relies on the surge of libido that, in his experience, frequently occurs when death is near.

It could be said, therefore, that Michel de M'Uzan always works on the side of life, convinced that the organism is endowed with a biological "life programme" that, in favourable conditions, ultimately leads to self-extinction. And if illness and suffering occur along the way, then our task is to give the life programme as much freedom to operate as possible by helping our patient shuffle, so to speak, and recombine his libidinal investments thanks to the work of analysis, so as to allow for the optimal channelling of libidinal energy in the service of elaboration and sublimation. So, one should not be surprised to learn that in the work of this exemplary French analyst there is no reference (or reverence) to a death drive, although de M'Uzan is probably the analyst who is the most consistent in taking into account and putting to use the unbinding forces that are usually associated with that ever controversial concept. For him there is only one sort of instinctual drives, the sexual; the rest pertain to what he recently called the *vital-identital* programme of development whose ending in death does not require a special instinct, since the end is part and parcel of life. This may seem unfaithful to Freud and perhaps it is. But few analysts have noticed, as de M'Uzan did, that when Freud (1920g) first introduced the idea of a death drive, he briefly equated it with self-preservation. He finally changed his mind, which in de M'Uzan's view is regrettable, for that was to him the only correct conception: that the necessity of death is inscribed in the genetic programme of self-preservation and that the organism strives towards living through the programme in its entirety, until death naturally ensues. To put it in the words of the mother of one of de M'Uzan's patients, the idea is that one dies after having finished living.

* * *

While most of the time in agreement with Freud's and many contemporary theories, de M'Uzan often reaches original and somewhat provocative conclusions. For instance, he advocates that patients with "borderline" psychic organisations are not only analysable, but are actually the best indication for analysis. The *economic point of view* here again plays an important role. Michel de M'Uzan indeed expects analysis to be effective inasmuch as some "economic turmoil" can occur, followed by a rearrangement or redistribution of libidinal cathexes. Given that analysis works by way of unbinding the psychic structures that were conducive to some impasse, the relatively more mobile structures of borderline organisations are more easily changeable than those of the more strongly bound neuroses. Mind you, this does not mean that the work is any easier, for it requires on the part of the analyst an equivalent disposition to being unsettled in his own identity. For de M'Uzan, indeed, what happens in analysis must involve both members of the dyad. This well illustrates how the two main threads to which I referred earlier, identity and economic point of view, are intimately linked. Indeed, if the libidinal turmoil and the change that ensues is provoked by the analytic method, this means that it rests in part on the contribution of the analyst. For this, the analyst is expected to be working as closely as possible to the primary processes as he listens and formulates interpretations. But this can only be achieved if the analyst is willing to let go of his own resistances regarding his mental functions and even his own identity. That is, the analyst's libidinal *cathexes* (economic point of view) and his personal *identity* status must be flexible enough to allow for novel, even if provisional, arrangements to happen *in himself* during the analytic hour. De M'Uzan writes:

> ... we are really analysts only at certain moments of our listening, when the stratified resistances that we usually raise against the changes in our mental functioning and in our identity status finally give up. (2001, my translation)

If the analyst can achieve that kind of availability to unconscious processes, then he will find himself participating with his patient in the formation of a new entity that de M'Uzan dubbed the *chimera*. This "fabulous being" born in the consulting room will lead a life of its own and evolve in the course of the analysis, combining the elements brought up in the transference by the patient and those contributed by the analyst. The analyst will thereby be subjected to a *paradoxical* form of thinking where it is not clear whose thoughts he is thinking, and the interpretations that come to him are inflected accordingly. Thus, de M'Uzan is here again making quite a provocative statement, asserting that a measure of *depersonalisation* is necessary, both in the patient and in the analyst, for change to occur in analysis.

* * *

It is worth mentioning that, in de M'Uzan's view, if identity is to be satisfactorily achieved, including the creation of an unconscious double, it should rest not on a rigidly defined and single identity, but on a *spectrum of identities* entailing a certain flexibility in the capacity for identification. I have had the opportunity (Scarfone, 2008a) to compare this notion of de M'Uzan's to Daniel Dennett's "multiple drafts" theory of consciousness (1991). In the same way that, in Dennett's model, there is no "final" or "official" state of consciousness but multiple drafts of a work that is always in progress, so we do not have a unidimensional, straightforward, and unmodifiable identity; rather, we play on a kind of keyboard of identities, none of which is truer than the others and in whose middle there is a zone of *floating individuation*. Therefore, while "identitarian" ideologies purport the notion of a clear-cut, unitary, and rigid identity—entailing the exclusion of the other, of the stranger— Michel de M'Uzan is clearly pointing in the opposite direction when he writes:

> … if it is true that man loves only himself, I would add for my part that he can only be himself if he is capable of including that which is not himself and of allowing his narcissism to dilate in order to absorb the objects of the world; in other words, if he is also capable of becoming an other. (See closing passage of Chapter Four)

* * *

For all the rich and innovative ideas that de M'Uzan brings to psychoanalysis, he has not tried to start some new "school of thought" or a new chapel. Throughout this book the reader will be able to appreciate how de M'Uzan pays due tribute to other authors while not sparing them his occasional criticism, as any serious scientist should do. His theory is open and capable of interconnecting with the works of other significant authors. In this respect, we have a rather rare occurrence where a major author such as de M'Uzan is ready and willing to link his theory to that of another important thinker: Jean Laplanche. When it comes indeed to making space for the insertion of infantile sexuality in the course of the "life programme" he describes, de M'Uzan simply calls upon Laplanche's theory of generalised seduction (1987). No "narcissism of small differences" is at work in him, but a clear sense that psychoanalytic theories, when adequately carved out, can and should be simply brought together.

For some reason, de M'Uzan seems to have a particular gift in this respect, as shown by two other examples. The first example regards the concept of the *chimera*. Readers familiar with Thomas Ogden's work will probably find a striking resemblance between his "analytic third" (1994) and de M'Uzan's *chimera*. There is, however, no problem of priority between the two authors; although de M'Uzan's idea was put forward earlier than Ogden's, it is quite obvious that the two authors produced their concepts independently, starting from different theoretical perspectives. The similarity simply indicates, in my view, how rigorous clinical descriptions and theoretical formulations can eventually converge. The second example is what had happened many years before, regarding another of de M'Uzan's (and Marty's) discovery of the early Sixties. In the wake of their research in psychosomatics, Marty and de M'Uzan (1963) described a particular state of the mental apparatus they baptised *pensée opératoire* (here translated as "mechanical thinking"), in which the function of the preconscious stratum is poorly developed, language is impoverished and lacks the usual metaphoric depth, there is paucity of dreams, affect is blunted, etc. A clinical picture similar to what Nemiah and Sifneos (1970) would later and independently describe under the label of "alexithymia". The two descriptions, though not strictly identical, referred to states considered by both teams as the harbingers of possible somatic decompensation.

Michel de M'Uzan is thus, at least to my knowledge, one of the rare authors in psychoanalysis who produced concepts and made clinical descriptions which would be later more or less replicated independently by others. This is encouraging for psychoanalysis as a whole, showing that we can, after all, agree about concepts and clinical findings across theoretical, cultural, and linguistic barriers. But it also speaks highly, in my opinion, of the extraordinary value and universality of de M'Uzan's clinical and theoretical contribution to psychoanalysis.

* * *

The present book contains a selection of texts that is well representative of de M'Uzan's trajectory during his long career as analyst and writer. The reader, however, should be aware that many other important pieces had to be left out. Let us hope that in the future the English-speaking public will be given access to these and that de M'Uzan's place in world psychoanalysis will become proportionate to the immense stature of his original and rigorous *œuvre*.

Dominique Scarfone

PART I

FROM ART TO DEATH

CHAPTER ONE

The same and the identical* (1969)

It is worth drawing attention to a contrast that each of us can readily identify with: analysts generally agree on the *clinical* notion of repetition, whereas interpreting this phenomenon always stirs up controversies, not to say passionate confrontations. The ambiguities, and even the contradictions that can be found in *Beyond the Pleasure Principle* (1920g) which Freud in no way tried to hide, are themselves part of the situation. We know that only Ferenczi, Eitingon, and Alexander welcomed unreservedly the highly speculative views developed in this work. For his part, Freud had no hesitation in writing: "The third step in the theory of the instincts, which I have taken here, cannot lay claim to the same degree of certainty as the two earlier ones" (p. 59).

In *Inhibitions, Symptoms and Anxiety* (1926d), he explicitly upholds the clinical value of the previous duality of the instincts. Finally, in the 1920s, when it emerged that there was enormous disappointment about the therapeutic range of analysis—a fact we perhaps

*This chapter first appeared as an article in French in the *Revue française de psychanalyse*, 34(3): 441–451, in 1970. It was translated into English by Richard Simpson with the assistance of Monique Panaccio, and published in *The Psychoanalytic Quarterly*, 76: 1205–1220, in 2007. (It is slightly revised for this volume.)

underestimate—a very agitated Wilhelm Reich personally questioned Freud, asking him if he really intended to introduce the death instinct as a clinical theory. Freud reassured him that "it was only a hypothesis", advising Reich not to let himself be bothered by it and just to continue with his clinical work (Reich, 1927, p. 138).

In making these few preliminary remarks, I already find myself going against the trend of current positions taken on the compulsion to repeat. This puts me in a somewhat delicate situation for, if I may say so, the death instinct is alive and well. However, and I want to stress this point, my intention is neither to acknowledge nor to challenge the notion of the death instinct, which, in fact, is often an act of faith. But I do want to get it out of the way before starting to examine clinical facts. In fact, the stipulated connection between the compulsion to repeat and the death instinct, which has perhaps become conventional, especially when made prematurely, is responsible, in my opinion, for quite a lot of the difficulties which often confront us. To avoid any misunderstanding and to clarify the standpoint that I am adopting here, I would say that I do not reject the existence of manifestations and forms of behaviour on the fringes of the pleasure principle. On the contrary, even in the context of a compromise, I believe there are phenomena that have nothing to do with the fulfilment of a repressed wish. For me, there are actually good reasons to distinguish repetitions governed classically by the pleasure principle, such as those found in neurotic symptoms where there is a return of the repressed, from other forms of repetition, admittedly of a different order, which should not be linked from the outset to a fundamental characteristic of the instinct, or with the activity of a death instinct, even if these repetitions have a lethal effect.

The thesis that I want to set out is based on a clinical observation that I would readily describe as an opposition between the *same* and the *identical*. Such an opposition is only artificial in appearance, for Paul Robert's *Dictionnaire de la langue française* already distinguishes one of the meanings of *same*, defined as an approximate identity in the order of similarity or of resemblance, whereas *identical* refers to perfectly similar objects and, according to this dictionary, constitutes a sort of superlative of the similar. We would not, for instance, confuse a situation where we go back constantly to the same text, to the same narrative, in order to rewrite it, with a situation in which, like Bouvard and Pécuchet (two characters in a novel by Flaubert, who are both copyists), we would be limited to recopying it indefinitely. In the first case the repetition always implies a change, however minimal it may be. The "perpetual recurrence of the same thing", which Freud refers to, has nothing to do with the unlimited repetition of the identical. In the analytic situation, the change that appears in the new version of what has been announced previously, even if it is extremely limited, always reveals the existence of a considerable amount of work, the insistent call of unflagging desire.

I will come back later on to the profound economic modification that occurs in the act of repetition. For the time being, I shall just recall one aspect of it, the mobilisation of the countercathexis, in other words, the *objective* alliance concluded between the preconscious refusal and the attraction exerted on the representation in question by unconscious prototypes. In this respect, I would suggest that this attraction should not be conceived of simply as an expression of the compulsion to repeat (Freud, 1926d, pp. 159–160). The representation does not return to the unconscious to agglutinate there with the said prototypes; it first returns to a place where energy circulates more freely in order to gain fresh momentum. We are therefore entitled to speak of a recovery of energy. This retrogressive movement, moreover, provides the necessary time for a redistribution of representations by means of condensation and displacement, which implies the presence of several terms. Faced with this distortion of the figures whose destiny it is to return in order to express the dynamics of desire, we may reasonably speak of a veritable dramatisation, entirely governed by the pleasure principle. In our *practice*, at least, it would be perilous to think prematurely of the situation in any other way, even in those cases where everything that we observe apparently results from those resistances which lead us to speak of a negative therapeutic reaction—resistances we attribute not to the superego but rather to the compulsion to repeat, a fact emphasised by Maurice Bouvet and Glover alike.

When clinical illustrations are absent, misgivings are expressed, but when they are supplied, they are criticised and diversely interpreted. Nevertheless, I will take the risk of presenting one. The patient in question was a young woman who had been in analysis for a long time, and who had developed a stubborn resistance of the type we are inclined to associate with the compulsion to repeat. I shall describe one aspect of it here. Constantly, or rather, repetitively, the patient would start counting inwardly: one, two, three, and so on. Sometimes she would tell me about this, but not always, far from it; and she repeated this operation indefinitely. In order to be faithful to what happened and to stress the role of the countertransference in these situations, as well as the factor of chance or luck that governs its form and intensity, I will disclose a sequence of a poem by Armen Lubin (1903–1974) that started going round and round in my head, just as repetitively. In it there is a mythical being who counts. "He counts, counts, and begins all over again," writes the poet, who then adds, "All sorrows are called absence, sorrows bearing lances" (Lubin, 1946). The repetition did not seem distressing to me at all.

One day, after this scene had been played out many times, the patient said to me, "I counted up to eight; usually, I count up to ten." This is exactly the sort of change I was referring to. I responded to her immediately, saying: "There are two missing, who are they?" "The father and the son," she replied. Now one was missing, the Holy Ghost—in the colloquial sense of the term—and I pointed this out to her. Now this young woman was expecting a baby for the second time in her analysis— a pregnancy which she had never clearly referred to. But from that point on, as you will imagine, the tempo of the session accelerated in a manner that is characteristic of such situations. The underlying fantasy became clearer: she had got pregnant through the intervention of the Holy Ghost, in other words, without any physical contact. So, in fantasy, it was the analyst who had made her pregnant. Soon after, there appeared the figure of her absent father who had died prematurely during the patient's childhood ("sorrows bearing lances").

It is not possible to dwell on the rich developments that followed this sequence, but I can say that it was a decisive turning point in the analysis. It would certainly have been regrettable if chance had confirmed the understandable feeling that what I was dealing with here was a manifestation of the compulsion to repeat. So I do not believe that we can always follow Freud when he declares that the tendency of neurotics to repeat in the transference is independent of the pleasure principle (1920g, p. 22). What we are dealing with here, then, is not, it seems to me, a pure and unlimited repetition, but rather a fresh elaboration of the same thing which, moreover, is capable of integrating a whole new section of reality within its ambit.

Another illustration of this can be found in *Beyond the Pleasure Principle*. To introduce this *tendency which asserts itself without taking account of the pleasure principle, overriding it*, Freud turns to Tasso's romantic epic, the *Gerusalemme Liberata*. However, when the hero Tancred slashes a tree in two in which the soul of his beloved Clorinda has taken refuge, he did not repeat, strictly speaking, what had happened before. In fact, he did both the same thing and something completely different from the murder he had committed when he killed her, not knowing she was clothed in the armour of an enemy knight. What the poet wanted to represent, more or less deliberately, through this changing of masks and mutation of substances, was a series of transformations ranging from the figure of the raw fact to the figure of its symbolic representation.

By way of concluding the first part of this chapter, I would like to emphasise that in clinical practice the domain of what is situated on the fringes of the pleasure principle must be reduced as much as possible from the outset or, better still, displaced. There are different ways of imagining this. I am thinking here, in particular, of a remark Maurice Bouvet once made: "What would we analysts do", he asked, more or less, "if we did not believe in the notion of progress, and thus of change?"

There remains, however, as I have just noted, a separate domain, an order of repetition situated beyond, or rather prior to, the pleasure principle. I will approach it without making any initial reference to the death instinct, solely from the angle of the opposition between the *same* and the *identical*. To do so, I must briefly recall the positions I presented in papers during the 1966 conference on "Analyse terminée et analyse interminable" (de M'Uzan, 1966) and the Congress for French-Speaking Psychoanalysts of 1965 (de M'Uzan, 1965) and of 1967 (de M'Uzan, 1967).

At that time, I distinguished two main orientations of the personality based on the idea of whether or not the *category of the past* had been solidly elaborated. By the term "past", I do not mean the sum of lived events, but their internal rewriting—as in the family romance—based on a first narrative. I use the term narrative on account of the homology of form and structure between this internal story and a novelistic elaboration. The first narrative, the first real "past" of the individual, is elaborated at the Oedipal stage; that is to say, when all the earlier stages are taken up again and reworked within the framework both of desire, which is henceforth constantly mediated, and of the castration complex. It is as though the real events, once they have been lived, have less importance than the internal narrative that is elaborated and re-elaborated from them. From then on, and throughout the greatest part of his existence, the subject continues day in day out to elaborate his "past", that is, the precedent of truth for times to come. And he does this on the basis of the description he gives, through the style of his activities, of his situation in the world as a person who desires. This would be the natural fate of so-called normal or neurotic organisations, those that form and develop a real transference neurosis in the analytic situation, whose evolution follows a path that eventually leads to an ending. When, however, this category of the past has not been elaborated properly, and a kind of chronology has prevailed over a novelistic past, we observe, in extreme cases, those *scattered island (archipelago) personalities* which I have described elsewhere (de M'Uzan, 1966). In such situations we witness either sudden eruptions of conglomerates of affect-representation or the predominance of a mode of mechanical thinking (*pensée opératoire*), or alternatively a mixture of both. These situations are in any case unfit to enter the narrative or novel of the transference-neurosis. It is no longer a question of transference but of postponements; the analysis may then become interminable, punctuated by incidents of direct, mechanical, and reduplicative acting out, since it is always identical, with the result that one has the feeling one is witnessing a repetition of the repetition.

I think I am in a better position now to define the thesis I am defending here. I will summarise it schematically as follows:

> It is useful to distinguish two types of phenomena among those that are associated classically with the compulsion to repeat. The first of these is characterised by a reproduction of the *same* and involves structures in which the category of the past has been elaborated sufficiently. The second is characterised by a reproduction of the *identical* and involves structures in which this elaboration of the past is defective.

I have already distinguished the *same* and the *identical* clearly enough to be able to pass fairly swiftly over the formal characteristics of these two sorts of repetition. So I will add just a few words before going on to examine them from a metapsychological point of view. There is no doubt that the repetitive return of what has already been formulated leads us to neglect, and even ignore, the changes that it conceals. But this repetition of the same, which, in its hidden form, involves a process of remembering that finds expression in a variety of circumstances—sometimes in subtle ways—can not be confused with the repetition of the identical. In the latter, remembering has no status at all. A strange resemblance can be detected in the tone of voice and the inflections: we find verbal stereotypes, language tics, and even the use of a strictly reproductive direct style of speech, giving the impression that the subject is permanently ready to change place with the object topographically. Notwithstanding first appearances, this form of repetition is fundamentally different from the kind that Verlaine alludes to in one of his poems which involves a dream—to be exact, a repetitive dream in which a woman constantly returns, an unknown woman whom the poet loves and who loves him; but each time she is neither quite the same nor entirely different.

It is time now to examine the situation from a metapsychological standpoint, even at the risk of presenting things somewhat schematically. I will begin with the repetition of the *same*. The forces in operation here give the impression of being somewhat nuanced in their intensity and, above all, variable in their direction. Those that emanate from the unconscious, encounter, as if in a dialogue, those that belong to the countercathexis. This interplay not only assumes the appearance of a developed story, but is also situated entirely in the psychic sphere. The change that is observable at the heart of this complex dynamic stems less from a simple addition than from the elaboration of a fresh narrative from two existing narratives, even though all three resemble each other closely. While the economic necessity is undoubtedly present, it does not seem spectacularly compelling and, above all, the presence of counter-cathexes gives a more complex and more progressive rhythm to the repetition, as if it were primarily in the service of temporisation. The way the tendency to discharge is handled plays a key role in the formation of repetitions, which could be seen in terms of a very discrete and progressive redistribution of cathexes.

As for the *sequence* of repetitions of the same, along with their inherent discharges, they follow a certain trajectory, by which I mean that we are not dealing with a simple series of perfect movements back and forth but rather with a progressive displacement that occurs with each repetition, marking out the trajectory just referred to. From one repetition to another the economic configuration is imperceptibly modified, but it is modified none the less. This somewhat arid metapsychological conceptualisation is simply another reading of what can be observed clinically. Thus if I return to the clinical fragment presented above, we see that dynamic and economic redistributions can be detected in the patient's discourse and behaviour. She counted, and then either spoke about it immediately or at a later point. A few seconds or minutes before, she might have made a statement such as "I have nothing to say"; the action of counting could be accompanied or replaced by a gesture of the hand, as if to say, "Oh well", or "I don't want it". Her tone of voice, which at first seemed perfectly even and similar from one repetition to another, was in fact marked by very subtle variations ranging from defiance to resignation—variations that were so discrete that they were only noticeable after the event, for instance, when a more important variation—almost a difference—occurred. Such was the case when the patient announced: "I counted up to eight; usually, I count up to ten." As we have seen, this situation expressed a truly novelistic elaboration, the narrative of a desire in which successive figures who call each other and overlap each other had remained hidden. In short, it was a real labour of which the author, whose own volition was wholly excluded, was nevertheless the field. This is why, in order to evoke the driving force of this work, I do not hesitate to adopt the expression *compulsion to symbolise*, proposed by Groddeck (1969, p. 274) to define a force that truly belongs to the subject but is not available to him or her because it is the unconscious; or, as I would say, is in the unconscious.

Let me turn now to the repetition of the *identical*. The contrast is striking. To begin with we notice an erosion of topographical distinctions. Actually, repetition occurs here within the scope of a transference that is quite different from the transference-neurosis, which is in the realm of the repetition of the same. The repetition of the *identical* can be part of a denuded id, which must not be confused with the psychical unconscious, as well as part of a sort of sensible reality in which the frontier separating inside from outside remains uncertain. Repetitions may result from this which I would venture to call imitative, where a particular characteristic of the object's perceived activities is incorporated and later faithfully reproduced. In "Analysis Terminable and Interminable" (1937c), Freud speaks of resistances that can no longer be localised, but which seem to depend on fundamental relations within the psychical apparatus. I think that this remark applies particularly well to the topographical erasure to which I am referring here.

The forces at work in this repetition of the *identical* may be distinguished by their insistent orientation in one and the same direction. We do not find here the dynamic I described earlier in connection with the repetition of the same, namely, a momentary resumption of a free circulation of energies in the higher systems, which is soon followed by a linking up with unconscious representations in a mode that constitutes a narrative. In repetition of the *identical*, it is what is closest to sensory-motor functioning that always seems to be the target. The foregoing is expressed as it is, openly, without beating about the bush. And if it were necessary, none the less, to refer to a phenomenon in the nature of a countercathexis, it would have to be located outside the subject, or in his physical organism, which to some extent always has an ambiguous situation of extra-territoriality.

Michel Fain's (1969, p. 933) formulation that "poverty of elaboration is the companion in suffering of the repetition automatism" is particularly applicable here. In view of the impoverished activities of representation and symbolisation, combined with the rudimentary nature of condensation, displacement, and dramatisation, one has the impression that the energies that are already very imperfectly bound could easily be unleashed. The tendency towards discharge in repetition is thus accentuated. The repetition in question is, so to speak, the repetition of an experience of discharge, where the economic dominates entirely; there is a sort of turning back to zero that is often expressed by a state of exhaustion. The principle governing this state of exhaustion is clearly the principle of inertia or, if you like, nirvana. In this connection, I have to say that I do not subscribe to the interpretation of the nirvana principle that sees it as the psychoanalytic equivalent of the constancy principle. If one wants to establish equivalences or filiations, I would say that there is an equivalence between the constancy principle and the pleasure principle on the one hand, and between the inertia principle and the nirvana principle on the other. From this point of view, the distinction is once again clear between the repetition of the *identical* and the repetition of the *same*, where the interplay in the balance between cathexes is limited and differential discharges are an expression of the effect of the constancy principle—that is to say, of the pleasure principle.

I think it is worth making a few remarks here concerning the use of the term *viscosity of the libido*. I shall overlook the difficulty of defining the quality of a substance. In any event, although the repetition of the *identical* can be seen as evidence of what would be the equivalent of fixations maintained owing to a particular viscosity of the libido, we can see by the way it erupts in the act of repetition that this libido is particularly fluid. Furthermore, it seems problematic from a logical standpoint to attach the compulsion to repeat to a definite quality (viscosity) of energy (the libido), while linking this same compulsion to repeat to the death instinct, which is no doubt another form of energy. Admittedly, the aporia is probably not as stark as I seem to be suggesting. But it prompts me in turn to suggest that, in the repetition of the *identical*, what we are given to observe, alongside the change of the energetic system described, is more a sort of mutation in the qualitative status of energy (we find ourselves in a similar situation to the one posed by the comparison of the topographical and functional definitions of the unconscious). In speaking of the *mutation of the qualitative status of energy*, I am referring to a more or less important and sometimes extreme alteration in the libidinal characteristics of energy and not to the employment of a different form of energy. This is how the tendency to discharge along the most direct paths is established.

Furthermore, the question arises as to what energies remain available for maintaining or bringing about a cathexis of representations capable of playing a role in the elaboration of desire. The critique of the notion of the viscosity of the libido no doubt requires a much more thorough examination. None the less, it seems to me that this notion applies more to those fixations that can be accounted for on the basis of the pleasure principle alone. In the compulsion to repeat, situated beyond the pleasure principle, energy, with its meagre libidinal characteristics, seems relatively unsuited to forming part of a representational complex and of *staying* there long enough for the expected process of dramatisation to occur. Here, energy simply accumulates and is discharged. It would be more appropriate to speak of excessive fluidity. Lorenz's model, cited by Hollande and Soulé (1970), provides a rather good illustration of this system in which the language of economic dynamics is the only one that is apparently valid, for the return of the charge to the zero level has become the dominant mechanism. Here we are dealing with a compelling demand in the form of need, with the repetition of an experience of discharge; this need is always identical in its lack of differentiation from a previous need, and short-circuits memory.

It is not possible to discuss the compulsion to repeat without dealing with the problem of memory, which is always deeply involved. I will only make a few remarks on this, however, especially as I would first have to undertake a thorough examination of Freud's text "Remembering, Repeating, and Working-Through" (1914g), which would be out of place here. So I will simply say that if it is legitimate to oppose repetition and remembering, it is equally important to ask ourselves about the value of remembering assumed by repetition, whether in the form of behaviour or acting out. In other words, we are entitled to speak of remembering when what is repeated takes up a sequence of the "past" elaborated in narrative form.

This is the case, for instance—and here I am quoting Freud—of "those experiences that occurred in very early childhood and were not understood at the time, but which were *subsequently* interpreted and understood" (p. 149). I would add that these experiences were the object of successive dramatisations for which the screen memories prepared the way. When this organic reference to the *theatrical past* is lacking, we cannot really speak of remembering. This is the case for repetition of the identical for which Freud, in my opinion, has given us a sort of model. In "Dreams and Telepathy" (1922a), he writes:

> A dream without condensation, distortion, dramatization, above all, without wish-fulfilment, surely does not deserve the name ... There are *other* mental products in sleep to which the right to be called "dreams" would have to be refused. Actual experiences of the day are sometimes simply repeated in sleep .... The conception of a purely "telepathic dream" lies in its being a perception of something external, in relation to which the mind remains passive and receptive. (p. 208)

Since I have just cited Freud again, I will acknowledge and accept a new repetition by referring to him once more in order to give an overview of what I have described so far. You will perhaps have noticed that the opposition I have described between the *same* and the *identical* coincides in many respects with an opposition that Freud defined, but to which he never returned—namely, between the psychoneuroses and the actual neuroses. Now the actual neuroses are closely associated with traumatic neuroses which, precisely, constitute one of the clinical anchoring points of Freud's last formulation concerning the compulsion to repeat. The same deficiency of representational activity, and the same prevalence of the quantitative factor, represented either by powerful external stimuli or by somatic excitation, exists in both cases. Thus traumatic experience and actual factors may be regarded as equivalent, and there is the same danger in both cases of the *Reizschutz* (stimulus barrier) being breached.

Could it be said, then, that the compulsion to repeat, in the full sense of the term, is a characteristic of a type of personality at risk of developing actual neuroses? Such a formulation is no doubt too radical; moreover, there is a clinical argument that can be set against it: there are authentic neurotic structures in which real repetitions of the identical can sometimes be observed, or at least a tendency leading in this direction. But it is not difficult to counter this argument, and it is once again Freud who provides the material for doing so when, for example, in his *Introductory Lectures on Psychoanalysis* (1916–17), he suggests that "actual neurosis is often the nucleus of a psycho-neurotic symptom" (p. 390). However, it was left to Reich (1927) to develop this thesis more fully.

For Reich, libidinal stasis, constant yet variable, constitutes a real and actual factor. It operates in two ways: first, by inducing parental fixations from which incestuous conflicts will develop, thereby providing the content for psychoneurosis; and second, by directly feeding, along another path, the nucleus of actual neurosis which provides the psychoneurosis with its essential energy (see Fig. 1 by Reich). It seems to me that the link, so to speak, between the neurosis with its actual nucleus is likely, under certain circumstances, to come undone, more or less. And this nucleus will then express itself directly (Fig. 2).

I think it is true to say that the existence of so-called actual symptoms alongside classical neurotic symptoms has frequently been observed in almost all the neuroses. This dissociation—essentially an energetic phenomenon—between the actual nucleus and the neurosis, remains a possibility that can occur at any time, for instance, under the impact of traumatic factors. However, personality structures exist that are based on this dissociation which constitutes, as it were, their fundamental trait of personality.

In any case, certain clinical facts can be accounted for by this schema. I am thinking particularly of those analyses that unfold in a paradoxical

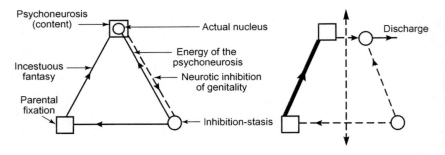

Figure 1. Reich.   Figure 2.

mode. They appear to progress normally as far as the elaboration of the complexes of representations is concerned, but in other respects they seem meagre, as if emptied of substance. The analytic work simply touches the superstructure which is scarcely cathected, and we would be tempted to say of such patients that their available libido is not very rich while, at the same time, at a much deeper level, considerable energy is accumulated and discharged, often obscurely, or in a completely hidden manner, in behavioural or even organic repetitions of the identical.

The question arises, then, as to the origin of these personality orientations which are dominated by repetition of the *identical*. I will simply form a schematic hypothesis here, which I will attempt to develop further on another occasion. I would say that in those cases where we can legitimately refer to the decisive effects of the compulsion to repeat, there is no obvious reason to appeal to a special quality of the libido, viscosity, any more than to the intervention of a death instinct. In fact, we are dealing with a certain type of organisation, and, more precisely, with something that forms part of an individual's development. We can imagine that this comes about in two phases at least. The second, as we have seen, is the confrontation with the Oedipal configuration and its destruction, when the first real past of the individual is constituted. The first phase, on which all the others depend of course, should be located at the point when hallucinatory satisfaction fails, giving rise to the gradual establishment of the reality principle. We know that with the appearance of the reality principle, a particular activity, fantasmatic activity, separates off, which is independent of reality testing and subject to the pleasure principle alone. It is my contention, then, that a traumatic factor, which is probably real though of variable nature, intervenes decisively in this phase. Through the agency of a precise mechanism—perhaps repudiation (*Verwerfung*) (what I have in mind here could be compared with the Lacanian notion of *foreclosure*)—this traumatic experience dissociates the necessary relation between representation of reality and fantasmatic activity, while destroying or severely inhibiting the latter. From there on, the dynamic foundations of the constitution of the past, as I have defined it, are altered. It will no longer be possible, for example, for a true family romance to be elaborated: the neurotic path of the repetition of the *same* is barred, while the reduplication of the *identical* becomes ever more dominant.

CHAPTER TWO

Countertransference and the paradoxical system* (1976a)

"I am true to the promptings of the life that is in me."

—Jack London (*The Sea-Wolf*, 1904, p. 104)

In examining the countertransference, one often begins by locating the question in relation to the various interpretations of the concept. At times the focus is on its narrow definition restricted to unconscious reactions to the analysand's transference, with their frequently pejorative accents; at others, a broader definition is adopted encompassing every aspect of the analyst's person that intervenes in the treatment, perhaps even to the point of playing an instrumental role in it. Michel Neyraut (1974), as we know, has pushed the limits of this concept back still further by positing that the countertransference, insofar as it includes psychoanalytic thinking and an implicit demand of the analyst, even precedes the transference. There is perhaps no need to choose; for, in fact, it is a question of circumstances. In our practice, though, I think it is advisable to follow the first definition, as the second

---

*This text first appeared in French in the *Revue française de psychanalyse*, 40(2): 575–590, in 1976. It was translated into English and published in Lebovici, S. & Widlöcher, D. (1980). (It is slightly revised for this volume.)

is more conducive to speculative work. For the purposes of the present chapter, however, the broader usage of the concept is more appropriate, as will become clear, I hope, as my argument develops.

For a long time now I have been struck by a peculiar phenomenon—though every analyst has undoubtedly experienced it—which occurs in the analyst's own mind in the course of his or her work. While listening attentively to his patient, the analyst perceives in himself psychical activity that is different from all other forms, affects included, that he is used to experiencing in this situation. All of a sudden, the analyst is invaded by strange representations, unexpected but grammatically well-formed phrases, abstract formulae, colourful images, more or less elaborate reveries, and so on. The list is in no way exhaustive. But what is most significant is the absence of any comprehensible connection with what is currently going on in the session. One would thus be tempted to say that the analyst is avoiding the situation, which amounts to a countertransference manifestation in the narrowest sense of the term. This supposition is corroborated when the fantasy explicitly concerns the patient, and when, in addition, it has more or less regressive features. In this case we are dealing with the analyst's transference on to a patient who has come to represent for him a figure from the past. It is also worth noting how this situation is likely to mobilise the "polymorphous pervert" dormant in each analyst, with all that this implies for his or her mental functioning.

However essential they may be, I am not going to dwell on these considerations here because they have already been studied at length by numerous authors. It is my belief, then, that confining ourselves to the limits of classical countertransference does not allow us to grasp all the aspects of the psychical activity going on in the analyst, precisely because certain aspects clearly seem to lie outside the realm of both personal issues and doctrinal positions.

The representations in question arise, then, unexpectedly, at any given moment of the session, sometimes right at the outset. What is remarkable is that they arouse neither anxiety nor unpleasure, regardless of their content. The analyst finds this most surprising, particularly as he or she is naturally led to wonder about the possible interference of some unconscious conflict whose affects may have been inhibited in their development. What he experiences, then, is a subtle change of state, something akin to an experience of floating, ever so slightly, which, paradoxically, is not accompanied by any flagging of attention. The similarity of this experience with certain mild states of depersonalisation is evident. But in this case the change seems to be a direct product of the discourse or attitude of the analysand—an analysand who is both emotionally affected and imperious, and who has induced a modification in the analyst's narcissistic cathexes.

Later, when the analyst has the possibility of reflecting on what he experienced at such a moment, he notices that two things were involved: he had been in a state of alert towards the object, and his own sense of identity had changed. It was as if he had evacuated what was most personal in him, while, at the same time, his psychic apparatus had become particularly permeable and open towards new fantasy activities. But if that is so, where do these thoughts, these images, and these words, which produce a sort of momentary experience of alienation in the analyst, come from? There is good reason to suppose that they correspond to psychic processes *occurring in the analysand* but which are as yet undetected. This might explain the most remarkable trait of the phenomenon in general—namely, that it precedes both the analyst's understanding of the material itself, insofar as such understanding is derived from logical deductions, and the fantasies that the patient is about to formulate.

You may recall that Paula Heimann (1950) read a paper at the 16th International Psychoanalytic Congress, in which she clearly asserted the value of the countertransference as a tool for understanding the patient. According to Heimann, the analyst has an unconscious perception of the patient's unconscious that is keener and quicker than that which might flow from any conscious conception of the situation. Heimann is chiefly interested, though, in the analyst's *emotional state*, in the feelings that the patient arouses in him, hence her recommendation that analysts should associate evenly hovering attention with a sort of free emotional sensitivity. This was in keeping with her wish to challenge the idealised image of an unruffled, detached, and—why not?— insensitive analyst.

This paper unquestionably marked a milestone and, moreover, many authors have pursued the same path. But the phenomenon I am referring to is something quite different from this sort of "emotional resonance" which, by leaving the specific nature of what is actually going on in the psychical apparatus rather vague, does not allow for a really rigorous conceptualisation. Another author who went a step further in this direction was Annie Reich (1951). She pointed out that insight into the material often emerges suddenly, as if from somewhere within the analyst's own mind. The analyst discovers equally suddenly what his or her interpretation should be, and how it ought to be formulated.

This type of understanding, Reich adds, is experienced passively: *it just happens.*

I should also like to draw attention here to two remarks of Neyraut (1974) which seem to be particularly germane to my argument. He observes that "... in a way, the analyst is paid to suspend his own train of thought and to surrender to associations that are not his own" (p. 40). Further on, in the section on *transference psychoses*, he adds that the "massive transference" of these patients is indicative of a "psychic stranglehold, an imprisonment of the therapist within the subjective space of psychotic thought. As this space ... no longer possesses the notion of the limits of its own interiority ... the internal contents belonging to other subjectivities, notably those of the therapist, may seem to be included within one and the same space" (p. 76). It remains to be seen, of course, whether these indeterminate frontiers are an exclusive characteristic of psychotics, and whether psychotics necessarily and consistently lose the symbolic meaning of the internal mechanisms that actuate their subjectivity. I am far from being certain of that. It is a matter of opinion but, for my part, I think that this lack is much more conspicuous in some psychosomatic patients. Furthermore, this disappearance of the boundaries of the internal world can be observed, at certain times, in many subjects who are neither psychotic nor psychosomatic.

It is clear that many analysts are attracted by those areas in which the phenomenon that I am studying can be found. However, to remove any possible ambiguity concerning the specificity of the factors involved, I would like to illustrate my remarks with two clinical fragments. I have scarcely any illusions, of course, as to the significance of such illustrations, which usually prompt a dozen other interpretations that are far better than those one has come up with oneself: their main value lies in their power to convey an experience whose significance was keenly felt at the time.

From clinical material that is too extensive to be reported in full, I will select those elements that are directly related to my purpose, while hoping that their somewhat incongruous nature is not too disconcerting. These incongruous features are not without significance, however, since they clearly comply with the same archaic mechanisms that govern puns and jokes.

A young woman, who had been in analysis for about two years, one day expressed the fear that she would not be able to settle her account with me on the due date. She dreaded falling behind with the payment, and remembered a similar situation that had occurred in the past. Her discourse was broken by long silences, and it was only gradually that she was able to muster and express her thoughts. She was disturbed to see how far her fears of abandonment and her intolerance of any situation of dependence were connected. Owing me money constituted for her precisely such a situation of dependence, which in turn evoked for her the image of an alarming fusional relationship. At this point, I was struck by the idea that she was deriving pleasure from this situation, which tied in directly with my reflections on the problematics of identity. There was nothing particularly troubling in all that; it might even be regarded as part of everyday "psychoanalytic routine". And then all of a sudden there was a moment of rupture, of surprise. I had the impression I had switched off; something had changed, I was no longer the same. While noticing this, an extremely clear image forced itself upon my mind. Before my eyes I could see an engraving or, to be more exact, the bottom left corner of an engraving that had been torn off. In this corner I could see a woman's leg emerging from a thicket and pointing downwards to the left at an angle of forty-five degrees. The leg was bare, and only visible from the calf downwards, but what struck me most of all was the fact that the ankle and the foot were hyper-extended. This image did not remind me of anything, and even later on I was unable to say where it had come from. On the other hand, scarcely had the image emerged than the thought entered my mind: *boys are better off*. At this point I immediately interrupted, saying, "So you think boys are better off." The phallic significance of this leg emerging from a tangle of weeds, bushes, and shrubs is quite obvious, but the associated image and words forced themselves on me first, before there was any possibility of understanding them.

Almost immediately the patient brought bitter associations to the conflictual aspect of her relations with her mother. Until then this conflict had always been linked to the twin fear that I have already mentioned—namely, the fear of absolute rejection and abandonment combined with a horror of finding herself in a state of abject fusion. This time she talked about her mother's forbidding attitude, and about her disastrous education. While her brothers had been allowed to do whatever they liked and had enjoyed real freedom, she had been watched over very closely by her mother. One day she had been severely reprimanded because she had returned from school arm in arm with a boyfriend. At this juncture in the treatment a significant amount of material emerged related to phallic issues rather than to the more archaic conflicts which had been in the foreground almost constantly up till then, to the point of conditioning the analysand's behaviour to a large degree.

I now want to consider an incident in another case, which is equally curious.

At the beginning of the session, a woman patient reminded me of the uncustomary "*Au revoir, Monsieur*" with which she had left me at the end of the previous session. This made her think back to an incident in her early childhood. She was certain as to when this took place, saying that she must have been two and a half years old at the time. Certain precise elements, which she did not specify, allowed her to pinpoint the event: "Not before, not after," she declared. The anecdote was the following: she had been walking along the street when she suddenly found herself in the police station. The policemen made her stand on a table and were questioning her. At this very point in her narrative, I once again experienced the same phenomenon of "switching off" that I described earlier, and at the same time a strange thought came to my mind: *"I would gladly gobble you up, Handsome Sailor!"* Needless to say, although I was far from lacking in experience, I was somewhat taken aback. Adding to my perplexity was the fact that the expression made me think immediately of a literary reference. It had to do with Billy Budd, the hero of Melville's short story, which I had last read some fifteen years or so earlier. It also seemed to me that there was a link between the "*Monsieur*" with which she had greeted me and the expression "Handsome Sailor". There was no spontaneous explanation for this bizarre association, though this did not prevent me from feeling that it had to be taken into account. Let it be said in passing that I have only just remembered today, while writing this chapter, that it is customary in the British or American navy to address officers as "Sir".

Meanwhile, the patient went on with her account of her childhood memory. She was still at the police station when she saw her uncle Pierre enter. She then spoke of how she had experienced intense feelings of shame, and stressed the peculiar quality of her experience. From there, she moved on to a dream she had already told me before, but which, for some obscure reason, I had wanted to hear again. I will just single out the main element in this dream: there was a sort of slab of stone covered in black fabric, which made her think both of a tombstone and a table. Her father had once offered her a marble-topped table. She had wanted to get rid of it as soon as possible and to replace it with another table that she would choose herself: a dining table (*table à manger*), she said. Then she turned to the theme of food, telling me about a local dish from her own country that she found absolutely distasteful; "And yet", she added insistently, "*j'étais de bonne composition*" (i.e., not fussy). At that very moment, my strange mode of thinking came back to me, and I said: "When you say, '*de bonne composition*', perhaps you also mean '*bonne à manger*' (good to eat)."[1] She was taken aback, and perhaps a little anxious; then, remaining somewhat dreamy, she replied: "Yes, that's true! I'm thinking now of that Uncle Pierre who used to frighten me so. He used to say to me: 'I'm a lion, and I'm going to eat you up!' I was fascinated, excited, and terrified all at once." It was not until the next day that I thought I had understood the meaning of my association with Melville's character. The support for the analogy was provided by the patient's neck which had been conspicuously bare on that day: in fact, Billy Budd, nicknamed the "Handsome Sailor" ended up being hanged from the ship's main yard where, as Melville says, he "took the full rose of the dawn", suggesting a close link between the tombstone and the condemned hero.

It goes without saying that on this occasion, as on all occasions of this nature, I did not fail to examine both the thoughts that came to my mind and my interventions. And I think I can say that the representations in question did not depend specifically on my inner life, with the interwoven desires and anxieties that determine its course. Neither did they in any way constitute a *personal* reaction to the patient's transference. Not that I am above such reactions, far from it; indeed, when I first experienced this phenomenon, I was inclined to attribute it to reactions of this sort. But to interpret the phenomenon simply in terms of the countertransferential interferences and the famous "blind spots" of which Freud speaks would, under the circumstances, have been too easy a solution. Why? Because it would have meant ignoring the original character of the phenomenon, that is, its astonishing polymorphism on the one hand and its anticipatory value, giving it a dynamic role, on the other. Indeed, it is so polymorphous that one would have to be presumptuous to believe one was inhabited by such a plethora of images and verbal forms, which proceed, moreover, from all possible levels of development. In this respect, I should like to note in passing that pregenital representations are particularly involved in this phenomenon, which confirms my contention that today the best indications for analysis may not always be found in the neuroses but the rather in the ill- defined group of *borderline* states. Given this really striking "proteism", even the presumptuousness just mentioned would not allow me to say that personal fantasy plays an unquestionable role in what occurs. But the most important feature of all this is perhaps to be found elsewhere. In my view, it lies in the almost prophetic character of these compelling productions, which is frequently borne out.

Generally speaking, within one and the same session—but *after the fact*—the patient will recall a more or less distant dream or event that he or she has never thought about since, or has repressed, which resonates perfectly with the thought that emerged in me. This thought has the particularity of both *anticipating* and *articulating* important fragments of the analysand's unconscious world in such a way that it leads directly to an intervention by the analyst of real dynamic value. I must say that I would never have dreamed of isolating the phenomenon in such a clear-cut way had I not been regularly struck by the predictions to which it unfailingly led me, and by the decisive role that it thereby played in interpretation.

All this only became intelligible when I understood that in the formulations that came to my mind, it was necessary to change the speaker: I had been thinking in terms of *I*, representing the subject, whereas I should have understood *you* or *he*, something I vigorously resisted—in the psychoanalytic sense of the term—for a long time. Who, in fact, was speaking when the thoughts and images were going through my mind, and when I subsequently used them in my work? Who else but the patient, for neither my inner life nor a personal reaction to the transference was involved? But then the inevitable conclusion to be drawn from all this is that at a precise level of his functioning, *the analyst's psychical apparatus literally becomes the analysand's*. The latter has "invaded" the analyst's psychical system, taking possession of it momentarily in order to trigger original mental processes in it. More precisely, it is by interposing his or her representation in the analyst's psychic space that the analysand "takes possession" momentarily, or more permanently, of the analyst's mind. In doing so, the analysand is seeking once again, as always, to be understood; but his primary need is to know that what he perceives fundamentally within himself as an economic exigency—or an inaccessible fantasised potential—will be elaborated and fully represented through the work of a psychical system he has annexed. For his part, the analyst seems to have withdrawn as an individual with his own passions and history, leaving behind him nothing other than active functional capacities that are more in the order of fantasy-making than logical thinking—capacities he fuels with his own energy.

This original psychical activity of the analyst, which duplicates those we are already familiar with, deserved to be given a name. In order to contrast it with the functioning characteristic of the waking state, as well as that of dreaming, and bearing in mind certain well-known studies on sleep, I chose to call it *paradoxical thinking*. This form of activity is certainly not limited to analysts; but I think that they are particularly disposed to it owing to the nature of their work. What is the importance of *paradoxical thinking*, quantitatively speaking? Is it constantly operative? *Paradoxical thoughts* only occupy a limited space. They only cross the analyst's mind fleetingly, and certainly do not manifest themselves in every session of each patient. But even though they manifest themselves in isolation, and apparently entirely out of context, I find it difficult to say they have any real discontinuity. As a matter of fact, I have noticed that some of these *paradoxical thoughts* were indeed homogeneous and sometimes interconnected. So I have come to think that they are probably only the visible part of an infinitely larger phenomenon which, more often than not, unfolds secretly, in the background in relation to other mental activities, and is endowed with a sort of continuity. This is what I have called the *paradoxical system*—a system, it is true, that is somewhat inaccessible, but one which we are sometimes privileged to get a glimpse of. We can make out, as if peering through a veil, a stream of pulsating images or figures, in a constant state of flux, which pass by, disappear, and return (on the descriptive level, these productions may be compared with hypnagogic images). Taking into account that fragments of incongruous or incomprehensible sentences sometimes seep through into this theory of representations, I would be inclined to attribute an intermediate position to the *paradoxical system* on the limits of the unconscious and the preconscious.

Characterising the *paradoxical system* in this way will undoubtedly give rise to perplexity and criticism. For instance, it might be objected that the phenomena described are comparable to those artefacts that alter the course and perception of an experience and, as such, should be regarded as insignificant factors to be eliminated from the field of reflection. That may be so, but in psychoanalysis, as we know, the most reasonable course is not always the most sensible one.

The reader will probably already have thought about the role that projection and introjection may play in the *paradoxical system* or, more precisely, the mechanisms of projective identification and, on the analyst's part, particularly, introjective identification. The intervention of these mechanisms in the countertransference has been widely discussed. Neyraut (1974), for instance, readily recognises that the countertransference—like the transference—in some ways resembles animistic thinking, which is partly identified with a projection of the unconscious. It is only a short step from there to say that my conception of the analyst's activity is somewhat paranoid. In fact, I do not go as far as that, having persuaded myself from experience that the appropriation and invasion of the analyst's psychical apparatus are not linked to destructive aims. The analysand is not trying to injure the analyst or to control him closely, or to deposit split off and bad fragments of his personality into him. What is much more at stake, in my view, is the fate of the narcissistic libido of the two protagonists present. If the analyst were to experience this situation as persecuting, it would be evidence of a countertransference reaction in the ordinary and negative sense of the term. Still, it must be conceded that these *paradoxical thoughts* are somewhat disturbing.

How can the analyst recognise, alongside the conscious and unconscious processes that take place in him, the existence of another register of psychical activity of which he is not strictly speaking the subject? He experiences, identifies, associates, understands, and transmits—all of which constitutes the nuts and bolts of his technique. He considers the famous communication from unconscious to unconscious as self-evident, but he is naturally unwilling to make room in himself for something that is indefinite, uncontrolled, and radically foreign. The sense of reticence inspired by the *paradoxical system* may therefore be explained primarily by the threat that it represents for the stability of our sense of identity. As our narcissism is badly shaken, we feel we are being attacked and so try to defend ourselves to the hilt, preferring to attribute the blame to some sort of personal problem, even though it may result in a technical blunder. In this respect, it is entirely plausible that the most rigorous classical technique has the secondary function of protecting the analyst against such instability. On the other hand, the tendency to drowsiness, which sometimes permits the analyst to withdraw narcissistically, may be another way of protecting himself. This means, though, is so extreme that there is a risk of it overstepping its aim, for by inhibiting the analyst's functional capacities, drowsiness paralyses the free play of the *paradoxical system*, precisely where one must let oneself go. Fortunately, however, it is not so easy to escape these dynamics: the enormous power exerted by the object-representation, which is all the more solidly entrenched in its host in that it has a hold on a portion of his narcissistic libido, prevents the analyst from ever really being able to keep the analysand at a distance.

In examining the resistances that are normally erected against the *paradoxical system*, I am now convinced that they are only so tenacious because the system itself depends both on very archaic experiences that are contemporaneous with the formation of the subject and on an elementary mechanism that is profoundly rooted in our being and inseparable from our flesh. From the standpoint of this primary mechanism, the *paradoxical system* leads us directly into the realm of biology— a realm into which we are still reluctant to venture, even though Freud clearly showed us the way.

A team at the Institut Pasteur, led by F. Jacob and R. Fauve, has recently made an important finding which gives cause for reflection (from the report by Dr. Escoffier-Lambiotte published in *Le Monde*, 7 December 1974). These researchers establish a parallel between two particular cases in each of which the immune defences, which are normally highly vigilant with regard to foreign intrusion, cease to function. In one case the organism shows tolerance for malignant cells and in the other the mother's organism shows tolerance for the foetus so that it can develop. In other words, both cancerous cells and the cells of the embryonic placenta alike defeat the defence system of the organism in which they are going to develop. This means that some special function must exist from the beginning of life that is capable of inhibiting the activation of the immune defence system, for were they to intervene normally, they would hinder the growth of the foreign body, that is, the foetus, as is perhaps the case in certain spontaneous abortions. (According to the same article, half of the genetic inheritance of the embryo—and of the trophoblasts—come from spermatozoa. Half of the surface antigens carried by the embryonic cells are thus incompatible with those of the mother.) But this function will also have to be inhibited in turn at a later stage so that the subject will be capable of *recognising foreign bodies as such and of protecting himself.*

On the basis of this biological model, we may assume that the analysand's representation behaves in the analyst's psychic space rather like a trophoblast—that is to say, it prevents the analyst from recognising its full alterity. If this were indeed the case, it would be easier to understand those situations in which one no longer knows who is where and who is who. The development of the *paradoxical system* probably would depend, then, at least in part, on the momentary or partial inhibition of the functions that allow one to recognise others and to protect oneself. I would say that this inhibition fortunately counters the activation of one of the most harmful, and perhaps fundamental forms of the countertransference, namely, the need to eliminate and to reject the analysand.

These considerations may seem rather audacious; but, after all, we analysts are hardly lacking in audacity when we link the most archaic mechanisms of the child with the physiological models of the incorporation of the good and the rejection of the bad; or when we show how these mechanisms are at work in fantasies that may be put into words. Once again, I would like to refer to psychosomatic practice which, by making us aware of the indistinct origins of fantasy activity, constantly reveals the extent to which the boundaries between subject and object, between mental and physical, are fragile and shifting. In this no man's land, power is shared and organic alterations frequently appear and develop as if in response to the most varied and often tiny modifications occurring in the other person, but which are experienced by the patient as changes affecting him or herself. In my view, this constitutes the model of *acting in*. What is more, there is every reason to suppose that a deep homogeneity of structure exists between the most elementary mechanisms and the most highly developed ones.

There are other arguments in support of the *paradoxical system*, however, to which the analyst should be more sensitive. I have already pointed out the affinity between the *paradoxical system* and depersonalisation or, more precisely, the dependence of the *paradoxical system* on a particular vicissitude of the narcissistic libido, which involves a relative uncertainty of the sense of identity. By sense of identity, I mean, following Greenacre (1958), the sense of uniqueness experienced by an integrated organism that is able to recognise others without ambiguity.

I have already explored these views in an earlier contribution on the theme of *"Le dehors et le dedans"* ("The outside and the inside"), where I took as my point of departure a study of the fantasy: *"Si j'étais mort"* ("If I were dead") (de M'Uzan, 1974). There I argued that strongly cathected objects can neither acquire real alterity nor obtain the status of a totally independent subject. Similarly, the ego, partly lost in the representations of its love-objects, never acquires an entirely distinct and unequivocal identity. Furthermore, I suggested that there is no true boundary between the ego and the non-ego, but a vague transitional zone, a *spectrum of identity* defined by the diverse positions that the narcissistic libido occupies, ranging from an internal pole to an external pole coinciding with the image of the other.

These remarks could equally well have been derived from an examination of the analytic situation, which provides a particularly apt illustration of what I am referring to. The analyst always attaches a greater or lesser portion of his narcissistic libido to the image he has of his analysand, and if this process develops, it creates a favourable climate for both evenly suspended attention and the emergence of the *paradoxical system*. Concomitant with this diminution of his narcissistic libido, the analyst observes an alteration in the obscure and indefinable image he has of his own identity. Theoretically, this movement could lead to the actual transposition of one into the other; but actually there is hardly any risk of this occurring in practice, for the narcissistic libido always continues to circulate and oscillate between its extreme poles. If one wanted to identify certain traits characterising the analyst's personality, one would have to include, together with a special disposition for primary identification, comparable to that of the psychotic or the pervert, a combination of maternal fantasy and an aptitude for depersonalisation.

With respect to the uncertainty affecting one's sense of identity, in my opinion it also derives from early experiences that have had a direct and lasting effect. The following experience provides a striking illustration of what no doubt constitutes one of the anchor points of the *paradoxical system* and, for some individuals, at least, a pivotal moment in their development.

A woman patient told me that when she was about two and a half years old she happened to be standing with her mother in front of a wardrobe mirror which reflected both of them standing side by side. This was the first time the child had seen the two images simultaneously. She then experienced two different feelings, which, though they were separated by a certain period of time, were none the less closely connected. The experience was ambiguous and, in any case, far from joyful and triumphant. Initially, though, there was a positive aspect to it in that it allowed her to make a prodigious mental leap. She inferred from this sight that her mother did not know what she was thinking, which even allowed her to hurl mental insults. Later, casting her mind back to the juxtaposition of the two images, she was overwhelmed by deeply distressing feelings. In a total state of panic, she rushed up to her mother and bombarded her with questions, crying, "Mummy, why am I me, tell me why I am me!" It is not difficult to imagine how awkward the mother felt; irritated by the child's insistence, she was first evasive and then rough, sending the child away without any answer. The patient recalls that she then threw herself down on the floor in a tantrum; her sister, who was a lot older than her, had apparently witnessed this scene several times and told her about it subsequently.

This brings to mind Lacan's mirror stage, where there is also a relationship between identity and specular image. But, in fact, the experience reported by my patient is something altogether different: it concerns a much later period—around the age of two and a half—and its affective colouring is quite different. At that age, the child is no longer plunged into the state of helplessness and lack of motor coordination that is characteristic of the infant. The older child has a certain sense of bodily unity and exerts a relative degree of mastery.

But even though this new step leads the child to a clearer delimitation of his ego, he none the less experiences a sense of disarray, for he senses that the price to pay for it is a "rift" in his libido. Although the "I" is beginning to assert itself, his whole being resists the necessity of pulling back within itself, of assigning a definite place to the narcissistic libido, and of drawing boundaries around it. The child protests violently against this restriction which involves a twofold loss: the loss of his former grandiose self and that of a narcissistic object, the mother of the earlier period of life. And as he is going through the painful and distressing experience of having to exist not only for the first time but for the rest of his life, the child puts up a struggle and so retains deep down within himself the memory of this period of adjustment. As it is too painful and harsh to be accepted, the experience drives him to reject, or at least defer a victory which he feels is diminishing, and even a defeat.

In spite of everything, however, the child has come a step closer to reality, and since reality asserts that the object is other, he will "eat" this other, if only so as not to lose the part of himself that is contained therein. It may well be that the rudimentary elements of every object-representation are formed and developed in the subject's space in this way. Furthermore, it is conceivable that the experience may leave a functional residue with the result that the narcissistic libido shifts constantly between the subject's representation of himself and that of his love-objects, so that the ego is never able to establish a firm and unshakeable sense of identity.

Finally, the question needs to be examined from the angle of the functions of the *paradoxical system*. The thoughts that are associated with it, as we have seen, give new access to latent material and lead to interpretations that are a little unusual, admittedly, but still not totally foreign to the classical way of seeing things. With this exception, however: the *paradoxical system* concerns more particularly the patient's fantasy-making powers which, either due to the occasional intervention of an economic factor, or to the role played by primary repression, cannot be fully deployed, at least for the time being. This state is not limited to a certain type of patient exclusively; in fact, anyone can be affected by it more or less severely, and for varying lengths of time. Interpretations connected with *paradoxical thoughts* confer a verbal form on the excluded representations which would not otherwise have received any preconscious cathexis, even at the price of major alterations. The virtue of these interpretations resides partly in the fact that, as they are formulated by another person who is at the same time oneself, they serve to shake up a rigid economic status quo: first, because their timing and content is appropriate and, second, because they are often the fruit of displacement and condensation. A portion of the energies that are normally bound up in the higher systems acquires a momentary capacity to circulate freely, and becomes available for cathecting those productions of the unconscious that have been excluded. This mobilisation, which probably occurs at the point at which thing-presentations are connected with word-presentations, is bound to generate a certain amount of anxiety.

Besides the very particular effect of the *paradoxical system* on interpretation, I must also mention one of its most remarkable effects on the patient's situation. I have always noted with a great deal of interest how patients sometimes say to us, "You're not there," or "I can't sense your presence any longer, where are you?" They may even think that the analyst is quite simply dead, behind them, in his armchair. Remarks of this kind do not necessarily express aggressiveness on the analysand's part; neither should they always be attributed to distraction, to an evasion of the analyst. The fact is that they tend to occur especially when the analyst is invaded by *paradoxical thoughts*, thoughts that concern the patient to the highest degree. Thus, although at this very moment the analyst is completely preoccupied with himself, *the patient experiences for a moment an authentic experience of mourning*, which brings to light another function of the *paradoxical system*. Doubts concerning the analyst's existence stir up a violent relational appetite in the analysand.

Having retained something of their initial status of extra-territoriality, instinctual impulses are suddenly mobilised, no doubt with the aim of obtaining satisfaction, but above all in order to be taken up again and assimilated organically—in other words, introjected in the Ferenczian sense of the term. In this respect, I concur, as I have already done in the analysis of the fantasy "If I were dead" (de M'Uzan, 1974), with the point of view that Nicolas Abraham and Maria Torok have set out so well (Abraham & Torok, 1972; Torok, 1968).

When *paradoxical functioning* is set in motion, the analysand may have the feeling that he has lost a portion of his instinctual energy because the other carries it away with him by effacing himself. But once the analyst has recovered most of the narcissistic libido he had lost, once he has reassumed his value as an object and articulated desire, what had been a threat now proves to be an opportunity for the analysand to recover some of the instinctual strivings that were activated in the situation of mourning, and to integrate them organically into his being, thereby enriching its quest for authenticity. It is this that leads me to think that the subject's construction owes much to an uninterrupted succession of fantasised experiences of mourning.

It is generally assumed that the ego is formed by virtue of its successive identifications. That may be true as far as its strictly instrumental functions are concerned. But I sometimes wonder if it is not also in this way that it becomes false in relation to itself, for the truest "I" cannot lie anywhere else than in the development of instinct, that is, in what is most fundamental and, like the unconscious itself, most unacceptable for the mind.

Note

1. The expression "*être de bonne composition*" might normally translate as "good natured", but here the meaning, as indicated, is more of not being fussy or difficult regarding food. There is obviously a play on words, though, because the analyst takes up the formulation "*bonne composition*" at the literal level by asking if the patient perhaps meant "*bonne à manger*".

CHAPTER THREE

The work of dying* (1976b)

"*The terrible thing about the dead is their gestures, which live on in our memory. For then they are dreadfully alive, and we are at a loss to understand*"

—Albert Cohen (*Book of My Mother*, 1954, p. 62)

It is often said that what a person goes through in the last moments of his or her life can only be understood in terms of physiological or biological processes, as if the changes that occur in the psychical apparatus necessarily elude every effort to understand them. The analyst, like the philosopher, should thus simply give up. This way of seeing things is typical of our modern sensibility. In ancient times, notes Kurt Eissler (1955), people sometimes thought they could see in the last agony the struggle of a god or an angel with the demons. In short, they did not hesitate to tell stories and create phantasmagoria describing allusively what goes on in the mind *in extremis*, during this stage of transition or passage which is the topic of this chapter.

---

*This chapter was first published as a paper in *De l'art à la mort*, pp. 182–199. Paris: Gallimard, 1977.

33

In fact, I had already been interested in this subject for some time (see de M'Uzan, 1974, p. 151) when, in 1974, three Nobel laureates, J. Monod, L. Pauling, and G. Thomson, published a manifesto in *The Humanist* in support of euthanasia (reproduced in *Le Figaro* on 1 April 1974). I have kept a copy of this text which, at the time, caused something of a stir, and reading it again now has reminded me of something one of my first analysands used to say to me. From time to time, this man, who was completely unacquainted with psychoanalytic knowledge, would remark: "I think that ... but my intuition tells me that ...", the second part of the sentence, of course, almost always contradicting the first. The thesis presented in the manifesto immediately plunged me into a comparable situation. On the one hand I thought I shared spontaneously and without any reservations the ideas in question; and, on the other, just as I was on the point of giving deeper thought to this theme of dying, my "intuition", as the patient would have said, led me to think along quite different lines. So I will have to try to reconcile what are partly contradictory thoughts.

Moral principles, the signatories of the manifesto assert, cannot prevent anyone from putting an end to their life when they are suffering from a horrible disease against which the known remedies have no effect. It "would be barbarous and cruel", they claim, to keep a person alive against his or her will after the "dignity, beauty, promise, and meaning" of life have vanished; and they go on to say that the "imposition of needless suffering is an evil that should be avoided by civilised society". From this point of view, when "living fully" is no longer possible, euthanasia should be a hope and even a right for each person. This line of argument seems irrefutable; in any case, generally speaking, only very conventional moral or religious principles such as the merits of courage, the value of confronting the tragic dimension of existence, the virtues of suffering, and so on, are set against it. In the manifesto, however, there were two points in particular that gave me food for thought: first, the impossibility of living fully, a notion that is at once categorical and imprecise, suggesting underlying narcissistic problems such as the fear of not being able to meet the demands of the ego ideal; and second, the ethical consideration that "death should be seen as part of the life-continuum". But how is one to reconcile this conception, which, by the author's own admission, is of a moral or philosophical order, with the purely material act that is supposed to give life and death alike their full dignity? If death is no longer only an ultimate biological accident, the final effect of somatic degradation, then we are bound to consider it as a psychical event and to act accordingly.

Psychoanalytic reflection, as we know, has approached the problem of death essentially through the phenomena of repetition and aggression—that is to say, through phenomena that are observable in life. One could equally well, by going in the reverse direction, start from death and turn towards life—or more exactly, towards a very particular aspect of life that has reached its term. It is not that I wish to make a projection of death into life, going right back to its very origin, as certain ontologies have proposed (Heidegger, 1927). My purpose here is simply to reflect on the terminal phase of the existence of the subject who is irremediably condemned, in other words, dying in a broad sense. You may well object that the infinitely varied forms of the process defy all analysis. Moreover, if analysts have dwelt at such length on the subject of mourning which, for its part is very accessible, they have had little opportunity to draw on death in the form of "clinical material" as a basis for reflection, unless they have worked in a general hospital, where the most diverse aspects of the experience of death can be observed. Furthermore, those who have seen opportunities for research in this domain, and have partly oriented their work in this direction, often seem to have stopped short for reasons which would merit examination in themselves.

Analysis is nevertheless the best way of not missing out on this essential psychical activity, this final task that each person has to accomplish during the transition or passage, literally speaking, from life to death. If the manifesto of the Nobel laureates left me so perplexed, it was because it expresses the belief that death should be seen as part of the life-continuum; but it does not take into account all the logical consequences that this implies. Who would not recognise the need to curtail the suffering of a person so as to guarantee him or her a dignified ending? But one cannot overlook the fact that this position leads indirectly to neutralising the psychic work that the dying can accomplish naturally. On the other hand it is no less certain that physical suffering can seriously affect mental activity, but who is to decide? By right, the person who has to endure it, yet when a person is on the point of dying, they are plagued by contradictory thoughts. So, when they ask the medical staff to hasten their end, they are silently expressing an altogether different request which needs decoding. Deep down, people who are dying do not want those around them to withdraw from the relationship emotionally, from the relationship of mutual commitment that they are proposing almost secretly, sometimes unwittingly, which will in fact determine how the *work of dying* unfolds. In fact, owing to what I imagine to be a sort of instinctual knowledge, they enter into an ultimate relational experience. While the ties linking them to others are on the verge of dissolving absolutely, they are paradoxically elevated by powerful and, in some respects, passionate stirrings. They hyper-cathect their love-objects who are indispensable to their final effort to assimilate everything in their instinctual life that has not yet been assimilated, as if they were trying to put themselves into the world completely before leaving it.

The reader may be astonished that I have as yet made no reference to the death instinct. It is a deliberate choice for which I have already given an explanation elsewhere (de M'Uzan, 1974). I think, in fact, that if we want to examine the clinical facts with an open mind, it is better to put this issue aside provisionally. In other words, however useful it may be at another level, getting bogged down in an interminable discussion on this subject exposes us to the risk of losing contact with reality. Further-more, clinical experience has always led me to put less emphasis on a death instinct than on modes of instinctual functioning, or if you prefer, on its *destiny* (see de M'Uzan, 1972). Rather than expressing an opinion on the instinctual nature of certain apparently lethal tendencies, I prefer to preserve the functional oppositions—for example, the antagonism between the principle of constancy and the principle of inertia—which, in the case we are concerned with, seem to me to provide an adequate theoretical framework.

* * *

Analysts who have had the opportunity of following terminally ill patients in psychotherapy, or even of observing them for a sufficient length of time, are few and far between. Their experience is especially valuable, particularly when they have captured it in detailed case pres-entations, as is the case, for example, with Kurt Eissler (1955), Janice Norton (1963), and Elisabeth Kübler-Ross (1969). The latter, moreover, was a professor of psychiatry at Chicago University, where she set up a research seminar specifically focused on this category of patients. Now, notwithstanding the fact that the authors all take rigorous case obser-vations as their starting point, carried out with an acute sense of clini-cal work, each of them comes to conclusions that are sometimes very contradictory. One has the feeling that contrary thoughts exist side by side, some of which depend essentially on countertransferential findings and theoretical references, while others are derived from a deep emotional attitude, an obscure but profound intuition. And while intuition makes it possible to really understand closely what is going on, it is relegated to the background as soon as it comes to formulating a theory.

Kurt Eissler, for example, rightly points out that the therapist of such patients must recognise and fulfil their wishes even before they have been expressed (1955, p. 126). Citing Jones (1911), he stresses the significance of this absolute availability which, for the therapist, amounts to making a gift of his own life to the patient. In this way, the patient can transform the horror of having been "chosen" by death, while life goes on in the world, into a death that is shared with another person whom he takes with him—corresponding perhaps to a new birth. Eissler is thus fully aware of the intense transference of these patients who, far from separating from their love-objects, seek substitutes for them as soon as they are absent. That does not prevent him from writing a bit further on that, as death draws near, the agony would be eased if the patient were capable of a sort of work of mourning vis-à-vis his love-objects. By enabling him to decathect the world prior to his demise, this would lead him to accept death as a "natural consequence of the energic constellation in that moment" (p. 181). Eissler sees very clearly that as long as the existence of the objects is clearly perceived in reality, such a decathexis is not likely; but this does not diminish the contrast that exists between his clinical observations and his theoretical commentary.

The remarkable work of Janice Norton raises similar criticisms. The case in question, moreover, is nothing less than exemplary. It concerns a young married mother of two children, who Janice Norton took into psychotherapy during the terminal period of a metastatic breast cancer. The patient, we are told, was not particularly neurotic and was perfectly aware of her condition. She knew she had very little time left to live, a few months at the most. As is frequently the case, the perspective of her impending death had seriously disturbed her relations with those who meant most to her. Thus her husband, her parents, and a sister, who all loved her tenderly, "had so decathected their relationship with the patient that it proved impossible for them to help; to them, in many respects, she was already dead or had in any event delayed her dying too long" (1963, p. 544). In spite of the defection of her loved ones and the progression of her illness with its accompanying infirmities—for instance, intermittent blindness—"her need for people, far from diminishing, had in fact increased" (p. 547). Janice Norton seems to have been immediately sensitive to this need; she responded to it spontaneously and soon noticed that a very intense transference had developed which she was able to follow into its most regressive aspects. Quite rightly, these were understood as a means of maintaining a constant and intensely cathected object relationship with the therapist at all levels. This process went so far that although the patient would speak about her "silly illogical imagination" she sometimes had the feeling that Janice Norton was with her twenty-four hours a day and that she was constantly talking to her. During her regressive transference, the patient repeated something that was connected with her relations with her mother, and Janice Norton quickly understood that she had to take on certain functions of her patient's ego, just as the mother's ego functions as an external ego for her developing child.

Janice Norton claims, moreover, that the essential aspect of the psychotherapy, its major objective, is to facilitate the development of this regressive transference relationship as much as possible so as to *protect the patient against any feeling of object loss*. As a result, when sufficient support from the family and medical staff is lacking, exposing the patient to what he or she fears most, namely, dying alone, it is the therapist who is in the best position to contain all the patient's cathexes. In the case presented, the patient, we are told, seems to have resolved the problem of the inevitable separation from the therapist by taking her with her into death, in her fantasy, sometimes adding, "although not at this time". This incorporation of the object, which is of the same nature as that which enabled the patient to hallucinate the constant presence of Janice Norton, is comparable up to a certain point with what can be observed in the work of mourning; but up to a certain point only, for the work of mourning is only accomplished completely if it allows the cathexes of the lost objects to be retrieved. Although the young woman had indeed withdrawn emotionally to some extent from those who meant most to her, the libido thereby liberated, and even exalted, was immediately re-employed in her relationship with her therapist, someone whom she had no intention of separating from and of mourning. And, as she was practically sure that her last object would not turn away from her, she had no reason to withdraw the libido placed in her representation. All that is clear in the case report, but then why does Janice Norton subscribe to Eissler's views concerning the benefits for the dying patient of mourning his or her objects prior to death? Why does she seem to think that the main characteristic marking the last months of the life of her patient was the work of mourning she carried out in relation to her family love-objects, when the real object, on whom everything was concentrated, was actually herself? How could she help the young woman to die by helping her avoid any experience of object-loss, and believe at the same time that it is easier to die when one has withdrawn emotionally from one's objects, in other words, when one is already emotionally dead?

All these contradictions are present, of course, in the therapist's self-analysis, and I am only emphasising them so insistently because they seem to me to be inevitable, especially as, given the importance of real people and of their actual presence, which is absolutely decisive, we tend to underestimate the role of object-representations and of the fantasies in which they are enmeshed. Likewise, the vividness of what occurs at the level of conscious processes prevents us from understanding clearly the fantastic topographical upheaval that occurs in these ultimate moments. Finally, by concerning ourselves almost exclusively with the vicissitudes of affects—understood, moreover, in the most restrictive sense—we tend to neglect those of the instinct, whereas the "new structural processes" of which Eissler himself speaks might well depend on them. But it is also that the theme of death fascinates us so much that we forget to examine the fate of the libido whose movements, towards the end, are just as worthy of attention as those that prevailed at the beginning of life. For my part, I have always been struck by the fact that what escapes us so often is perceived and understood perfectly well by caregivers or attentive medical staff (see de M'Uzan, 1974). The day before their demise or in the hours leading up to it, the behaviour of some patients suggests the presence of a surprising amount of instinctual energy, a regressive avidity that is positively *uncanny*, which might almost induce one to speak of a flaring up of desire.

For example, one patient who had completely lost her appetite suddenly started eating voraciously. While one would have expected an accelerated extinction of all the life processes, all of a sudden, the life urge seems to ignite again, albeit in a rather unusual form that makes one feel somewhat uneasy. And as those who are still present are gripped by anxiety, they are in a complete state of denial. Blind to the significance of the fatal prognosis concerning their condition, they begin to believe in a miraculous remission. It will be said that this does not happen very often, which is true, but statistical arguments have no significance when one is seeking to determine the remarkable nature of a fact. Furthermore, the "passion" I am speaking of is not always spectacular, and it is easy for anyone who wants to put their head in the sand not to see it. We should not lose sight of the relational aspect of the phenomenon though, in which the cathected love-objects are, as it were, surrounded by innumerable pairs of arms and invited secretly to participate in a sort of manic celebration.

I can recall a case very similar to the one described by Janice Norton, involving a young woman who was also in the terminal phase of a metastatic cancer. Until the end, her behaviour astounded all those around her, me included; at the time, I must admit, I could not understand it at all. In the awful condition she was in, as you can well imagine, with diffuse metastases in her bones, affecting even the spinal column, she formed an authentic loving relationship with one of her surgeons, the same one, in fact, who had informed her clearly of her condition, and consequently of the prognosis. Although no one was in doubt as to the genuine nature of this relationship, some were none the less somewhat shocked by the surgeon's attitude, for he was a person of great intelligence and high moral values, who, after being caught up in the transference movement, had obscurely sensed that there was something fundamental involved. But the young woman's surge of energy was not limited to this expression of love; she also managed to bring some personal work of art to a conclusion; and, to ensure its success, she took part just a few days before she died in an artistic happening to which she was taken by ambulance. On that day, everyone saw her smiling, elegantly dressed, and brilliant, while her doctors and nurses were trembling at the thought of the foreseeable accident that might destroy this intensity of life in an instant.

Before meeting Janice Norton, her future patient had had a very similar experience to that of this young woman. A Protestant minister had been visiting her regularly, during which time they engaged in philosophical discussions together on immortality. Although she was highly sceptical of standard religious doctrine, the patient took pleasure in these meetings. Gradually, these conversations with the minister took on a more personal turn and, sure enough, the day came when she confided to him that she might be falling in love with him. One can imagine the minister's reaction which, as it turned out, was less profound than the surgeon's. He responded by telling her that all this was unrealistic, that she was ill, and so on. He began to visit her less frequently, and then took flight altogether. The impending perspective of death had in no way diminished the patient's need for others; on the contrary, it had increased it. Her creative faculties were also revived, and in the months following the appearance of the metastases, she began writing poems again. Another small detail, amid these strange transferences, provides a good illustration of the tenacious strivings of the libido. One day, the young woman asked Janice Norton if, after her death, she would wear a red dress for her that she had bought just before the onset of her illness in the hope of making herself more attractive.

* * *

These observations which, incidentally, are by no means exceptional, clearly show the two essential traits that are characteristic of the terminal phase, namely, *libidinal expansion* and *an exaltation of the desire for relationships*. These two closely interrelated tendencies govern the particular psychical activity that I have called the *work of dying*. I am naturally thinking of the work of mourning but also of the dream-work which, in its own way, obeys an exigency of the same order. This comparison is in no way arbitrary and is borne out by a remarkable fact that proves that these two aspects of the same work are practically indissociable. Having witnessed helplessly the death of a man who was the victim of a cataclysmic haemorrhage, a colleague told me that he had seen the unfortunate man suddenly emerge from a state of unconsciousness into which he had fallen, crying out, just before dying, "I have just had a strange dream." In this dramatic episode, the man was quite clearly making an ultimate effort before dying, as if he wanted or felt obliged to make something out of what was happening to him.

There is a common belief that a human being sees his or her entire life unfold in images at the very moment of dying. But how is this so, and why? What meaning should be attributed to this sort of sacrifice of one's past life which is now accomplished? To come to a better understanding of this extreme contraction of the last moment of life, we no doubt need to return to observation, to enquire into the purpose of this psychical activity whose effects are perceived more or less clearly, and to take account of an essential aspect of the problem, namely, temporality. In the parallel that can be made between the work of mourning and the *work of dying*, there is none the less one major difference that should not be overlooked. Unlike the person who is in mourning, the person who is dying has very little time at his disposal to accomplish what amounts to his last task. It is true that the way in which this "short space of time" is lived bears no comparison with what such a period of time would normally represent in life. For my part, I am inclined to think that at the very end there occurs an extraordinary condensation of temporal facts, as if consciousness were progressively affected by the law of timelessness that reigns in the unconscious. Furthermore, it is likely that the *work of dying*, in the sense which I am giving to it, begins well before the last agony. For Janice Norton's patient, as for the young woman whose case I have reported, it had certainly begun several months before death intervened; partly, perhaps, because they had been clearly informed about their condition. From my point of view, moreover, this creates the most favourable situation.

Elisabeth Kübler-Ross (op. cit.), who has studied more than 200 cases, at least partly shares this viewpoint, when she proposes to replace the question, "Should I inform my patient?" by "How am I going to share this knowledge with him?" At any rate, she adds, whether they had been informed or not, most of them, if not all, "knew". Does *the work of dying* begin, then, from the moment the patient "knows"? I am inclined to think that it begins very early on, for the morbid processes taking place in the body are always identified by the psychical apparatus at some level or another; after which, they are given shape, related symbolically, and dramatised like in a dream that is destined to be forgotten, which already implies that the libido is involved to a certain extent. For Elisabeth Kübler-Ross, who is above all mindful of what affects the conscious ego, patients who have been informed of their condition go through several phases from refusal and denial to acceptance, or the abandonment of impossible hope, via intermediary stages of anger, bargaining, depression, and resignation. If the *work of dying* begins quite early on, as I believe it does, it is possible that it only really takes place once the patient has gone beyond the phase of depression and reaches a sort of acceptance of destiny which, as I was given to observe on one occasion, can occur within a very short time.

With some people, the representations of their love-objects are so powerfully cathected that the *work of dying* is initiated all by itself, but more often than not—and the cases I have cited are good examples of this—the presence of a real person is indispensable. Whether it is a loved one, a doctor, or an analyst, what is important is that this person is genuinely available, trustworthy in the patient's eyes, and capable of meeting the patient's elementary needs, which means that he or she is able to accept that a part of him or herself is included in the funereal orbit of the one who is dying. I prefer this formula to that of empathy or identification, which is always selective, because it takes more adequate account of the essential fact that, when the love-objects or their substitutes fall disastrously short of expectations, withdrawing emotionally from the dying person, what is at stake in reality is the ancestral fear of being carried off and devoured by the one who is dying. These fears are abundantly illustrated in folklore, but even in everyday experience it is not uncommon to hear a survivor affirm that the deceased is still trying to snatch him from beyond the grave.

I will return later to the consequences of the failure of objects; for the time being I simply want to point out that when the object is no longer able to assume his or her role, the representation of this object alters in the patient's mind; the latter substitutes the relationship with the object by an identification, or to use the expression used by Fuchs (1937, p. 269) in his study of introjection, by the edification of a *monument*. As the transference capacities of the dying person increase, owing to the *paradoxical* movement I have described in Chapter Two, they gradually concentrate their deep interests on just one person who, moreover, is not necessarily among those who are dearest to them. What is important, in fact, is that the chosen object is capable of exposing him or herself, without excessive anxiety, to the broad captivating movement that tends to envelop them entirely; in other words, that there is not too great a difference between what they are and the representation of them in the patient's mind. The dying person thus forms with his or her object what I shall call their *last dyad*, in allusion to the mother of whom the object might very well be a last incarnation. The cry of a man calling out for his mother just before expiring, be it an appeal for help or an announcement of their forthcoming reunion, is the most striking example of this synonymy of the mother and death, which becomes patient when certain limits of the struggle for life have been exceeded. In any case, the dying person and his or her *key object* constitute a sort of organism, almost an independent body, which, in order to grow, requires physical contact between its elements. I fear that we always underestimate the importance of this elementary contact, even if it is limited to two clasped hands, when all verbal exchange has become impossible.

There is something comparable here with the organism formed by the mother and her newborn baby; or alternatively with the developing bodily schema, when the global and integrated image depends on successive moments of contact between the diverse segments of the body. At the heart of this organisation, any movement affecting one of the protagonists has repercussions on, and is amplified in, the other person; the slightest countertransference withdrawal is translated immediately by a more or less subtle modification of behaviour that dislocates the *dyad*. This relationship is so fragile that any emotional withdrawal is fatal to it; furthermore, to maintain it, the key object should not be constantly subject to an overriding need to maintain the stability of his or her identity. In other words, they should be able to provide and guarantee a reliable presence and tolerate a certain vagueness of their identity, living almost in a state of absence. This is by no means an easy task, but not an impossible one; for, in fact, we never achieve a sense of identity that is indubitable, perfectly stable, and definite, without ambiguity. For the most part, though, this relative status of *a-personalisation* is perhaps only accessible in certain extreme moments, and results naturally from the primal non-differentiation of the "I" and the "non-I" which, in my view, is never completely reduced and is always ready to reappear, even outside the field of psychopathology. If, in the organic unity formed by the dying person and his or her key object, the "I" is always partly deposited in the other person, while moving about in the transitional space that I have described elsewhere as the *spectrum of identity* (de M'Uzan, 1994), it is because the narcissistic libido remains caught in the object-representations, which may be *other* without losing their familiar character. In this respect, the end of life profoundly resembles its beginning, something that is confirmed by observation and which would probably also be familiar to us instinctually if it were not for our preconceived ideas. This analogy, of which popular wisdom and the poets have often had a premonition, can even be said to have a dynamic value of a sort, insofar as death participates throughout life in the construction of the human subject and in the process of individualisation of which he or she is capable. This hypothesis sets me in contradiction with what I was saying earlier about the retrogressive projection of death into life, but should not be excluded entirely.

It is easy to conceive how the processes that I have in mind here are disruptive at the topographical level. At a certain moment the ego of the person who is going to die both knows and does not know this; the id, for its part, continues to desire and to manifest itself, with the unexpected consent of the ego, which has none the less been alerted by instinctual exacerbation. The proximity of the inevitable end causes a sort of split in the ego, which results in two lines of contradictory thought existing alongside each other, each expressing itself independently of the other. According to one, death, by virtue of a veritable denial, simply does not exist; according to the other, which is asserted equally clearly, there is no other solution than to resign oneself to the inevitable or even to hope that it will all be over as quickly as possible. In short, we find ourselves faced here with a situation that is very similar to psychosis, except for the fact that it does not derive from a mental disorder. In such cases, however, the position is more akin to the neurotic schema, for the attitude of resignation barely masks a perfectly conscious appetite for relationships, while the instinctual foundations are either completely ignored or perceived indirectly, at a moment when the displacement on to the transference-object makes the latter the representative of the dying person in the world, where experiences of satisfaction are lived. It is in this sense that the gift of the red dress that Janice Norton received from her patient could be interpreted.

Such an impulse does not, however, prevent the ego, which is no doubt partly governed by its ideal, from sometimes proudly claiming its right to die, but even then, it has no real power over the transference process. We would still have to agree on the sense to be given to the notion of transference; for my part, I have adopted here, as I have done elsewhere (de M'Uzan, 1974 and 1976a), the definition proposed by Ferenczi and taken up by Maria Torok (1968) and Nicolas Abraham (1972).

In Janice Norton's case report, we saw how the patient's interests were concentrated on just one object, and how a past relationship was repeated in the process; but, above all, how the analyst found herself gradually incorporated and digested. Thanks to the progressive distension of her psychic being, the dying person absorbs the object into his or her erotic space, sometimes so totally that he or she no longer senses the absence of the real person. This disturbance of internal and external perceptions, linked to a profound regression of object relations, can, of course, disappear during free periods when the ego's functions are entirely exempt from regression. But this period when the boundaries between inside and outside tend to be erased can also last for a long time. And when the object-representation is almost entirely charged with the narcissistic libido with which it is cathected by the dying person, one can say that the subject's boundaries no longer have any stability. It is precisely this "phagocytic-like" movement that those accompanying the dying person find increasingly difficult to tolerate.

Other people are unable, in fact, to understand the meaning that this indefinite expansion of psychic life can have in someone who, they clearly feel, tends to include them in himself and to dissolve them. How can they possibly realise that, as *"incorporated objects"*, they are in the service of a final passion thanks to which the dying person may be able to repossess and assimilate a whole mass of instinctual desires which, hitherto, he or she had only been able to integrate incompletely? Janice Norton's patient is certainly not the only one to have feared that she was no longer attractive, and to have mourned all the experiences that she was unable to have and would never share with those she loved. Escaping the ordinary limitations imposed by the laws of temporality, those that govern the higher systems, the prodigious expansion of the ego that accompanies the last agony is thus in the service of an instinctual introjection which, in return, enhances the subject by dilating indefinitely his narcissism.

PART II

THE MOUTH OF THE UNCONSCIOUS

CHAPTER FOUR

The person of myself* (1983)

*T*he person of myself. This was how a famous patient of Jean-Pierre Falret, the French psychiatrist (1794–1870) referred to her *other me* (*autre moi*), born of a split in her personality. Everything that proceeds from this strange double, its voice, sensations, etc., is endowed with a singular status: it belongs to the subject, as nothing else can do more; and, at the same time, it forms part of the outside world, since the subject's ego has in a certain way been objectified in it.

Can any ordinary form of speech be considered to be as self-evident as a delusional idea? Yet as analysts we dream of provoking this sense of self-evidence, so that we may wonder if the chances of an analytic interpretation being successful do not rest on the potentially active and utilisable presence in every patient of those psychic processes that determine the most morbid pathological evolutions.

* * *

Every analyst has had the following experience on any number of occasions: confident that he has grasped the deep meaning of what

*This chapter was first published as a paper in the *Nouvelle Revue de Psychanalyse*, 28: 193–208, in 1983.

his patient has said, he has given an interpretation which has gone unheeded. Once again, the interpretation has not been *taken up*; it has had no effect. Whatever the patient's attitude may be, it is as if nothing has happened, even though there can be no doubt that he or she has heard the interpretation. Worse still, the situation has sometimes changed in subtle ways: the resistance, for example, has become more tenacious, or has taken on a new form that is difficult to detect. The irony of the situation is that what has just happened constitutes the exact opposite of the famous efficacy of an inexact interpretation (Glover, 1955).

This very ordinary situation is, as we know, not a new one. It seems that analysts became particularly aware of it just after the First World War. At that time, psychoanalysis was certainly still regarded as a prodigious instrument for understanding psychic processes but, in a more or less indirect way, its therapeutic power was already being called into question. Recently, André Green (1983) has emphasised the role played by this doubt in the elaboration of the new structural conception of the psychic apparatus.

In an attempt to go beyond the limits of their activity or, at the very least, to understand these limits better, analysts pursued their investigations by examining in greater depth, and even revising, their ideas on mental functioning, and further by submitting their technique to critical scrutiny. Coming up against the stumbling block of neurosis, they turned their attention, as if in headlong flight, to pathological entities which, on the face of it, concerned them less, but whose study contributed a great deal to the theory—with the risk, since the role of sexuality was seen as reduced here, of ensuring the victory of repression.

The introduction of a new drive dualism, arising above all from a critical study of the phenomena of repetition, undoubtedly represented an original speculative effort, but it also sought to explain the negative therapeutic reaction. Since then it has been primarily through the study of narcissism that the most important theoretical contributions have been made (I am thinking in particular here of the work of Heinz Kohut and Bela Grunberger). These contributions have undoubtedly helped us achieve a better understanding of certain structural characteristics that are responsible for the failure of many treatments. But then we almost have the impression that we are dealing with a sort of fatality specific to the human mind (a line of thought inspired by André Green's work on narcissism: he has proposed that the concept of negative narcissism be set alongside that of positive narcissism). Both in the "normal" subject and in the psychotic, the ego finds itself both split and affected directly by the death drive, and is thus exposed to the consequences of a prevalence of the principle of inertia (Green, 1983).

Speaking of fatality, I am led to comment on what I regard as an extreme position held by Christian David (1983). For him—and his arguments count—the analyst necessarily comes up against something irreducible in his or her practice. He or she is confronted by an insurmountable obscurity that is characteristic of "every situation that brings into play the fundamental elements of the mind and notably affectivity" (p. 15). The means at our disposal, he says, are scarcely a match for what we are seeking to discover. In actual fact, and in opposition to the helplessness that he denounces, Christian David is already opening up a domain for future exploration when he emphasises the role of the dissociation between affectivity, a veritable instrument of knowledge, and the intellectual tool proper. But this opposition soon leads back to obscurity, for it is responsible for the eruption of "material which seems to elude every attempt to understand it" (p. 15). The counterpart of this failure is situated on the ethical level, since "awareness of the probable impossibility of crossing certain limits … goes hand in hand with a genuinely emotional approach to suffering" (p. 15). Such an approach is desirable, but is equally marked by helplessness.

One would have to be very presumptuous indeed to deny that impenetrable darkness reigns at the bottom of the mind and that suffering and conflicts are in part inextinguishable. I would suggest, however, paraphrasing Jaspers, that there are always grounds for pushing back as far as possible the point at which we are faced with the incomprehensible and, if I may say so, the intractable, which requires us to ignore temporarily and tactically the fact that the power of analysis has limits.

On the other hand, to suggest, as has been done, that our failures result either from a hypothetical quality of the libido, viscosity, or from an unshakeable resistance of the id, or again from a Machiavellian subjection to repetition, almost amounts to incriminating the patient; unless, that is, we acknowledge that the analyst himself can be affected by these perverse effects, which naturally requires him or her to engage in a permanent process of self-analysis.

And yet these same negative phenomena could lead us to undertake a critical review of our technique which, as we know, is eminently perfectible. Why should we not endeavour to make its rules clearer or even to introduce innovations that would remain metapsychologically coherent? This second path of investigation was one that analysts took a long time ago already, sometimes exposing themselves to the risk of seeing new technical operations lead to certain excessive revisions of the theory.

The work pursued by Reich from 1925 to 1933 (see Reich, 1933), as well as that of James Strachey (1934), among many other equally important contributions (I am thinking, in particular, of the symposium on the variations of the classical technique at the 20th International Congress of Psychoanalysis in Paris in 1957), constitute, it is well to bear in mind, a basic reference in our ordinary practice. But I want to turn my attention in particular to Ferenczi's contribution. We know that Ferenczi was particularly sensitive to a divergence between the way certain treatments evolved and the degree of theoretical understanding attained by the patient and his or her analyst, and that this led him to introduce technical innovations. His "active technique", which was heavily criticised, even though the indications for it were considered to be exceptional, sought to "enable the patient … to comply more successfully with the rule of free association and thereby to assist or hasten the exploring of the unconscious material" (Ferenczi, 1920, p. 198). The artefices specific to this technique tend to irritate the ego's sensibility, leading to heightened resistance, increased violence at the level of the internal conflict, and thus to an exacerbation of the symptoms. For Ferenczi, new states of tension then emerge and the quietude of remote or deeply repressed psychic domains is disturbed. But the "active technique" should only play the part of an *agent provocateur*. The injunctions and prohibitions that characterise it assist, first and foremost, in obtaining repetitions that must then be interpreted (p. 217).

Very many causes have been invoked, both circumstantial and structural, for the disappointing outcomes of certain treatments. I cannot mention them all, and furthermore it is not central to my argument. So I will confine myself to those that seem to me to be essential, the study of which led me to formulate the following thesis.

The chances of an interpretation being successful are greater when it meets two *obligations*. The first is of an *economic* order. It is important that both in its formulation and its "timing" the interpretation takes full account of the status and the regime of energy in the different psychic systems. The second, I would say, through an extension of meaning, is of an *immune* order, meaning that the interpretation should be homogeneous with the ego (as I have done elsewhere, I maintain a certain semantic indeterminacy that must be clarified by the context) without which there is a risk that it would not be assimilable, in the literal sense of the term.

The fulfilment of these two obligations depends on a prior condition: both the status of the energy in the system Pcs/Cs and the sense of identity must first be subject to a disturbance. Both these changes occur in one of the two registers of the activity of the psychical apparatus, that is to say, the quest for satisfaction, and the construction and preservation of identity.

The peace of the conscious mind is never so well assured as when everything that stands in the way of the free circulation of energy triumphs. While the linking up of ideas or groups of ideas constitutes one of the positive functions of the ego, this act of binding, by fixing a certain quantity of energy, resists both the eruption and cathexis of new ideas. Cohesion militates against change; that is the downside of the benefit it procures. Such change is never easily accepted, for violent emotions always emerge when, even for a limited period of time, the preconscious begins to function in a primary process mode. Thus, although the operations of binding protect against any influx, and even more so, against any disrupting surges of energy, thus against any recognition of guilt- and anxiety-laden ideas, they do not leave much room for progress.

Just like the patient, the analyst—perhaps too often—avoids these storms, either because he fears that he will not be able to control them or, more obscurely, as if by contagion or in a mirror response, because he is afraid of being affected by them himself. He then runs the risk of becoming, against his will, the ally of resistance, which has an immediate impact on his interpretative activity. It will be remarked that as interpretation is constituted essentially, though not only, of words (C. David, in the text cited earlier, rightly confers a structural value on vocal inflection, its tone and rhythm), it primarily addresses or concerns the ego. That is true. But it is not enough to have brought the different terms of a thing-presentation into relationship with the corresponding word-presentation; it is also necessary for these terms to be able to combine, that is to say, to live, which in turn is only possible if the cathetic energy circulates freely, at least momentarily. Now, as the activity of interpretation has been affected, as I have just stated, it is expressed in excessively rational, explicative language. It is no longer even a message but a piece of information, a logical explanation that is addressed to the most differentiated levels of the ego where it will combine with the most intellectual forms of knowledge. Ultimately, the analyst addresses his patient as he would anyone else and lapses into textual explanations. He is very fortunate when anxiety does not induce him, unwittingly, to make recommendations. It is not that long and very elaborate interpretations should be rejected systematically; some are wholly justified and even necessary. I am thinking in particular of certain major reconstructions which bring an important phase of work to conclusion and are aimed at consolidating what has been acquired. They only become doubtful when our reasons for formulating them are unclear.

Metapsychological considerations, especially regarding technique, can so easily be abstract and arid that they may make us fall into a sort of mechanistic process that is quite alien to the phenomena we are faced with. Not to mention the fact that in the analytic situation we scarcely have the opportunity of indulging in complex metapsychological elaborations, given that the affective fabric of the exchanges is so resonant. We also know that many interventions come spontaneously to the analyst's lips, without prior reflection. It is often after the session that one comes back to this or that aspect of the material, first of all associatively, and then in order to construct its metapsychological architecture. In the long term, this work induces a sort of second nature that functions economically. Hence, and notwithstanding the reservations I have just expressed, it is natural that the analyst is constantly led to define metapsychologically what he observes and what he does.

That energy is essentially bound in the systems Pcs/Cs is a fact that the analyst experiences almost physically through the resistance. He is tempted to think that the lifting of this resistance depends on his efforts alone—that is, on an important expenditure of his own energy. One thing is certain, in any case: a full cathexis of the interpretations can only occur at the expense of the countercathexis, which must therefore be dismantled. Otherwise, the resistance will become more tenacious by feeding on a new knowledge which belongs to the reality-ego alone.

Furthermore, the most classical technical recommendations—I am thinking in particular of the contribution of Strachey (1934)—acknowledge implicitly that an interpretation of content should be accompanied by a modification of the status and regime of energy in the ego. The change in question, corresponding to the breaking through of primary processes into the preconscious, can also be considered as a phenomenon of *unbinding*. On the other hand, the increase of integrated knowledge won over from the dark regions of the unconscious, which is the aim of analytic work, belongs to Eros whose instrument is binding. Binding and unbinding thus stand in a dialectical relationship as the indissociable partners of one and the same process: unbinding follows on from sterile binding, but precedes fruitful binding.

Binding, an *economic scandal* in the higher systems, is the first of the two obligations I have defined. Multiple factors play a role in triggering it. In principle, this role should be entrusted once again to interpretation, and especially to interpretation of the defences. It is a classic question, although recommending that interpretation of the defences and interpretation of content be associated in one and the same sequence suggests, paradoxically, that interpretation of content could protect the ego from the economic disorder engendered by a disorganisation, albeit limited, of the countercathexis. I have always found it striking, moreover, to see how far any alteration in the economic status of the ego arouses a sense of uneasiness in the analyst. It is as if he or she feared being incapable of mastering a sudden influx of excitation, in short, being faced with a traumatic situation. The analyst is almost tempted to assume the functions of a protective shield, while in fact there is usually sufficient time to reduce the excitation to a level of activity that is more in line with the principle of constancy.

The analytic situation is in itself a factor of unbinding. While the fundamental rule structures an intersubjective relationship in an original way, when associated with free-floating attention, it also participates in the dismantling of economic blockages. It is therefore not surprising that this pairing causes anxiety, which then tends to become a source of fear that is inspired by the analyst, independently of classical projections.

The singular climate of the situation also owes much to another pairing uniting words and silence: discourse against a background of silence, silence that is broken by unexpected words. It is the unforeseeable manner of their distribution, encountered in no other circumstances, which, as it were, "trips up" the logic of the interpersonal exchanges. In his work, the analyst is not only concerned with understanding and transmitting what he has understood. He experiences the situation, perceives its "respiration" as if it were an organism, and strives to maintain its secret functional continuity and fertile fragility. He is sensitive to the suspension of psychic processes which are ready to resume their course, either by virtue of something the analyst says or thanks to the silence that conceals thoughts. The organic intertwining of silence and words preserves the energetic fluidity that is expressed by an agile and uneasy disposition of consciousness. The analyst should not be permanently preoccupied with decoding the material, as this would scarcely be compatible with the need to maintain a sufficient degree of free-floating attention. The encounter between two well-individualised persons, the analyst and the analysand, with everything that goes on between them, gives birth to a distinct entity of its components which I have referred to as a *chimera* (de M'Uzan, 1978b). This is why the analytic situation resembles an original creation in which the *characters* confront each other, as in a classical drama whose structure and development follow their own laws, relatively independently of the roles played by the actors. This is why one often feels disconcerted and dazzled immediately after a session.

Taken in its restricted sense, interpretation is thus just one of the instruments that play a role in the development of an analytic treatment, even if it is the main one. It must still correspond to the demands of what I have called an "original grammar". In order to thwart excessively rational and explicative interpretations, which always risk blocking the movement of the process, the type of interpretation that I have in mind here can neither be complete nor devoid of ambiguity; indeed, that is precisely why it plays a positive role in the economic disturbance that is necessary. What is more, I think it is beneficial, depending on the situation, to formulate the interpretation by using primary mechanisms such as displacement and, in particular, condensation. An additional advantage of this procedure, which essentially involves the analyst's "inspiration", is that it is sound from the topographical point of view. Thanks to the mechanisms that it employs, it has an effect at the level of the preconscious, at those frontiers of the unconscious that are still dependent on primary processes. It follows that thing-presentations have much more chance of becoming linked up with word-presentations, especially as, since interventions of this kind are in the nature of witty remarks, they allow for an economy in the expenditure of energy.

From a slightly different point of view, but based on experiences that are no doubt comparable, Kutrin A. Kemper (1965) contrasts direct and immediate interpretation with *allusive interpretation*. Relating either to current or past manifestations or to modes of reaction, this form of intervention consists of isolated words, incomplete sentences, or even illogical constructions. It makes use of symbols and analogies and is sometimes limited to mere syllables, or even sounds, which, in principle, should be in harmony with the emotional climate of the session. Allusive interpretation could also, in certain cases, and at certain moments, mobilise perceptions or representations corresponding to preverbal stages. It has the advantage over direct and immediate interpretation of not explaining everything, thereby allowing archaic ideas to be established and developed. The author cites, moreover, a passage from the general study of neuroses by Fenichel (1945), which I am going to reproduce here because it corresponds to a large extent to the criticisms that I have formulated. He writes:

> Many patients have retreated from the world of emotions to that of concepts and even beyond this world to a world of empty words. As psychoanalysis wants to influence emotions with the help of words, one can understand the danger, in particular with obsessional patients, that the words exchanged between the doctor and the patient remain isolated within the sphere of the word and the concept. (Cited by Kemper, 1965, p. 92)

Kutrin A. Kemper's "allusive" technique, which is somewhat impressionistic in my opinion, is not unrelated to my own conception, although I have not found in this author's work the economic references that are essential for me. Indeed, they are so essential that if I were to radicalise my position, I would readily see the permanent reorganisation of energy as the fundamental aim of analytic work. Apart from the power I confer on this technique with regard to the patient's capacity to invest interpretations fully, not only does it have the merit of imposing nothing, as Kemper says, but it also avoids the risk of introducing into the patient's mind heterogeneous and falsifying ideas. That would not be so harmful if they merely served to feed the countercathexis.

Analysts generally acknowledge that the best interpretations are often those that the analysand formulates himself. I am not thinking of rationalisations, which are frequent and easily identifiable, but of authentic interpretations that the patient formulates first in a dubitative tone, a little uneasily, before pursuing them with more assurance, expressing a bit too much satisfaction as if he had just made a profit. Yet the climate of the session still retains traces of the preceding moments: a slightly disordered associative drift or, alternatively, a surprising degree of concentration on one idea; or, on the contrary, a sort of dispersion of psychical activity. One could multiply the characteristics of these phenomena, but what is certain is that they all attest to an erosion of the resistance, that is, to the presence of a certain degree of unbinding in conscious activity.

The orientation of the analytic work towards a permanent modification of the economy might suggest that the analyst is not always capable of managing the situation. This could then result in a veritable unfurling of excitation that would be responsible either for a traumatic situation or for deep regressions that are uncontrollable and the source of severe decompensations. Theoretically, this is not impossible, especially in cases that are initially very regressive, though in such cases one would act differently. It would be out of place to accuse the analyst of pursuing, as it were, a policy "on the brink of the abyss"; for, in any case, effective analytic work cannot take place without the patient going through such difficult moments, which are often states that are more or less marked by depersonalisation. Andrew Peto (1959) drew attention to this fact long ago. Interpretative work, then, does not only affect the vicissitudes of the object-libido by causing more or less serious regressions, but also those of the narcissistic libido. This results in transitory alterations of the patient's sense of identity and sometimes the analyst's too. It is by no means the case that these states are always spectacular, but it is rare that traces of them cannot be found—for example, in the sudden appearance of a singular and unusual mode of mental functioning in a patient, who is astonished by it himself and says that he does not recognise himself in what he is saying.

* * *

All these phenomena, characterised by a vacillating sense of identity, are a prerequisite for the second order of obligations imposed on interpretation. For a while, they seemed to me to be more or less disturbing, more or less preoccupying "hiccups"; but then I came to see them as a necessary accompaniment and condition of mutative interpretation. Closely linked to the psychic work that is achieved in the register of the search for satisfaction, they indicate the phase of unbinding that is necessary if new capacities for cathexis are to develop. Finally, their positive functional value in interpretative activity became clear to me. It seems to me that the expression "functional value" gives an imperfect account of the essential role of the processes involved in the *assimilative integration of what is new*.

To the experience of seeing an apparently adequate interpretation go unheeded, another may be added which can be likened to it superficially. The analyst again has the feeling that his interpretation is not only exact, but economically opportune. In making it, he may even experience the famous "ring of truth" that convinces him of its aptness. The patient hears the interpretation, recognises and accepts it without compliance, and without undue haste, which is usually considered as a positive sign. And yet, a moment later, the analyst has a rather disagreeable feeling. It is as if there were a hole in the session; the analyst and patient are sometimes both astonished by it, and in other cases silence prevails. The analyst may have the feeling he has made a blunder. Even though he tells himself, not incorrectly, that just a moment before there was a slight disturbance of consciousness, that the associative drift was of good quality, not too fluid, and with moments of suspension, the situation has none the less deteriorated. It is as if the protagonists have each been sent back to their respective places, and the patient keeps his own counsel. The disturbance of consciousness has been transitory. The patient is affected by a superficial sense of irritation, and in some cases the analyst, too, who begins to feel rejected. Everything he ventures to say then risks being repudiated. The patient shows, in one way or another, that he wants the session to end. It is under such conditions that the image of an immune defence imposes itself, for the patient's reaction closely resembles that of an organism in which foreign molecules have erupted. The analyst's words belong so much to the non-ego that they can neither be accepted nor assimilated. The analyst himself appears to be really foreign; temporarily he has become wholly other.

Retrospectively the analyst may wonder, for instance, whether the patient was worried by a direct interpretation made in a peremptory tone, or if the economic disturbance caused a state of depersonalisation without regression, leaving the analysand no other option than to withdraw autarchically. The analyst may also ask himself if in his habitus, his tone, and his style, he has not personalised himself to the extreme, to the point of discouraging oral needs of absorption. I am far from always putting the patient's subjectivity in question when, at the beginning of a session, he or she asks me, in a slightly anxious voice, "Is something wrong? You look awful. I hardly recognise you." It may be that they are right and that something has happened within me, without my realising it, which is now blocking the introjective movement. Examples of this could be multiplied, showing at the very least that a relative indeterminacy of identities is necessary for the patient to be able to "recognise" him or herself in the interpretation, which thus becomes part of the ego.

Quite some time ago now (see de M'Uzan, 1974), the famous notion of the "strict delimitation of bodies" gave me much food for thought. Certainly, the definition of the sense of identity advanced in particular by Phyllis Greenacre (1958) retains its value. But it seems to me that her notion of the uniqueness of an integrated organism that recognises others without ambiguity is too rigid and needs correcting. The notion of identity, as I envisage it with regard to the adult in his relations both with others and with himself, suggests more the idea of oscillation. "I am me and not someone else" seems self-evident, and yet nothing is guaranteed, even if the ambiguity only manifests itself obscurely when everything is going well, and when one can trust in the boundaries of one's body and mind. In fact, everyone knows that it does not take long for this fine sense of certainty to crumble—for instance, when one loses oneself for a bit too long in the contemplation of one's own reflection.

The initial uncertainty as to what belongs to the external world and what belongs to the ego never disappears completely. It is not only a moment but a *motor* of development, thanks to its capacity to include and engulf objects or fragments of objects. By objects I mean both the external object and the parts of the subject's body, his instinctual world and even his thoughts. The activity of thought, Tausk (1933) points out, was experienced as coming from the external world before it was attributed to the ego as a function. From another perspective, since he has in mind the destructive processes directed against anything that seems to link one object to another, Bion (1967) also emphasises the fragility and the problematic character of every boundary: "I will suppose that there is a normal degree of projective identification, without defining the limits within which normality lies, and that associated with introjective identification this is the foundation on which normal development rests" (p. 103). Elsewhere, he stresses that "[S]ometimes the boundaries of a person do not correspond to the person's anatomical structure .... There may well be some analogue in the personality to the capillary blood system which ... may dilate" (Bion, 1977, p. 30). One cannot underline better the continuity, even in the healthy person, of the initial uncertainty of the boundaries of the human being, and of its function, as much in the distant past as in the present.

There is no shortage of references of this order. But it is in Ferenczi's work that we find the notions that allow us to get a better grasp of the essential aspects of the question. I shall mainly refer to the contributions he made on introjection and transference. We know that for Ferenczi (1912) introjection involves "an extension to the external world of the original auto-erotic interests, by including its objects in the ego" (p. 316). Every transference on to an object is thus an extension of the ego, that is to say, an introjection. "Man", writes Ferenczi, "can love only himself." Introjection thus appears as a process of dilatation in which what is absorbed and included loses a notable part of its identity, since the sensations themselves of pleasure and unpleasure, of auto-erotic origin, have already been displaced on to it.

I would add in passing that Ferenczi's views help to clarify further the notion of the transference. Transference corresponds, in fact, to the activity of two different but organically linked processes. On the one hand transference is the classical reliving of unconscious wishes derived from infantile experiences in the analytic relationship and, on the other, the introjective dilatation of the ego. One thing should be made clear, though. The processes of the dilatation of the ego, during which the primary indeterminacy of the frontiers between subject and object are experienced again, depends essentially on the vicissitudes of the narcissistic libido. The other is never completely other, since he can only be encountered through his representation which is situated in the ego of the subject and thus narcissistically cathected. The other can only constitute himself as fully other by committing an act of violence, and we know that sometimes interpretation can be such an act. As for the ego, it is never absolutely itself, for it is partly lost in the image of the objects that it cathects; and it is also occupied by the representations of the other which shape it up to a certain point. Its only chance of being as authentic as possible resides in the constant pursuit of instinctual introjection.

It was these theoretical and clinical arguments that led me to replace the notion of identity with that of the *spectrum of identity*, defined by the *loci* and quantities cathected by narcissistic libido, from the narrowest view of the ego to the image of the other in his full alterity (de M'Uzan, 1974). Midway between the extreme poles of the spectrum there is a zone of *floating individuation* which, in the register of identity, could correspond to the preconscious in the systemic conception of the psychical apparatus. Introjection is thus reduced to a mechanism of shifting frontiers. André Green (1966–67), examining Freud's remarks on the vicissitudes of the object in introjection, proposes a solution that does not seem unrelated to what I am saying: "Introjection becomes merged with the inscription of the framing circuit, thereby constituting the matrix of identifications and coinciding with the object's disappearance" (p. 87). Although such extreme moments of the *spectrum of identity* as the disappearance of the phagocyted object or, on the contrary, the dilution of the subject in the image of the other, only manifest themselves fully in very particular psychotic structures, they are nevertheless present and active in the background of all psychic life, in the same way as pregenital conflicts. The faculty that the narcissistic libido has of shifting position and of occupying propositions that are far removed from one another, just as the image of the subject is far removed from those of its objects, constitutes, in my opinion, a fruitful source of tension. Though the avatars of the sense of identity are generally related to psychopathology, they nevertheless offer possibilities for positive action when they occur in the analytic situation, where they sometimes resemble phenomena of mental automatism. I am in no way ascribing a pejorative character to them. Analysts recognise without too much difficulty the underlying psychotic processes in each person's mind; they have more difficulty, though, in accepting that these processes intervene positively in analytic work, and also in the very conception of interpretation.

A woman patient anxiously exclaimed: "But what's happening today? I have the impression that I am not myself." I responded: "You have probably lost me." She added: "Yes, probably .... It's like those souls that change their bodily form or inhabit a different body. But does that mean my mind is no longer in my body?" My intervention may seem strange, but for the layman many of our interpretations, even the most ordinary ones, are utterly absurd. Analysts will certainly regard the comparison between analytic interpretation and delusional interpretation as questionable; yet if we consider the order in which the phenomena occur, such a comparison is unavoidable. In both cases, the subject has been affected in the first place by a disturbance of his or her sense of identity. In psychotics this is very evident, but it is much more discrete in the analysands, and often only noticeable from the slightest of indications. Interpretation proper only plays a role secondarily. Although they are sometimes similar, it is neither the content nor the structure of the interpretation that best distinguishes the subjects in question. Paradoxically, what separates them also brings them closer together in a sort of mirror relationship. If the delusional patient produces his interpretations entirely by himself, or almost so, and *objectifies* his ego by placing it in the object, the analysand, for his part, listens to the analyst's interpretation with a view to *subjectivising* it. One of the conditions of the mutative interpretation is precisely that it must first be subjectivised by a patient who is capable of accepting an inaugural and momentary disturbance of his sense of identity.

Is it necessary, though, to conceive of major technical innovations? Less so, perhaps, than one would imagine, for some have already been implemented to take account of the economic demands specific to the search for satisfaction. Sometimes it is simply a matter of reconsidering this or that technical arrangement from a different angle. In any case, the analytic situation—a factor of unbinding for the higher systems— also problematises the identity of the protagonists owing to the transferences that it provokes. We cannot therefore speak of it in terms of a technical manoeuvre, even when it intervenes rigorously in a way that is comparable to it.

Likewise, the moments of silence that disrupt the economy of consciousness also intensify the transference and consequently displace the narcissistic cathexes. In distinguishing them clearly from a disastrous state of mutism, I have proposed elsewhere (de M'Uzan, 1978b) that silence, which is better represented by spatial rather than temporal metaphors, constitutes not only a fundamental path of access to the unconscious mind of both protagonists but also a fruitful space of encounter. When he is silent, the analyst is no longer a totally independent and definite subject; he lets himself be included in the patient's orbit. Furthermore, the analyst's silence *creates* a void, as fascinating as a chasm, into which the patient tends to throw himself to avoid leaving any empty spaces.

Economic revisions in the preconscious, which, as I suggested above, modify the status of the protagonists as persons, also play a decisive role in the eruption of certain singularities of language. Although they are minimal in the first instance, they clearly reveal discrete vacillations in the analysand's sense of identity. When they manifest themselves more openly, these singularities betray the displacement of narcissistic cathexes towards that floating zone of individuation at the centre of the *spectrum of identity* to which I referred earlier. The patient's discourse now becomes particularly evocative. It is reminiscent of the parapraxal slips related to the position and identity of persons, or of the mechanism of the allergic object-relation described by Marty (1958). The affective context, which is very difficult to convey, passes from a state of apparent neutrality to the manifestation of violent emotions, sometimes accompanied by neuro-vegetative and visceral phenomena.

One woman patient said to me: "We are but one, owing to an effect of transparency. Each of us can be seen in the other; when each one of us is in the other, that makes but one." Then, somewhat less troubled, it seemed, she continued: "It's funny, I lose my sense of boundaries when I think about my relationship with you." Another patient said to me: "No, you are neither a friend nor an enemy, as might be the case in life ... [*then in an interrogative tone*] You are more an extension of me ... No, it's not that, you are not an extension of me; you are part of me, yes, that's it ...." I replied: "Can you hear me?" And she said: "It's when you are part of me that I can imagine you; otherwise I can't .... After all, it's also a way of being you."

On a day-to-day basis, however, sessions do not constantly produce such sequences, which is no doubt fortunate, for otherwise what would become of classical interpretation? But it is rare that their presence cannot be detected in a discrete form, as if in counterpoint to an almost banal discourse. Detecting such moments remains one of the essential tasks of analytic activity; for they not only indicate economic modifications and developments of introjective processes, but also the possibility and opportunity for making interventions.

It is never easy, or perhaps desirable, to systematise an interpretative approach. From my point of view, the difficulty is even greater due to the fact that almost all the interpretations belong to those positive inductions that emerge unexpectedly in the analyst's mind. It is often after the event, moreover, that the analyst is able to appreciate the importance of the work that has occurred in him, almost without his realising it. Reflecting on the situation afterwards, he notices that the way he had formulated his interpretation maintained a relative degree of indeterminacy regarding the speaker. Who completes or clarifies an ambiguous interpretation (see Chapter Two)? Who do the *paradoxical thoughts* that led to his intervention belong to? Who is the analyst, really, when he takes up in an interrogative tone what the analysand has just said? For Kutrin A. Kemper, repeating the material, "... as far as possible as if one was speaking during one's sleep, can be an opportunity for the analyst to perceive relations and connections that he had not grasped hitherto. For the patient, hearing what he has said repeated gives him the passive impression of being welcomed, accepted, and understood" (op. cit., p. 98). It is certainly a lot, but in my opinion it is far from sufficient; moreover, Kemper himself seems to sense this, for he likens the analyst's words to a dream discourse, that is, to something that is capable of modifying the sense of identity significantly. As in a dream, one character can represent another, and two characters can merge into one.

In this grammar of interpretation, discourse with a dreamlike tonality is not the only means of expression; the analyst can present himself not only as "I" but as a "one" (*on*) or as "he" (*il*). He can even take the ambiguity to the point of replacing "you" by an indefinite pronoun: *it is said that* (*on dit que*), etc. Sensitive to these nuances, the patient feels obscurely that he no longer knows for certain *who* is speaking or *where* the words have come from. He sometimes asks himself if he has not already said what the analyst has just said. When there is a doubt about identities, and when the words exchanged do not seem to come entirely from either one of the protagonists, or seem to come from both of them, the patient has the impression that the interpretation is proffered by the *person of himself*, that is, by his double—a double who speaks from a transitional space, in that uncertain zone of individuation that I would be tempted to call an *every man's land*. Under these circumstances, interpretation acquires a power of conviction thanks to which it has more chance of being assimilated.

* * *

At the beginning of this chapter, when I was referring to the role of structural elements in therapeutic failures, I wrote about a fatality characteristic of the human mind. Now that I am on the point of concluding, I am bound to recognise that in alluding to a subject who is uncertain of his essence, doubting the otherness of his objects, and functioning sometimes in anachronistic ways, I am proposing an almost schizophrenic vision of man. That is not incorrect, even if one takes into account the fact that the states and processes in question appear sporadically and in a very particular situation, that of analytic work. There is nothing surprising in the fact that deep and hidden traces from past times manage to manifest themselves in the course of an analysis. We have been quite convinced of this since the beginning of psychoanalysis, the doctrine of which rests to a large extent on this capacity of the past to return. In the conception that I am defending, the subject is no more a schizophrenic than the adult, in whom relics of infantile sexuality manifest themselves, is a polymorphic pervert. But even though we are ready to recognise these sorts of reminiscences when they concern the psychic figures and processes specific to object-related sexuality, we are infinitely more reticent when they are related to archaic modes of identity, that is to say, to the vicissitudes of narcissism. We are no doubt dealing here with another deeply rooted taboo, and one that is very difficult to overcome. Many are shocked by Ferenczi's dictum: "In principle, man can love only himself" (1912, p. 316). Analytic experience none the less confirms each day the reality of this essential egoism of the human being; but, if it is true that man loves only himself, I would add for my part that he can only be himself if he is capable of including that which is not himself and of allowing his narcissism to dilate in order to absorb the objects of the world; in other words, if he is also capable of becoming an other.

CHAPTER FIVE

Slaves of quantity* (1984)

In *M*, the famous film by Fritz Lang, Peter Lorre, as a sadistic murderer in a total panic, faces the underworld of the city united in a people's jury. Terrified, aggressive, pleading, he defends himself like a rat caught in a trap, and finally howls that *he couldn't help himself*. Less concerned with demonstrating the remote origins of the behaviour of his character than with showing him in the present, Lang has perfectly grasped the crucial function of the asensory element in a famous air from *Peer Gynt*, and above all depicts the uncontrollable pressure exerted on the murderer, as well as the inescapable character of his *passages à l'acte*.

Quite a long time ago, I had the opportunity to take the measure of a similar intrusion of unrelenting forces. It was in the course of two long meetings with a perverse masochist whose practices went beyond the extreme point of the imaginable (M'Uzan, 1973). Although the man

---

*Originally published in 1984 as "Les esclaves de la quantité" in *Nouvelle Revue de Psychanalyse*, 30: 129–138, and translated into English by Richard B. Simpson, MD for the *Psychoanalytic Quarterly*, 72: 711–725, in 2003. *Translator's Note*: Quotations from Freud are translations of the French version of Freud. The Standard Edition equivalents are annotated as footnotes.

gave the impression of having deliberately chosen his condition, he was not fundamentally in control of anything. He could not modify in any way the peculiar behaviours that shaped an essential part of his existence, and it was perhaps to try to get the upper hand on destiny that he paradoxically claimed a total annihilation of his will. The tyrannical demand of *jouissance* that dominated him diminished only little by little with the approach of old age and its biological alterations.

For M the accursed in the film, as for Mr. Maso (the name he used for himself), it was the incessant return of powerful and compelling excitation that irrevocably controlled the course of things, making them inevitable. The difference is almost tangible between cases like M and Mr. Maso and those people, neurotic or not, who, according to Freud "give the impression of being pursued by destiny" ("The impression they give is of being pursued by a malignant fate") (1920g, p. 21), reproducing in life, as in the transference, the same destructive attitudes. In tenaciously reiterating ad infinitum this kind of sabotage of the present, neurotics certainly present an image of a destiny independent of external events, "... but [these events] allow a link back to influences suffered ... in the course of earliest infancy" ("But psychoanalysis has always taken the view that ... [these patients'] fate is for the most part arranged by themselves and determined by early infantile influences") (p. 21).

It is all there: on the one hand, with M and Mr. Maso, one is dealing with a play of forces endowed with unequalled power and characterised above all by the *quantity of excitation* that they bear; and, on the other hand, with neurotics, one is dealing with the obvious, obstinate search for previously suffered frustrations and the "skilful" reproduction of "painful affective situations" ("Patients repeat all of these unwanted situations and painful emotions ... and revive them with the greatest ingenuity") (p. 21).

Considered from the perspective of a chain of repeated events, the two situations—the perverse and the neurotic—have not always been distinguished one from the other. Moreover, it is most often when thinking of the neurotic that one speaks about destiny. And Freud, precisely in regarding "neurotics and a large number of normal subjects", put forward his well-known formula: "We cannot help admitting that there is a tendency in psychic life for reproduction, for repetition, a tendency which asserts itself without taking account of the pleasure principle and puts itself above it" ("We find the courage to assume that there really does exist in the mind a compulsion to repeat which overrides the pleasure principle") (p. 22).

Actually, the tendency for repetition that we note with neurotics never has a really fatal nature and does not completely affect the subject's freedom in the realm of life's essential choices; by this I mean that many neurotic solutions remain possible. The subject makes bad choices repeatedly, which without doubt largely escape his will, but, contrary to what happens with M and Mr. Maso, his choices remain essentially dependent upon *psychic conflict*, upon the clash of desire and its opponents. The determinism involved is not at all irremediable. Besides, it is indeed in order to have access to potentially greater freedom that a neurotic undertakes an analysis. While he stubbornly transfers his past, he also has an obscure hope of allowing his internal conflicts to find the best possible outcome. Whatever point of view one has of it, with neurotics, the pleasure principle continues to fully direct psychic activities.

When destiny and repetition seem to have common cause, most often—happily—it is in fact only a façade. For even when phenomena have the mark of repetition and are forced to follow its law, repetition does not necessarily have an unequivocal meaning.

I have sufficiently explained myself on this point (de M'Uzan, 1969), so I will only briefly return to it. I have distinguished in their essence two kinds of repetition: the first I call *the repetition of the same*: it alone involves the importance of recollecting the past, and it is connected with the order of approximate similarity, of resemblance; the second, *the repetition of the identical*, deprived of the function of elaboration, refers to the realm of absolute similarity. The latter is what occurs with personalities deeply dominated by the narrowest and most immediate necessity; actually, they alone give a feeling that the course of events happening in life is unchangeable and has been decided long ago. In the text previously referred to (de M'Uzan, 1969), I have considered these questions and made conclusions about the origin of these stereotypes. Resorting to the role of a special quality of libido, "viscosity", or to the activity of a special instinct, the death instinct, appeared to me hardly acceptable. It seemed to me more economical to imagine the intervention of a *traumatic factor* very early in the life of the individual, and to do so in connection with a very special defence mechanism, *Verwerfung*. (There is a certain connection between my conception of *Verwerfung* and the notion of *foreclosure* introduced by Lacan, who specified the part it plays in fetishism and psychosis. The difference stems from the fact that in foreclosure, the accent is put on the expulsion of a signifier outside a register, the *symbolic,* whereas I mostly have in view the part *Verwerfung* plays in hindering the constitution of the functions of symbolisation, understood in the classical sense.)

This hypothesis is sustained by arguments drawn from experience with psychosomatic ailments and appeared to me sufficiently strong to be accepted, at least provisionally, while I reserved the right to re-examine it more closely one day. This opportunity is provided for me today and prompts my return to the case of perverse masochism touched on above. Thanks to its very marked characteristic features, it seems to me that this case should propel the discussion further.

Quite intelligent, Mr. Maso was not gifted with a very rich imagination. Even in the realm of his perversion, he had to resort to specialised reading material in order to think up new tortures. His fantasy life— I was struck by this—had a poverty totally comparable to what I had observed in certain psychosomatic patients. We would be mistaken to try to find in his fantasies the instigator of the *passages à l'acte*; the rest of the time, between these acts, he led a completely conventional life governed by very strict morals. In this instance, rather than fantasy, the determining factor that produces the *passage à l'acte* is the violent, unexpected arrival of a massive excitation, coming from nothing definable; and, in spite of appearances, sex is less the cause than a preferred instrument fully at the disposal of the discharge. One will understand that when I speak of *perverse sexual activity,* I have in mind, first of all, not its content, but the compelling irresistible nature that establishes its course.

The infinite need to "enjoy" stems, therefore, directly from quantity, which leads to the thought that a biological component is then at work at the depths of being. (In the case of Mr. Maso, a cousin who was to become his wife was herself affected by a serious perverse masochism, well before meeting him. He was to discover after the death of his father that he also had been a perverse masochist.)

But whatever may be the source of the excitation, the situation is not unrelated to what one observes in another morbid entity: the traumatic neurosis, where the subject is in no condition either to work out the excitation or to discharge it. (Whatever the origin of the surge of excitation, the inability to discharge it should not be understood in an absolute way, but rather as the impossibility of the discharge process's following the economic regime of the constancy principle.) The surge of quantity, which is reproduced continually, brings about in the psychic organisation a sort of trench, a rut, which the psychic apparatus, as soon as it is confronted with a fairly strong excitation, can no longer avoid. The nature of the trauma is almost indifferent; also, it little matters whether its origin is internal or external; it is not always possible to tell the difference. Only the quantity of excitation involved counts. Fritz Lang had an intuition about this; in the film, he made use of the rhythm and intensity of the air from *Peer Gynt* to bring out the progression of the sadistic compulsion. But he has also understood very well that the stimulus could not be clearly located: when the air goes round in his head, the hero feels it, however, as if it came from outside—in other words, like a hallucination. And for the audience, in part identified with him, the air is perceived equally as internal or external reality; the ambiguity must be sustained. Hence, with its frightening and at the same time fascinating character, the film puts to the fore, as no other film has done, a kind of diabolic possession where an intolerable excitation dominates with its fatal course and outcome. *Quantity is destiny* when it is constituted in actual *trauma*.

A notion principally of an economic nature, *trauma* is defined classically as an intense event or experience carrying a charge that overwhelms both the subject's tolerance and his capacities for psychic mastery and elaboration. In fact, the phenomenon is more complex than it appears, and in order to retain its specificity, numerous elements must be combined and organically linked therein. To begin with, I will speak in terms of narcissistic investments. The boundaries of the ego are always in danger of being altered by any excitation as soon as it reaches a certain intensity. But, properly speaking, there is trauma only if, pre-dating the mishap, there were a distortion in the ability to differentiate inside from outside—or, on the contrary, if there were a total intolerance of any blurring, however functional, between the ego and the non-ego (M'Uzan, 1978a).

When natural displacements of narcissistic investments are at this point intolerable, the psychic apparatus is hardly in a position to face the surge of excitation. This has two ways of being expressed: on the one hand, there is an inability to utilise the countercathexis in order to delay discharge; and, on the other hand, there is also a deficiency of the psychic apparatus, which is powerless to articulate the excitation with a conflict in order to elaborate, for example, a neurotic solution. All in all, such a solution would be reasonable and correspond to a genuine work of integration. One is faced with an actual traumatic situation when the subject, unable to find a response to the mishap, even in the form of a neurotic symptom, is condemned to *behavioural reactions*. In order for the essential narcissistic investments and the feeling of identity to be preserved as much as possible, the excitation, in this case, can only be discharged in a massive, brutal fashion by a *passage à l'acte*, in which the violence is proportional to the quantities at stake. (The violence should be carried out not only completely, but also in the shortest period of time possible. We could say that the process completely obeys the law of the principle of inertia.)

Such a solution decisively marks the person, insofar as it lays out his future by opening channels for further identical reactions.

The reader will perhaps point out that in a *passage à l'acte*, a perverse act in particular, the act itself has a meaning that cannot be disregarded. I am well aware that for some, this meaning, relating to a fantastic exuberance, is even decisive. Actually, the meaning that seems to be revealed in the act is only an addition, introduced secondarily and often dependent on the sociocultural environment. In some respects, this generation of meaning is comparable to frenzied intellectual activities that one observes sometimes in perverts, for whom these intellectual activities have a mainly behavioural value. During an act, when the signifying function is eclipsed by the evacuation of quantity, one can hardly conceive that a desire, an element of defensive conflict, has been at work. If one still wants to speak in terms of desire, even desire when it is freed from repression, one would see, after all is said and done, that desire is completely devoted to the handling of quantity.

If the perverse solution occupies a large place here, it is because it lends itself particularly well to observation. But other outcomes of the traumatic surge of excitation are conceivable, such as the spectacular or almost mute development of a severe somatic pathology. Everything happens as if the "somatosis" were the equivalent of an act, admittedly involuntary, but nevertheless conceived by the organism with a view to a desperate, sometimes lethal, defence. And in cases where the potential resistance of the organism is very limited, the force of excitation is not always obvious. In certain structures, the least modification affecting the object or what serves as an object is felt by the subject— without his being able to identify it—as having happened in the very interior of his person, where it triggers somatic, not hysteric, symptoms. This reaction itself constitutes the model of "acting in".

Violence, restrictive perverse sexual activity, and somatosis are closely allied and equally dependent on the same characteristic, which is quite intrinsic to excitation, and, I repeat, they are not dependent on a special instinct. As different from each other as they may appear to be, these slaves of quantity battle in a similar way to deal with what invades them: they oppose, sometimes in a desperate act, fatal developments, either direct or indirect, which from then on are foreseeable. And the repetition of these acts sometimes takes place with a rhythm that almost becomes a conduit, conferring a sort of style upon existence. Meanwhile, almost silently, the economic after-effects of each *passage à l'acte* add one to the other, finally causing profoundly disastrous biological alterations—for example, an immune deficiency.

Another trait common to all these personalities is the deep *disarray* that can be deduced behind a façade of restrictive defences. Immediately preceding the emergence of an up-until-then concealed somatosis, a state of disarray and despair develops more or less mutely. Although it is sometimes inconspicuous, this phenomenon has, however, received so much attention that it has been made into a genuine syndrome. The subject may complain only of a vague and unspeakable unrest; one senses his disarray and begins to be aware of very old deficits. The deficiencies affect multiple functions, the psychic in particular; one notes, for example, an attack on the capacity for symbolisation that normally plays an essential part in the economy of the subject.

When one observes the most representative of the somatoses, these deficiencies of symbolisation are directly linked to the prevalence of a defensive technique: rejection (*Verwerfung*), to which I alluded earlier. The mechanism is undoubtedly very archaic, but for me, the main thing is that it is itself an economic consequence of a catastrophic traumatic situation, initially responsible for an evolution in which the state of disarray is ready to be reproduced at any time. Afterwards, primitive rejection leads to an obsessional-appearing connection with external reality in which reality is overinvested. We recognise here one of the characteristics of the *pensée opératoire*—I will not dwell on it now, but will only recall how much, with the psychosomatic patient, an apparently normal and orderly psychic activity relates back, in fact, to profound anarchy that pervades the organism (Marty & de M'Uzan, 1963).

With the violent or the sexually perverse, disarray may be concealed, or, on the contrary, it may explode for all to see. In any case, such disarray is an expression of the intrinsic inability of the subject to escape from the law of excitation that forces him to expel the quantity to the outside. A prisoner of his internal inferno and completely at the power of explosive forces that assail him, the subject passes through the violent act exactly as if it were an "other" acting in his place from whom he would expect relief. Exhausted, unaware of the repercussions of his act, he can finally go to sleep. The discharge has been complete; it is a return to the zero degree of excitation; at no time has the pleasure principle played a role. It is not surprising, then, that this absolute retrograde movement towards a time when no excitation existed at all—and so there was no life at all—has been accounted for by the death instinct, or at least by the conservative tendency of every instinct. What is certain in these conditions is that the biological instinct, as much as one retains this notion, is outside the grasp of the psychic apparatus, and the biological does not become a drive. All that remains is excitation.

One seldom has a chance to witness such an annihilation of every freedom. Even though the neurotic's future seems to be already rather largely determined by conflict, he can all the same, as the physicist puts it, *take in information*, thanks to transference and symbolisation. Nothing like that occurs with the slave of quantity. In spite of the uncertain limits of his being, which could lead one to think that there was an infinite capacity for merger, he is inaccessible to information. Nothing can enrich his preconscious, and if by chance he undertakes an analysis, his prospects are appreciably reduced, since quantity prevails over every other factor and impedes the development of a true transference neurosis. In this specific analytic situation more than others, one cannot always immediately appreciate that the subject becomes comparable to a walled-in space, and it is not a great leap to think that he is in the power of a malignant entropy. Thus, as long as the organism still possesses living forces, the massive surge of excitation inevitably returns and all hope of controlling the rush of it is futile. To use another image, we could say that the energies, as if turned back on themselves, become the object of their own investment and increase their own charge.

A disarray that leaves the person in the same way impotent, facing the repeated return of the same traumatic rush, can only have a very distant origin—still more distant, of course, than that of neurotic states: it must date from a time when the human being is very poorly equipped physiologically. Freud found the model for this in the infant's situation, confronted by all sorts of aggressions, coming as much from the external world as the internal world (1926d). We note, nevertheless, that in their violence, the cry and gesticulation of the infant have a real efficacy during a phase of development in which brute discharge still has an adaptive value. And what is more, these vehement demonstrations arouse an intervention from the family circle that may eventually be beneficial, and that, like the triggering event itself, could be felt as coming from outside as well as from inside.

Be that as it may, at certain times, the infant's disarray can be quite severe—but how can we express what the foetus endures during delivery? Even if human beings are programmed to withstand it, it is an experience of unprecedented violence and is unavoidable.

In complete passivity, the small being is subjected over the whole of its body to considerable pressures that recur over a time that can be very long. Excitations of every order assail it and come to an end only when—thanks to a discharge of extreme brutality—a new attack occurs and air opens up the pulmonary alveoli. Freud adds that this act of violence constitutes for the foetus "a considerable disruption in the economy of his narcissistic libido" ("It [the foetus] can only be aware of some vast disturbance in the economy of its narcissistic libido") (1926d, p. 135), which is precisely what enters into the factors of destiny that I envisage here.

Some will object by noting that since each individual passes through the same ordeal, how could there be anyone left on earth except slaves of quantity? This is mistaken, if one understands it to mean that no freedom at all would exist for anyone. But it could be correct, in a restricted sense, if one considers that there is in each of us, like a seed, an intrinsic potentiality for subjugation to powerful excitations. This potentiality would be absolutely comparable with the core of the actual neurosis, which according to Freud is the basis of all psychoneurosis (1916–1917, p. 390). It goes without saying that birth can be identified with trauma only when it triggers a surge of excitations *radically* overwhelming the capacities for what has been programmed as tolerable. It is in this case that one meets either with fatal outcomes, which the external circumstances of the delivery are not sufficient to explain, or with psychophysiological deterioration, in which the future of the subject is more or less put at serious risk (let us note in passing, however, that an unfavourable sociocultural factor—destitution, underdevelopment, or the like—can also confer a pre-eminent role to quantity).

As I did in the case of perverse masochism, so here as well I am led to bring together two things situated in different spaces by looking at their influence on the unfolding of a process, namely that of birth: the purely exterior factors and the constitution of the newborn. It is indeed probable that, at the time of birth, the characteristics of energy depend mainly on biological givens, in other words, the constitution. And in a way, it is all the more complex in this instance. The energy is at the same time a product of the mother and a product of the child: two beings in one but not identical, distinct but at the same time overlapping.

In their theoretical systems, Rank and Freud assigned to birth the place that we know: marginal for one, central for the other. Thus, they arrived at a conception of trauma, its origins, and its consequences that differs somewhat from the one I am presenting here.

> After having explored all the meanings and all the directions of the unconscious—one finds oneself, both for normal man as well as for abnormal subjects, face to face with the source behind the psychic unconscious. We note that this source is situated in the region of the psycho-physical and can be defined or described in biological terms: it is what we call the trauma of birth ..., source of psychic effects of an incalculable importance for the evolution of humanity, making us see in this trauma the last conceivable biological substratum of psychic life, the core itself of the unconscious. (Rank, 1924, p. 9)

As early as 1909, Freud himself started to sense the role of birth as the first experience of anxiety (1900a, p. 400, footnote 3 (dated 1909)). Freud returns to it in 1925 in a review of the work in question, where, however, he points out "the indisputable merit of Rank's construction" ("The discovery of this extensive concatenation is an undoubted merit of Rank's construction") (1926d, p. 151).

First, Freud criticises Rank for having put too much emphasis on the variable intensity of birth trauma, while neglecting the role of constitutional and phylogenetic factors. (This criticism does not appear to be too well founded because it is true that birth trauma is subject to variable intensity, and furthermore, one cannot say that Rank neglected constitution, although he did not use the word, since he makes of trauma the last biological substratum conceivable for psychic life.)

Furthermore, Freud does not accept that the force of birth trauma is such that it prevents abreaction and, as it were, prepares the way for subsequent neurosis. As his thinking about the notion of anxiety progresses—thinking maintained precisely by the problem of challenging Rank's thesis, to which he returns several times—Freud tries to eliminate, little by little and as widely as possible, the role of birth trauma, the major importance of which he did, however, recognise as the prototype of the state of anxiety. And in continuing with his refutation, he is led to put the emphasis on the situation of danger, which is admittedly always linked to the repetition of the lived experience of birth, but still, it is linked even more to the economic disruption resulting from a considerable increase of quantities of undischarged excitation.

Finally, in the supplement to his work on anxiety (Freud, 1926d), the question is no longer one of birth at all, but rather of a distinction between the traumatic situation and the situation of danger. The traumatic situation arouses only disarray. On the other hand, the situation of danger allows for a position of expectation suited to trigger signal anxiety, with a view to the active and attenuated reproduction of an initial trauma. Indeed, when all is said and done, there is no longer any possible bridge between the two ways of seeing things. In terms of Rank's position, I would say that he wanted his discovery to explain too much (which is often the case for dissidents). In addition, he did not see that in certain cases, dominated precisely by an excess of quantity, his trauma led not to meaning and neurosis, but on the contrary, to a deficiency of meaning and non-neurotic morbid entities. Freud, in distinguishing first of all between the traumatic situation and the situation of danger, winds up making one situation the derivative of the other, since he maintains that "[A]nxiety, a reaction originating from the disarray of trauma, is reproduced subsequently in the situation of danger as an alarm signal" ("Anxiety is the original reaction to helplessness in the trauma and is reproduced later on in the danger-situation as a signal for help") (1926d, pp. 166–167).

For me, disarray is precisely what stands in the way of the development of anxiety in the full sense of the term. When the traumatic mishap puts at stake quantities of excitation, considering their enormity—their being impossible to integrate or to elaborate and totally unfit to be physiologically discharged—the situation becomes literally staggering. Disarray gets the better of danger, and the basis for subsequent release of anxiety as a signal of alarm is missing. If the trauma comes to be repeated, the subject, who is not warned by anxiety and as a result is defenceless, will feel its impact full force. From now on, the process of compulsive repetition is entered into: it is, in fact, the only "solution". Any excitation, whatever its origin, provided that it reaches a certain level, will inevitably reproduce the original situation.

Thus, the *psychoanalytic* notion of birth trauma must be divided up. On one hand, there are actually cases where the process, in spite of violence exercised upon the foetus, produces only physiologically tolerable quantities of excitation that are compatible with the biological programme. Real turmoil may ensue that is perfectly suited to becoming the matrix of an anxiety that will later be experienced at the time of each separation from the mother, then on the occasion of any loss, and finally, when the time comes, to confront the threat of castration. I mean by *turmoil* something that allows for a memory to be reworked, that can enter as a pattern into a history and provides the nucleus for fantasy activity in the future. On the other hand, there are those situations in which the birth process causes such quantities of excitation to erupt that no place for turmoil as such is allowed. It is only in the latter case that the individual's destiny is decisively *fixed once and for all* by the power of quantity.

It has been evident throughout this discussion that the figure of Destiny does not have for me the form, certainly terrifying but poetic, that the Greeks were known to give it, as personified in the goddess Moira. Destiny short-circuits all history, and therefore does not have any edifying meaning, lying outside the domain of tragedy. Nevertheless, it does share something with Moira beneath a play of conflict and passion, where Destiny represents the absolute casting of the die to which certain lives must submit before they have even begun. For that matter, perhaps Moira, the only deity with whom we have no influence, was also born out of a profound intuition about the ineluctable that we now situate in biology.

Note

1. Translator's note: *somatosis* is a word coined to correspond to the French word *somatose*, just as the French *psychose* corresponds to *psychosis*.

CHAPTER SIX

During the session: considerations on the analyst's mental functioning* (1989)

From time to time a patient would tell me about a fantasy she was having which—stretching the imagination a little—might cross the mind of any one of us in one form or another. She wished she had a hammer with which she could smash my skull and see what was inside. Many different motives could be attributed to this charming reverie but, as you may suppose, it was dictated primarily, I would say, by a playful movement. In fact, appearances notwithstanding, aggressiveness did not play an important part in it; on the other hand, the wish to reassure herself that I was exclusively preoccupied with her at that moment was present. All of this is familiar ground to analysts. But, to be more precise, the interest that she showed for the contents of my mind, among which she was supposed to occupy a prominent position, masked an obscure curiosity for my mental functioning that was perhaps more difficult to grasp. It is important to recognise that the analyst himself is much more at ease with discovering and apprehending the various forms of his fantasy life than with understanding his mental functioning and its diverse modalities while he is listening to

* This chapter first appeared as a paper in the *Nouvelle Revue de Psychanalyse*, 40: 147–163, in 1989.

his patient. It is this singular activity that I wish to dwell on in this chapter.

In doing so, I am following in the footsteps of a number of other authors, whose observations are worthy of our attention. I am thinking, in particular, of Paula Heimann (1977) who remarked that "[I]n recent times interest in the clinical situation has increasingly focused on the analyst, on what goes on in him ...." (p. 313). In fact, the subject had been treated advantageously well before that, though, to the best of my knowledge, usually non-systematically and within the strict context of reflections on the countertransference. Evidence of this can be found not only in the remarks Freud makes on the problem in "Constructions in Analysis" (1937d) or in "Analysis Terminable and Interminable" (1937c), but also in the contributions of Ralph Greenson (1960), Maxwell Gitelson (1952), Annie Reich (1951), and others.

As I was rereading these often profound studies on the functioning of the analyst's mental apparatus, it seemed to me none the less that they were almost always, at one moment or another, in a certain way *restrained*. It was as if there was something that acted as a brake on or served to deflect the course of reflection as soon as there was an attempt to give shape to what had been perceived during the sessions. In fact, the brake in question corresponds to an impediment that sometimes affects the analyst's activity in the analytic situation. What is it, then, that actually happens?

In order to give a more adequate treatment to a subject to which Serge Viderman (1970) and Michel Neyraut (1974) have also turned their attention, it may be useful to recall an idea that has now become familiar. It is often stressed that theoretical knowledge is insufficient and that an intellectual understanding of the material has definite limits. Although we are convinced of this nowadays, it perhaps still needed pointing out a few decades ago. That is no doubt what Ralph Greenson thought in 1960 when he emphasised forcefully the need for the analyst to have a sort of emotional knowledge of the other person. This knowledge was defined by the term *empathy*, that is to say, a capacity to share and even experience the feelings of the other person—let us say, a free emotional sensibility. When one takes a closer look at things, however, one quickly realises that no sooner had these truths been asserted than a number of small *adjustments* began to be made. It was with a certain degree of subtlety, for instance, that a distinction was introduced between identification, considered as purely unconscious, and empathy which was seen as figuring solely in the preconscious. This *separation of powers* led on quite naturally to a close examination—certainly necessary but somewhat hasty—of the notion of empathy. Empathy—I am retaining the term—had become almost a passion, and was seen as exposing the analyst to various dangers resulting from losing control of the countertransference. It was doubtless important to be able to feel empathically, the argument ran, but it was even more important to be able to revert to the earlier state again swiftly so as to avoid exposing oneself to instinctual temptations that were difficult to detect. It was in this way that value came to be placed essentially on the aptitude for understanding reduced to a "neutralized and autonomous ego-function" (Greenson, 1967; Hartmann, 1958). There is no need for me to spell out what this formulation implies.

Feeling and understanding, being involved and yet detached, participating while observing: nobody would dream of questioning the legitimacy of this. I am recalling all this because it led to the implicit acknowledgement of an essential fact—namely, that the compromise which is regarded as indispensable between these two attitudes undermines the idea that one can *listen to the patient directly*.

According to this new way of seeing things, the analyst listens to his patient by means of a sort of apparatus that he sets up within himself, combining several elements, which, as a whole, all contribute to a single aim, that of understanding. Listening is thus mediated, the analysand's discourse distorted, transformed, and reconstructed, with the aim of identifying a certain truth that can be communicated to the patient, thereby contributing to and furthering the analytic process.

Awareness of this fact certainly represented an important step in reflecting on the analyst's work. A very significant expression of this can be found in the aforementioned paper by Ralph Greenson, which I regard as an essential contribution. There the author describes, along with its functions, a sort of organisation of apparently composite findings which, he says, are constitutive of our *apparatus for listening to patients and of processing* their utterances. In this *working model*—Greenson's own expression—are aggregated not only the functions of the reality-ego—as described by Freud in his "Formulations on the Two Principles of Mental Functioning" (1911b)—but also the analyst's clinical experience and theoretical knowledge, linked to everything that he knows about his patient, his capacities for insight, his resistances and, for good measure, his own human experience. Thus, although the picture the analyst has built up of the patient through empathy plays an important role in the construction of the working model, this model is also a product of the analyst.

In the studies devoted to the question, many remarks show that it was no small matter to recognise the extent to which the analyst must let himself be submerged by the patient's most intrusive impulses and abandon the use of perception to ward off "adverse" stimuli. So it is all the more striking to see those who insisted so much on the role, significance, and effectiveness of empathy promptly restoring to the most differentiated and rationalised instruments of the ego their power, their faculties of control, in short, their absolute primacy. Admittedly, much emphasis has been placed on the fact that the analyst must be able to listen to others at several levels and to have at his or her disposal the famous *third ear*, once evoked by Theodor Reik. In other words, the analyst must be capable of regressing with his patient, of *hovering around* him, of allowing a silent running commentary to develop in himself based on elements emerging from the preconscious, or even the unconscious. It was even acknowledged that the analyst *should be ready to allow a part of him or herself transiently to become the patient*. But the fear of being a lasting victim of unconscious identification also made it imperative to be able to revert almost instantly to the most developed functions of the *working model*.

* * *

It is worth dwelling for a moment here on the succession of the diverse phases of the analyst's psychical activity, as they have been described. First, there is the observing phase where listening occurs in the most banal and ordinary manner. Next comes the phase in which signs of inadequacy emerge, when the analyst realises that he is listening to his patient as he would listen to anyone else, elsewhere, and in other conditions. The analyst feels ill at ease and has the impression he is not "*with it*"; or, alternatively, he sometimes feels tense while, at the same time, being more open to sensory stimuli. Then comes the phase of ego-modification when the analyst *agrees* to let himself be transformed by taking the patient into himself at the deepest level. It is here that the notion of empathy has its place. It is said, however, that this experience can neither be tolerated for very long nor too extensively; for, as it is prone to become more intense, it may lead to phenomena in the analyst that are incompatible with the development of the analytic process, for instance, uncontrollable instinctual reactions.

The fourth phase involves recourse to the *working model*. The latter may be compared to a compromise-formation resulting, on the one hand, from a regression of ego-functions in connection with a narcissistic cathexis of the representation of the analysand and, on the other, from the necessity of putting into words what has first been experienced and then thought about. But *processing* the material to which the working model has given access cannot take place without a new modification of the ego; this constitutes the fifth phase in the process. The ego has got the upper hand again, relinquishing the free emotional sensibility, an ally of free-floating attention, to which it had abandoned itself. By virtue of the intervention of a narcissistic factor, together with a capacity for object-cathexis, the analyst thinks he will succeed in giving clarity to what had been so obscure. Surely one can only recommend the virtues of, shall we say, a flexible transition from a narcissistic position to an object position and vice versa.

In fact, the problem cannot be considered simply from this standpoint. Attention must also be focused on what governs the creation of the working model, and particularly on the point at which it yields to the most developed cognitive processes. On the face of it one is convinced by the technical necessity of implementing this working model, and even of accentuating the functional aspects of it that are most associated with ordered verbalisation. It is necessary, is it not, to emerge from the depths of empathy in order to be able to communicate with the patient by using the specific instruments of language, and to leave the terrain of empathy for that of intuition, which, according to Greenson, has more in common with thought or ideas? Further, it is necessary, surely, to take one's distance from felt experience in order to draw closer to psychic activities that lead to ideation; for, the argument runs, this is how one enables the patient's ego to extend its empire. In fact, this sort of transfer of power to the ego-functions that are most dependent on the regime apt at binding cathexes is only partially justified by technical requirements. *This transfer of power is aimed more at protecting the analyst, who is a potential victim of the very practice of his art, and whose particular and constrained psychic functioning has made him a "person apart"*, a person whose capacities for understanding others leave him exposed.

The idea that the analyst runs certain risks is not a new one. Paula Heimann did not hesitate to say that we can only understand our patients by identifying with them, but that it was important to take account of the danger of a *"folie à deux"* (1977, p. 315). It will be agreed that what takes place none the less occurs within the framework of an object relationship, even if the transference conflicts of the patient have temporarily become the analyst's too.

I want now to mention the work of Robert Fliess (1942) who was, I think, one of the first to have taken a fairly systematic interest in the subject I am concerned with. In his study, he accords a central place to *empathy*, a notion that was taken up later on by Greenson. Fliess said that empathy, resulting from a transitory introjection, helps the analyst to understand the patient better. Thus, as Theodor Reik (1937) pointed out, observing the patient requires the analyst to observe his own ego or, more precisely, a part of his ego that is transformed by taking the object into himself. One could even say that at certain extreme moments of the process the analyst becomes the patient. In other words, the patient's instinctual tendencies change into narcissistic tendencies in the analyst. By withdrawing the most individual aspects of his own personality, the analyst allows his analysand to invade him. He thereby creates the conditions in which the patient's representation, which is now acquiring considerable power, can occupy him and, at the same time, become the object of a narcissistic cathexis.

The menace hanging over the stability of the psychoanalyst's sense of identity now becomes clearer. The boundaries between outside and inside tend to disappear. One could almost say that we are in fact faced with no longer knowing quite who is who. This is a situation that Michel Neyraut (1974) has discussed in connection with psychotic transferences. Incidentally, it seems to me that it is potentially present in *every analysis whose course takes a radical turn of direction*. The most extreme point of empathy—and of the regression that goes with it—may thus be said to constitute a *crucial moment* in the deployment of the psychic processes specific to the analyst's functioning. It is also crucial in that it is one of the greatest risks; indeed, Paula Heimann, evoking Searles, speaks about the capacity of "certain very regressed patients to drive another person crazy" (1977, p. 320). A further reason why it is crucial is that everything is articulated around it, while the continuation of the analyst's psychic activity depends largely on the way in which it has been confronted and dealt with. Robert Fliess had already recognised this moment as a *situation of danger*, precisely in the sense noted by Freud, presenting the risk of a rupture of the stimulus barrier.

The structural modifications required of the analyst when he settles himself into the armchair already involve an important alteration of the relations between his ego and his superego. His superego must display a tolerant attitude towards all the patient's productions, while being ready to assume the most atrocious roles that are thrust upon it. What's more, as Fliess points out, the analyst is caught painfully between two alternatives: either he must change tack and allow a completely inconsistent object-relationship to develop, or he must face the toxic consequences of an attack on his narcissistic libido. Under these conditions, the analyst is led, as it were, instinctively, to adopt attitudes or measures that are more or less acceptable or open to criticism. "Behind his mask of professional calm and detachment," says Glover, "the analyst's mental apparatus is going to defend itself ... and this protective system should be kept in constant repair" (1955, p. 90).

We are familiar with such elementary measures of self-protection ranging from excessive observation to distraction, from silence to interpretation-seduction, from the search for instinctual satisfactions, masochistic ones included, to the quest for narcissistic provender. The list is not exhaustive, and I am only mentioning it for memory's sake; for the real problem, in all its gravity, lies elsewhere.

If, as Glover says, we are justified in interpreting everything the patient says in terms of transference, then it must be accepted that everything that the analyst says or does, as a consequence of his countertransference, may be interpreted in terms of counter-resistances (p. 93). This way of seeing things is fraught with consequences, and leads me to put forward the following proposition: *the analyst's activity, as a whole, is not only likely to be affected by counter-resistances; to a large extent, it consists of a stratification, so to speak, of hierarchically organised resistances.* From this point of view, we should consider that each of these *resistances*, beginning with the elementary and superficial measures I have just mentioned, announces and then opposes the deployment of the following one. In all the phases of his activity, the analyst thus sets up sorts of mobile functional structures which certainly shore up his interpretative capacities, but also protect him against the possible harmful consequences of his relationship with the patient. The nodal point of this movement can be located at the point when his identification with the analysand deepens. The famous working model then appears to function as what I would call a *shield-antenna*: an antenna insofar as it orients the analyst towards another mode of understanding, towards gaining access to new contents that had been inaccessible hitherto, and a shield in as much as it blocks the pursuit of the movement of identification. In the working schema, then, the portion of narcissistic-cathexis allotted to the patient's representation gradually gives way to its object-cathexis. The patient's representation is thus less and less prone to be confused with the ego of the analyst for whom some of the most developed functions of the ego correlatively acquire increased importance in certain respects. What might have been considered as a progressive movement, since it leads to words, to the formulation of an interpretation, turns out largely to have the purpose of preventing the situation from taking a worrying turn. Worrying in what respect? Not because there would be an excessive risk of losing contact with the patient's unconscious, or because of the risk, highlighted above, of seeing the analyst develop a rapport of complicity with the patient which could bring him more or less obscure but rich instinctual satisfactions. No, thanks to an increasing affirmation of secondary process functions, the issue is to avoid the stability of the analyst's narcissistic-cathexes from being undermined beyond tolerable limits. All his capacities for *restraint* must then be brought into play. And now, as its role as an instrument of understanding recedes, a further function of the working model is affirmed when the space in which the representations of the protagonists move tends to become an *every man's land*. This function resists another mode of functioning that is felt to be worrying, that which is characteristic of what I have called the *paradoxical system* (see Chapter Two). I simply want to emphasise that it results from the conjunction in the analyst of an aptitude for using primary identification and a capacity to tolerate feelings of depersonalisation. It appeared to me, then, that this psychical disposition makes it possible to come to a different or supplementary understanding of the patient, whose representation continues to behave like an invader or a *mole* in the analyst's mind in a way that is difficult to detect because it is narcissistically cathected.

It is not surprising, then, that even when it is fruitful for understanding the other and for gaining access to new forms of interpretation, this situation makes the analyst feel so uneasy or anxious, sometimes almost without his realising it, that he feels the need to put an end to it. The *paradoxical system*, functioning at a different level than the *working model*, which opposed its institution, should, logically, in as much as it succeeds it, suffer a comparable fate, namely, of functioning itself as a shield-antenna. For the moment, the main point I want to stress is that the analyst's psychical activity describes a veritable trajectory, from its most intellectual forms which make maximum use of knowledge, observation, and judgement to the form in which *paradoxical functioning* manifests itself, preceded by the working model. In other words, a potential connection exists between the different phases of which it is composed, each phase being linked to the following phase to which it leads, while simultaneously opposing its institution. That is why I say that this activity describes a trajectory that is undoubtedly travelled several times during one and the same session. But there is something that precedes this instant that it is difficult for me to overlook, even when I have defined the context of the remarks I am making, namely, the session. Indeed, if we think once again about the "impossible" task that the analyst is faced with, and about the risks involved, we can see that he may, as it were, anticipate them, even before the session begins, and take precautionary measures (to be considered as belonging to the countertransference).

You will recall that Michel Neyraut (1974) has put forward the idea that the countertransference precedes the transference, as well as the possibility that resistance might be located in the analyst. I take a similar point of view when I speak of the precautionary measures that the analyst takes unwittingly. What is involved is a freeing up or liberation of tendencies in the analyst that are generally countercathected. The analyst knows what is awaiting him or, rather, he knows it without knowing it. But what he often does not realise is that he is ready to do anything, even to use his patient, in order to impede the course of the trajectory I have been referring to. The tendencies in question—personality traits, almost—doubtless exist in each analyst. They concern, *a priori*, any patient, irrespective of the nature of the provocations that he or she resorts to thereafter. That is why the idea of anticipating the uncertainties ahead is worthy of consideration. The analysand is felt to be someone who may become an intruder whom an analyst in difficulty would attack within himself in a similar manner to the way in which he may be attacked. *Even before this patient settles down on the couch*, he risks being received like an anachronistic object who offers himself, as it were, innocently to the analyst. The latter "unknowingly" perverts the situation with the sole aim of thwarting the play of mechanisms which he may not be able to control. I have chosen to call these tendencies: egg-laying, covetousness, and domination.

Egg-laying defines a need the analyst feels to deposit parts of himself, his own productions and ways of seeing things, in the analysand. A sort of projection may be recognised in this, but there is more to it than that because the analyst is then *prone to interest himself first and foremost in the fate of what he has deposited*. Have these deposits developed? Is the analysand really the right sort of terrain that is suitable for *germination*? Is cathecting his image enough for him to become an accomplice in the impregnation of his unconscious by that which emanates from the analyst?

Covetousness is aimed at the analysand's *psychic contents* with a view to making an egotistic use of them, for example, for furthering the analyst's self-analysis. I am thinking here of object-representations that are capable of being delimited, but also of something infinitely more elementary, comparable to raw material that requires processing. To give you an idea of what I mean, I will cite the example of a dream in which the patient represented herself with her parents. She had the feeling she was exposed to an extreme danger: her parents were about to pump out her substance and to pour it into little tubes of different colours.

Domination, lastly, is linked to the need to exercise tight control over the analysand's psychic functioning and to master it as if it should function in conformity with the principles that define the analyst's relations with his own objects.

If I have dwelt on this aspect of the countertransference, it is because the three tendencies animating it—it is even the objective in the service of which they are working—have the effect of opposing any transformation that the analyst might undergo as a result of his relationship with his patient. By making use of the other, by assigning him a place and a role over which he has control, he ineluctably blocks the play of processes affecting the feelings he has about his own identity, even when he has accepted the principle intellectually. How is it possible to imagine that we can identify usefully with a person whom, in other respects, we want to dominate, whose contents we covet, and whom we hope will provide a fertile container for our own conceptions and fantasies?

This pre-countertransference, which is liable to leave its mark more or less on the whole analytic process even before it has begun, intervenes in a manner that is very similar to that of the working model when it begins to resist the moment *paradoxical thinking* comes into operation. It is striking, is it not, to see that all available means are employed to impede the *identificatory movement*? In speaking of an identificatory movement, what I want to stress chiefly is that identification should not be seen merely as a phenomenon that can be described in terms of its diverse forms taken in isolation, but rather in terms of a series of moments (states) inscribed in time and animated by a dynamism that carries them towards a term where a destiny is accomplished. Generally speaking, when phenomena follow a predetermined course directed by an internal necessity, they are described as being inevitable in character. This gives the analyst a supplementary reason to take all the necessary measures to avoid being the victim of the process of which he is the theatre. This can most easily be detected when, as I have suggested, in the working model, empathy gives way to secondary psychical activity which, although it may make it possible to formulate an interpretation, mainly serves to thwart a different mode of functioning. The working model is a replica of the patient which not only possesses—albeit to a lesser degree—the same defences as he does, but is also nourished by his current utterances; and it reacts in certain respects like a *person* who has to be controlled in one way or another. It is conceivable, for example, that the analyst's failure to understand his patient's relationship with him intellectually constitutes for the analyst an object-loss that can be repaired by the model, since it contains an important part of the patient. In fact it soon becomes clear that something quite different is involved, namely, *the attempt to prevent the establishment of a new state of transference-neurosis*. This transference-neurosis no longer presents itself merely as a substitute for the clinical neurosis with which we are familiar, but as a consequence of the activity of a new entity, almost a *being*—a creation of the intertwined or interpenetrating unconscious minds of the pro-tagonists which I have referred to elsewhere as a *chimera* (de M'Uzan, 1978b). The *chimera* corresponds, though at another level, to the sort of *person* that the model has *represented* in the meantime.

You will recall that it was the *first signs of paradoxical functioning* that introduced a progressive change in the course of the model. What hap-pens, then, once this paradoxical activity has been set in motion? I will recapitulate the essential points. When this mode of functioning comes into play—the very mode of functioning that allows the *chimera* to take shape—the analyst is subject to a very special state of passivity; he is at the mercy of something that is happening within him. Some very curi-ous phenomena may now occur such as those, for instance, which can lead the analyst to intervene, believing that he is taking up something the patient has said, when in fact the patient has said nothing of the kind! This just goes to highlight the extent of the trouble that is affecting the analyst, bearing some similarity to certain hypnogogic experiences and states of depersonalisation. The sense of *change* that Maurice Bouvet (1960) considered to be an essential characteristic of depersonalisation is an apt description of what is taking place. The analyst experiences, witnesses, lives—all words conveying the extent to which he is caught up in this aggravated state of passivity—and undergoes an inner trans-formation. When he closes his eyes, he may even have the feeling that he has no responsibility for the images that well up in his mind, images whose aesthesia is so vivid that they are sometimes at the limits of sen-sation; or for the appearance of infinitely varied abstract forms or faces that continually change as one turns into another; or again, for the vari-ations in his sense of gravity. The phenomenon is generally fleeting, and I would add that it actually unfolds quite slowly, which suggests that contact with a form of very archaic psychical activity has not been lost. One might see the phenomenon as the trace of defective function-ing and attribute it, for instance, to fatigue. In fact, it is a very positive and prospective activity. It will be said that this kind of phenomenon is of limited frequency and ephemeral; that certain subjects are more exposed to it than others; and, what's more, that many patients do not even allow it to develop. Such arguments are undoubtedly worthy of consideration, but I cannot help thinking that they tend to caution the resistance that the ego puts up against this state of affairs, which constitutes a *second nodal point* in the trajectory of the analyst's mental functioning. It is well and truly a moment of transition, since the ver-bal formulation of what was initially inexpressible marks the interven-tion of secondary level activity, even if the content of the formulation is evocative of moments of identification and the other's alterity cannot yet be conceived of. Here, I concur with André Green's views on the knowledge-value of projection: he puts forward the hypothesis of an *isomorphy between the I and the Other* (1971).

I have no doubt that the *paradoxical system*, which takes over from the specific functioning of the working model after overwhelming it, can, once the *chimera* has been constituted, lead to another form of interpre-tative activity which, to use Michel Neyraut's expression, is fruitful for *understanding* the patient. But what I want to stress about the *chimera* is that apart from its real and effective power which has so far held my attention, it intervenes to put a stop to the worrying development of a topographical and economic anachronism. Strangely enough, the *chimera*, just like the working model, may, in its turn, see its activity taken over by the ego. This occurs when, right in the midst of the *paradoxical state*, as I have pointed out, words and sentences insert themselves that can undoubtedly lead to the formulation of interpretations, but also serve to help the analyst get a grip again on the consequences of passivity. The protagonists then find that acceptable boundaries have been re-established.

* * *

In order to give more concrete substance to these considerations, I am going to refer to a clinical sequence in which we discover, from the moment *paradoxical functioning* comes into play right up until the moment when the *chimera* takes shape and leads to an interpretation, an alternation between passive acceptance of the process underway and defence, albeit fruitful, against its extension.

As we know, any change, however small, in the setting or in the analyst's appearance can disconcert, trouble, or cause the patient anxiety. Likewise, a notable change in the analysand is capable of affecting the analyst. But, as a general rule, the analyst recovers his balance so swiftly, so automatically, that very often he does not recognise what has just happened in him. At other moments, he shows a greater inclination to accept identification, which is sometimes announced by a subtle change in his perception of the environment.

As I was ushering in the patient, a young woman whose regressive structure had already posed some difficulties, I noticed that she had completely changed her hairstyle: she had had her hair cut very short. Nothing had been said as yet, but in retrospect I think that I undoubtedly supposed that, once again, my patient was struggling with problems of identity.

It is not easy to give a satisfactory account of what happens in such cases. There is a risk of introducing too much clarity in presenting the facts. Nevertheless, I think I can say that I soon discovered a special disposition within myself that was conducive to the development of fantasy activity. At such moments, one has the feeling that a thought is about to emerge, though it is as yet unknown. This situation resides partly in the fact that the localisation of the phenomena occurring is extremely aleatory, given the fact that the destabilisation of the relation between object-cathexes and narcissistic-cathexes has become so pronounced. I would readily speak of *working intuition*, provided it is accepted that a form of knowledge or discovery can emerge in a place or in a mode that is not naturally accessible to consciousness.

This was roughly what was happening when the young woman began to tell me about what had happened to her since the previous session. She had ventured, and this was essential, she said, to take a livelier and more critical interest in a painting connected with a theme she was working on. The painting represented female or androgenous bodies, strangely interpenetrating or intertwined, whose respective forms were lost in a tangle of stray members. After a long, anxious silence, she appeared to change the subject. She had done something terrible, she had changed everything, she had "exposed" herself by having her hair cut, so that her forehead, which had previously been covered by a thick fringe, was now completely bare. Her discourse, however, became increasingly confused. She made a few tense or awkward gestures. Her anxiety became oppressive before she fell back into complete silence.

A number of hypotheses can be advanced to explain what happened. At any rate, in the communicative silence that was established, I witnessed, if I may put it like that, the slight emergence within myself of those bizarre sensory phenomena that I have described as *paradoxical*, though without experiencing a real sense of malaise. But it is quite possible that, without realising it, I had *got myself back on an even keel* again by recalling that, in an earlier session, she had noticed me glancing at a rose nearby and had cried out, citing Gertrude Stern: "A rose is a rose, is a rose, [etc.]." For me, things were back to normal again because ego-activity, remembering, had reasserted its rights, thereby blocking the development of the disturbance that was affecting me. My patient had seemed to follow a parallel path because, without my intervening, she began speaking again but this time in a different register that some would describe as *redeemingly neurotic*. She explained that she had her hair cut to punish herself, to expiate obscure feelings of remorse in connection with the sadomasochistic dramatisation of her relations with a friend (relations in which each of them seemed to be alternately dominating and dependent). This problem, it may be surmised, was much less trying than the one involving a disturbance of her sense of identity. Once again, and fleetingly, I noticed the appearance in myself of very slight phenomena akin to depersonalisation. I managed to pull myself out of this state with the help of a most remarkable thought that crossed my mind. It was remarkable in that it almost had the quality of an affect, but particularly because of its insistent nature; it was a sort of *fantasy-thought*: "I want to cut her head off." You will imagine the self-analysis that I immediately undertook in order to evaluate, for example, my eventual sensibility to a masochistic provocation. I did not insist with this because very soon a considerable amount of intellectual activity was triggered in me for the purposes of transmitting what I was in the process of understanding, but also, and much more obscurely, for my own protection. I persuaded myself that the sadomasochistic theme was indeed a *cover*, and that what was involved was chiefly related to the relationship that the young woman had with her own body. Nevertheless, I needed to recall Gertrude Stein's remark about the rose before feeling able to intervene. First, I pointed out the defensive value of the displacement of the theme of identity towards the theme of sadomasochistic relations with a man. Then I repeated Gertrude Stein's remark. Experience notwithstanding, I was surprised by the young woman's reaction: she started breathing heavily, seemed very anguished, and then, after calming down a bit, she said, rather emotionally: "Yes, I know." Another period of silence ensued and then I took the risk of making use of my fantasy as it had come to me, saying: "In fact you would prefer me to cut you up into pieces rather than to cut off your head" (thereby aggregating what was related to identity and to masochism). She started breathing heavily again and then, after a moment of silence, replied: "During my last analysis, I had a dream. I was guillotined, but it wasn't my head that came off, it was my body."

I will only write about those aspects of the following session that linked up clearly with the one before, revealing the progression of the work involved. My intervention had been heard, and the patient had thought about it at length. She spoke to me about it with a certain generosity (in good faith). Her associations led her naturally to Medusa and from there to her ambiguous and highly ambivalent relations with her mother. She then came back to the painting in question. She was preoccupied by a photograph that she found particularly disturbing. The photo was of the body of a little girl with the belly of a pregnant woman; her head, as if detached, was midway between the thorax and the hips; one leg seemed to form an extension of the body but was detached and cut into two sections; the other leg seemed to be supporting the head; finally one could make out the little girl's genitals, and then some small balls with an eye in one of them. She suddenly began talking about something else. I drew attention to the avoidance, adding that she wanted to distance herself from her own body, as her mother "saw" it, perhaps. She agreed. The atmosphere of the session began to assume, at the very least, the strange characteristics specific to the inception of *paradoxical functioning*. Although she was very troubled, my patient returned to the image of the little girl. She saw an allusion in it to giving birth. And it was at that moment that a new fantasy crossed my mind: if I made an involuntary movement of my head, I might displace one or two vertebrae and find I was quadriplegic, with just my face remaining really alive. I thought again, naturally, about Medusa and what had just been said about her. But I simply said: "In normal conditions of childbirth, there is a moment when only the head is outside." My patient was overwhelmed, almost terrified, and on the verge of tears. She none the less managed to pull herself together and to say that if one took a snapshot of this moment, one would discover a body with two heads, which was a horrible idea. Once she had calmed down again, she concluded: "A certain amount of trust is required to be able to experience fear."

A few brief remarks are necessary here. It will be noted that what I am describing here resembles Meltzer's (1984) definition, following Bion, of a singular feature of the analytic space. In fact, the value, in terms of acquiring an understanding of the patient that is comparable to that of a dream, of the overlapping of the concept container-contained with that of projective identification, is not unrelated to the functions of the *paradoxical system* and those of the *chimera*. The difference becomes clearer though if I stress the need to extend our tolerance for the wavering distinction between the identity of the subject and the object. Such wavering, Jean Bégoin (1984) tells us, would none the less expose the analyst to getting stuck in a narcissistic identification that would be a sign of a failure to elaborate loss. In fact, there is a still more fundamental danger for the analyst when he or she, experiencing the situation as a real intrusion, "expels" the patient and is subject to what Bion called "nameless dread". Nameless dread is a felicitous expression, but it also applies to something else. What is the ultimate nature of a danger that is so extreme that it leads the analyst, in the course of his or her work, to set up a succession of resistances that are increasingly difficult to detect and overcome, and to transform—as we have seen—the instruments, that he or she employs in order to get a better understanding of the patient, into a resistance against gaining access to other regions, against the discovery of other ways of doing things? How are we to understand that the analyst ends up neutralising his or her capacities for identification? Here we are touching on the deepest level of the problem.

As long as identification, in its full development, only—if I may put it like that—called into question the analyst's sense of identity, the defensive virtues of interpretation could intervene to a large extent; for, in spite of everything, there was a certain margin separating the representations of the protagonists. And, in this *every man's land* to which I have alluded, there was room for bits of objects with sufficiently distinct boundaries. But now we are dealing with something much more disconcerting. I had begun to evoke an aspect of this when, in connection with the initial stages of the functioning of the *chimera*, during the installation of *paradoxical functioning*, I pointed out that the psychical apparatus, which is its seat, could not *hold the representations*. This manifested itself, among other ways, through the stream or succession of intertwined images to which I referred earlier.

If we compare the modes of Freudian or Kleinian interpretation, I would say that the patient who is in a full state of regression does not so much attack the object or bits of the object as thoughts or psychic processes (de M'Uzan, 1988). It is a phenomenon of this order that occurs when identification attains its extreme condition. The patient does not have exclusive use of projective identificatory functioning or a similar model. The analyst can also be affected by it, not only in situations where a perverse countertransference has set in as a consequence of a libidinal regression of which he is unaware, but when, in identification, he is no longer *helped* by his capacities for cathecting objects, and *when he takes charge, without really realising it, of the dislocated mental functioning of his patient in order to be able to follow it*. And then, *everything gets out of hand*, the mind seems to be functioning at *breakneck speed* or as if it has lost its edges, its angles. This eventuality can occur in those moments, which are fortunately quite brief, when the analyst experiences not so much a sense of fatigue, or a propensity towards drowsiness, *as a state of annihilation*. Functioning in the same way as his patient, who is nevertheless restrained by his anxiety, the analyst is *led even further* along this path. In certain respects he is no longer the one who is thinking, for the ownership of the psychical apparatus in action has become ambiguous. I see this partly as the consequence of an attack directed no longer at representations, but at the links between them. The complicated system linking them to each other is more important here than their configurations taken in isolation. In fact, to construct is to articulate; to be more exact, it is only when the modalities of the articulations multiply and diversify that there is a possibility of seeing some sort of meaning being formed, invented, or created. In the situation I am referring to, constructing fantasies becomes impossible and, correlatively, the analyst's possibility of resorting to interpretation has, as it were, vanished into thin air, while distinctions of identity, even between bits of objects, become almost inconceivable. Can it be said that the inertia principle asserts its prevalence when the links between representations, that is to say, images and ideas, are broken, and that nothing seems capable any longer of restraining a tendency to an indefinite flow of attention, interest, and involvement? One could say that, but what needs to be emphasised particularly is that the real danger looming on the horizon is one that I would call a state of *psychical aphanisis*. I am thinking, here, of course of the expression used by Jones (1997) to define the disappearance of sexual desire which, he says, is feared more profoundly than castration. This outcome is among those that the analyst obscurely fears the most, no doubt more than that of discovering that he is momentarily fragmented, albeit well and truly alive among the fragments, however surprising that may seem. In order to curb the evolution that leads to a *loss of being*, going on the attack constitutes a last recourse; for, in the effort involved, there is the hope of maintaining or finding a point of impact, something that the attack can be directed against, a sort of anchor point. But, strictly speaking, there are no more objects. The identification has been taken so far that it no longer pertains to objects, to figures, but to modes of functioning that are constantly recreated and which arouse a quasi-immune reaction.

Continuing to function in the disunited mode of his patient, as if it were his own, and in order to avoid psychic aphanisis, the analyst ends up, as a last resort, attacking his own psychical apparatus, or rather those functions of it that sustain the identification. This finds expression in fragmented, disordered psychic activity, a veritable chaos in his thoughts, to use André Green's formulation (1989, personal communication). It may seem strange to see a positive value conferred on what proceeds from a sort of psychic anarchy, a pulling to pieces of thoughts to the point of breaking up the links between them. And yet this is precisely how the struggle against psychic aphanisis is carried out. Fortunately, the undertaking almost always succeeds, but at the price of a renunciation—the renunciation of another form of knowing.

Having avoided the worst, distinctions between images can now be detected. The analyst gradually recovers, along with the sense of his uniqueness, his recognition of the natural alterity of the outside world. Going back over the events that he has experienced, and following a topically and economically "progressive" movement, the analyst gives the most secondary functions of the ego the possibility of asserting their power again—no doubt due to the fact that the temporal factor has been taken into account. The process has followed its trajectory and has returned to its starting-point, though it may resume its course again a little later in the session … or on another day.

* * *

It may seem strange and even worrying to consider analytic activity from the standpoint of a succession of counter-resistances that are set up in correlation with the progression of identification and intended, first, to protect the analyst against a disturbance of his own identity, an upheaval in his narcissistic economy, and second, against a loss of being, a state of psychic aphanisis which can only be avoided by a fragmentation of the activity of thinking. Should the abrupt character of the formulation be nuanced? Definitely not; psychic aphanisis is a potential term, inscribed as a veiled form of the analyst's activity, and constitutes a negative pole activating the whole process. Sensed more than measured, and always covered over by less formidable dangers, it obliges the analyst to take all necessary measures to prevent its realisation. These measures are implemented in all the phases of his work as it progresses; furthermore, they possess therapeutic efficacy, even when they impede access to what remains almost unnameable but none the less active.

We are obliged to recognise that psychic aphanisis, which presents an extreme danger even though it can be extremely fruitful, can only be approached asymptotically and never asymptomatically, since the analyst's interpretations are his symptoms, symptoms that allow him temporarily to rediscover the meaning of the strict delimitation of beings.

PART III

AT THE FRONTIERS OF IDENTITY

CHAPTER SEVEN

The paraphrenic twin or at the frontiers of identity* (1999)

"Mummy, tell me, tell me Mummy: why am I me?"

This anguished and extremely violent appeal, which might hold a philosopher's attention for ages, was still a vivid recollection for my patient. At the time, she was only about three years old. And my patient added—this was a long time ago now, for I reported her case in a text I wrote in 1976 (see Chapter Two)—that this episode had followed shortly after a strange scene in which she had seen her own reflection *simultaneously* alongside that of her mother's in a large wardrobe mirror, and had realised for the first time that her thoughts were really her own.

When someone tells us about experiences of this kind, or when we experience them ourselves, they sometimes make such a powerful impression on us that we cannot avoid feeling that we have touched upon something essential, something fundamental, to the point that it even orients and directs our thoughts which, at moments, continue almost independently, making their own way, so to speak, beneath the

---

*This chapter first appeared as a paper in French in the *Revue française de psychanalyse*, 63(4): 1135–1151, in 1999.

most elaborate and rational levels of thought. We only really become aware of the issue retrospectively as a result of gradually discovering the organic link connecting the successive phases of our work. The little girl's account of the crucial event she had experienced was undoubtedly of this nature, and I remember it because *problems of identity* have constituted a theme of special interest for me.

I could see here that the child had been faced with two phases of a scene of capital importance—both of which she had created—bringing together in a spectacular and specific way the themes of identity, the double, and fidelity to oneself—for lying to her mother and insulting her in her mind, without her knowing it, had now become a possibility.

The clinical material on which my argument is based is not limited, however, to this episode in a child's life, however exemplary it may be. Indeed, I have encountered many others which reveal, particularly clearly, what I have called a *vacillation of identity*.

As it happens, I am thinking, first and foremost, of a patient's repetitive dream—a dream, on the face of it, that is very ordinary. *In a deserted street, at night, the young girl in question heard someone walking behind her. As the footsteps were getting nearer, she quickened her own step before waking up in a state of acute anxiety.* Commenting on her nightmare, she told me that she hoped that one day she would turn round and be able to identify her pursuer. This indeed was what happened—and what she then saw, with a mixture of horror and terror, was herself, very old, like her insane mother, with her dishevelled white hair falling across her face.

How, in this context, can I fail to recall the words of a patient suffering from generalised cancer, who, only a few days before her death, told me about a phenomenon that she had been observing recently? "You see," she said to me, "it is not me who is ill, it's the other person ... No, I'm not schizo, believe me. It is something light and tenuous; a sensation I feel beside me. How distressing it is to have something beside one" (this episode is reported in de M'Uzan, 1981 and 1994).

Quite recently, an analysand was speaking to me about her father's death. It was the very end; she was at his side and heard him say: "Don't worry, I am two, and I'm 'playing up'; so we can communicate in another way."

Finally, another analysand told me that one day she had experienced something strange and frightening that she preferred not to think about any more: she had had a vision of some rabbit heads. She said: "It was a part of me that didn't belong to me but which was none the less me; an unknown zone that is me, but does not belong to me. When it emerges, I have to hide. If I continued to look at that part of myself, it is as if it would take precedence over the other part, and then I would be nothing more than that, in this anxious state."

The thesis that I am going to put forward is based in clinical facts such as these.

You will perhaps be thinking that this is "yet another story about doubles"—a theme that has already been explored extensively in psychoanalytic literature. But it is also a theme that has an important place, to say the least, in fictional and poetic writings; and if I had to mention one in particular, I would cite Joseph Conrad's *The Secret Sharer*.

Incidentally, to the best of my knowledge, neither the theme of the double nor the theme of identity has been studied much from the point of view of its relation to the *notion of authenticity*—that is to say *fidelity* towards the most essential aspects of oneself. This is precisely the focal point of my argument. I will explain.

The subject's status of identity, as we know, is infinitely more complex and uncertain than its most accessible definition, locating it as closely as possible to consciousness, would suggest. Thus this first—or last—level of the status of identity corresponds, according to the formulation proposed by Phyllis Greenacre (1958), to the sense of uniqueness experienced by an integrated organism capable of recognising others without ambiguity. Such a statement, in spite of its awkwardness, is intended to express what should be the ultimate stage of the complete evolution of the ego—constituting, in short, a sort of certificate of mental health.

Since my study of the fantasy "If I were dead" (de M'Uzan, 1974), and with the introduction of the concept of *paradoxical psychic functioning*, it is well known that I do not recognise a precise, certain, and permanent frontier between the ego and the non-ego, and that in its place I locate an intermediate space that I have called the *spectrum of identity*. Thus the *I*, the *ego/I* is specified uncertainly within this space both as that which is most intimate and that which is most foreign, and in relation to the displacements of the narcissistic libido all along the fringes of this spectrum, from an internal pole occupied by the subject's own self-image to the external pole which coincides with the image of the other.

It would seem that these views can be reconciled, up to a certain point, with those extensively developed by one of the authors who has been most concerned with the subject, D. W. Winnicott (1971). Winnicott also makes use of the notion of an intermediate space in which the ambiguities of human problems of identity are played out. For him, and this is the essential point, the *transitional object*, different for each person, is a *reality*—an external reality that takes the place of the breast but which, he stresses, *is not a hallucination*; a reality that announces the object to come, while benefiting, as a result, from a cathexis that is fundamentally object-related, even when certain characteristics of this cathexis allow them, in certain respects, to be qualified as auto-erotic.

With the notion of the *spectrum of identity*, things present themselves differently, for the "question of identity" is not specified in terms of the relationship with a pre-object whose material reality is maintained to the extreme limits of what is conceivable, but in terms of the displacements of the narcissistic cathexis of representations.

That being the case, and in spite of their respective differences, the three formulations of the status of identity (Phyllis Greenacre's, Winnicott's, and my own) have one very important feature in common: according to each of them, identity is accomplished *at the heart of the sexual organisation* and, as we have just seen, within the framework of a *relationship with a non-ego*, whether in reality or imagined, when "I is an other" ("*Je est un autre*").

It is important to bear these propositions in mind as I attempt to consider the question of identity from quite another angle. I want to stress that the views I am putting forward in no way invalidate the ones above, even if they are radically different with respect to their foundations and to the drive order to which they belong. For the sake of clarity, I will begin by giving a somewhat blunt presentation of it.

If the *self* can no longer be specified only in terms of its transactions with a non-self, even delimited haphazardly, from what must it differentiate itself initially? Faced with this question, I shall put forward the following proposition: *before progressing in the acquisition of its own identity, drawing on an antagonism with the non-self by way of support, the archaic self must first differentiate itself from itself. What does that mean?*

Well, this archaic self, the essence of the future subject, first has the task of emerging from an indistinct syncretic entity which I call *primordial being*, a basic state of being of the very earliest stages of life, or rather, a state of being from which both the ego and the non-ego in the ego proceed. It is an entity that cannot be perceived distinctly and can only be apprehended globally. It is a "that" of which one would readily speak as if it were a space, with the "where" taking precedence over the "who": a space permeated by enormous quantities of surging energies that only obey the principle of discharge; a veritable chaos which can be found, moreover, though in a different way, in the field of the drives when no overall organisation has been able to impose itself. It is a state of being that is perceptible in the very first phases of the life of a new-born baby.

Such a fate would be incompatible with the continuation of life or, more precisely, with the accomplishment of the genetic programme in the service of which the drives are employed, if it were not thwarted, as we know it is, by the object-cathexis, at first partial, and before that by a fabulous "discovery", namely, *the creation, the invention, of a double, of an authentic twin*. This creature, a double because it is strictly similar to the subject, and like a twin because it was born at the same time as the subject, originates from one and the same entity. A complex psychical operation is involved because it is by virtue of the creative advent of a twin and an antagonistic relation with it that the *archaic self* will be able to emerge from primordial being and forge the beginnings of a distinctive identity. This double/twin, emanating from primordial psychic activity, is the expression of a work of *personalisation* to which one can only gain access subsequently during experiences of depersonalisation.

I will be forgiven, I hope, even if it is somewhat fashionable to do so, for borrowing once again for rhetorical purposes notions belonging to disciplines foreign to our art, in this case physics. I am willing to do this because, in connection with the problematic of identity, I speak of *primordial being*, the entity from which the *paraphrenic twin* originates—the justification for this term will come further on, rather like the physicist who, referring to the quantum void, speaks of a *nothing* that is both saturated with energies and at the same time the matrix of the universe. The point of resorting to this sort of metaphor will become clear when I come back to this state of nothing. For the moment, it suffices to point out that the *paraphrenic twin* must not be confused with the early stages of a subject who constructs himself by discovering in hate bits of objects before finally finding his place, as Freud says, in castration anxiety; neither must it be confused with Winnicott's transitional object which, as you will recall, is endowed with an unquestionable external materiality that is essential in preparing the way for the full cathexis of the object.

Under these conditions, I will propose the following statement: *the paraphrenic twin is not a transitional object; it is a transitional subject*. It is a psychic being whose place and nature can be inferred from the traces of it that remain throughout the individual's history. These traces are admittedly less flagrant than those of the pregenital phases of libidinal development, but they are none the less clearly identifiable when the figure of the double suddenly appears in one of its frequently evoked forms. The beginnings of psychic life proper are then celebrated and commemorated in a powerfully original and even stupefying mode. We are a long way here, it should be said, from Rank's (1932) conception, according to which the double in the form of shadows or reflections is created to give an energetic denial of the power of death. Likewise, the views set forth by Bion (1967) in his article "The imaginary twin", albeit less foreign, are still quite different. If, for Bion, the invention of the twin can be traced back to some of the earliest experiences, it primarily expresses the subject's incapacity to tolerate an object that is not entirely under his control. This shows the importance of the defensive aspect, for Bion even became "the twin of the patient who encouraged him in his evasion ..." (p. 8).

If we turn now towards literature, we can see it is swarming with stories of the double, some of which, owing to their linguistic specificities, lend themselves to being interpreted in the light of the thesis I am defending. I will come back to this point later, but first I must situate my conception of the double and of the status of identity in relation to the question of the drives, the theoretical repercussions of which are far from being negligible, as we shall see. A long time ago, while I was visiting one of the wards of a psychiatric hospital, a very ill and frightfully malnourished female patient called out to me. With her arm outstretched, pointing to the person in the bed next to her, who was not far from death's door, she cried out: "Regardez, regardez, elle meurt de *ma* faim" ("Look, look, she is dying of *my* hunger"). *Faim, F.A.I.M.,* it was clear ... although, today, I am ready to hear a different spelling (i.e., *fin*/end).

If I am evoking this desperately tragic episode which has never been very far from my mind, and which, I would say, has even accompanied me throughout the years, it is not on account of its profoundly moving character; neither is it only because the poor woman specified her status of identity by designating the person next to her as a double of herself, but rather because in uttering the word *faim,* she clearly indicated the nature of the instinctual drives involved. And this eruption of the word *faim,* in such a context, obliges me to reintroduce, in relation to the question of the double, the old debate concerning the oppositions between the instinctual drives.

If the *elementary self*, edifying itself with the help of the intervention of a double, has no need to differentiate itself from a *non-ego*; if it does not belong to a non-ego on the path towards objectalisation; if, emanating purely from itself, it is fundamentally distinct from the world of objects, narcissistic objects included; and if it is the *transitional subject* I am writing about, then the energy with which it is charged is equally of another nature than that which cathects the world of objects. In other words, the *elementary self* and its double are not cathected by a sexual, libidinal energy but—let's retain the expression—by the so-called non-sexual ego-drives. So it can be said that the establishment of what I have called the first strata of the status of identity must take place under the authority of the drives of self-preservation insofar as they are opposed to the sexual drives. And the theme of identity supplies arguments that are capable of underpinning the value of the first theory of the drives. After all, there is nothing inconceivable about that, since Freud himself, not only in *Beyond the Pleasure Principle* (1920g), but also in *Inhibitions, Symptoms and Anxiety* (1926d), explicitly upholds the clinical validity of the first drive dualism. That being so, this line of argument calls for three remarks.

To begin with, and I think I have already explained myself sufficiently in this respect, the pertinence of libidinal conceptions of the construction of identity are not affected by the one I am presenting here; for, even at the price of a slight temporal disparity, the two paths towards an emerging identity, one sexual and the other non-sexual, in fact develop concurrently. I will come back to this proposition when I deal with the relations between identity and authenticity, mentioned earlier. But a thought has just come to me in passing: the capacity for libidinal, object-related cathexis might merely be the consequence of an accident comparable to a tiny random fluctuation of the primordial quantum void at the origin of the universe; physics once again!

My second remark concerns the so-called drives of self-preservation. They should be understood as the economically charged, psychical representative of those instruments whose task it is to accomplish the plans of a *general programme of creation, development, and preservation*. The essence of this programme can only be genetic ... which, it is worth noting in passing, saves us from having to speak of instincts.

Finally, and this is my third remark, if reinstating the first drive dualism were to pose some embarrassment—though that is not the case for me—it would suffice to recall that before guaranteeing a place to the ego-drives (or the drives of self-preservation) among the life drives, Freud, once again in *Beyond the Pleasure Principle*, had briefly but explicitly intended to classify them on the side of death (1920g, p. 44), which, in my view, was a stroke of inspiration.

* * *

"'Know thyself' does not mean 'observe thyself'. 'Observe thyself' is what the Serpent says. It means: 'Make yourself the master of your actions.' But you are so already, you are the master of your actions. So that saying means: 'Misjudge yourself! Destroy yourself!', which is something evil—and only if one bends down very far indeed does one also hear the good in it, which is: 'in order to make of yourself what you are'."

This apophthegm, uttered by an expert on the subject of identity, Franz Kafka (*Notebooks 20*, 1991), underlines the irrefragable connection between identity and authenticity. According to the perspective I have adopted, authenticity and fidelity towards oneself, in their quasi-iconic relationship, reside in the subject's total allegiance to his innermost *self*, that is, to the basic entity which has extricated itself from primordial being by virtue of the intervention and intercession of a double. The label of authenticity applies unequivocally only to those exchanges that unite the fundamental self and its double. Consequently, strictly speaking, it is impossible to recognise a real, total, and undeniable authenticity in everything that constitutes the web of interpersonal relations, in the remarks that are made in this field, in what is said and transmitted, in short, in everything that nourishes object-relations, from the most archaic to the most developed. And the degree of authenticity of any manifestation varies in a proportionate inverse relation to its engagement in the field of objects! Is there only room, then, in relational life, for sorts of more or less triumphant *false-selves*?

It goes without saying that such a provocative proposition calls for substantial clarifications. How am I to accept, when an analysand says to me, right in the midst of an uncanny experience, "I am no longer myself", that this in fact means that she has been thrown back on the most basic aspects of herself, at the heart of the *paraphrenic realm*, a realm of truth? How does one integrate the idea according to which the interpretative spiral, specific to psychoanalytic work, has the vocation of thrusting the subject, retrogressively, unremittingly, as if she had been catapulted, through a whole series of existential loops, mechanical or neurotic, end-points or stages, towards a place of "madness", the residence of the truth? How can the analyst accept to be nothing but the mere agent of the adventure that leads a person to make contact again with their twin/double, with the perspective, admittedly, of gaining something in terms of authenticity, but at the risk of entering into a sort of macabre dance with it? And the analyst may have to identify with this twin—one cannot help thinking of Bion here. How are we to understand that the most authentic aspects of a person are to be discovered in *one* of the "psychotic" areas of his mind? How convincing melancholia is! But we still have to agree to separate the "psychotic" from psychosis.

But we cannot leave things there, for the ambiguity affecting the notion of authenticity requires us to take our critical examination of it further by approaching it from a different angle.

I will not dwell on the case (for it is evident) of an individual who, from the outset, gives the impression of being totally devoid of what is ordinarily called authenticity to the point of making us speak of a false-self, in the usual sense of the term. This would imply—without going into the matter further—spurning the idea that there is nothing but false-self. Everyone, in the depths of his own conscience, can make up his own mind.

Less clear, but still accessible, is the case where the sincerity of what someone says is quite simply doubtful. A friend, who was not an analyst but more than well acquainted with our art, said to me one day, on the subject of the psychic agencies: "It's true that there is the conscious and the unconscious, but there is also bad faith!" (What has become of the false-self?)

And if we consider a neurotic patient, who is well settled into his or her analysis, we take it for granted that the derivatives of the unconscious are considerably more authentic than the content of his manifest discourse, especially when he or she is speaking about love and hate.

As for a transference-object, we know that it is never recognised for what it is. By the same token, the one who forms the transference is not the person he thinks he is, for to a greater or lesser extent his current identity is problematised by the identity that he had at the time of his infantile neurosis.

Now, notwithstanding the commonplace nature of these remarks, with which we are all familiar, they deserve to be reiterated, if only briefly, because they allow us to reserve the place of the defendant for libidinal cathexis. And the reign of mendacity, even if unconscious, is assured. It was such mendacity that Ferenczi (1912, p. 78) recommended the patient to give up ... *hypocritically* ... in order to gain access, so to speak, to full individuality.

Throughout this necessary argumentation, which I must cut short because the essential point lies elsewhere, we have remained, as can be seen, within the field of the object-related libidinal drives and their destiny.

An examination of the criteria of authenticity is, in fact, deferred only a little. This was already what I thought when, following Tausk (1933), I argued that mendacity, and even the first successful lie, was not enough to ensure the promotion of the individual's identity, and further that this lie would still remain impenetrable and inaccessible (de M'Uzan, 1988). The case of the child with which I opened this chapter shows this well enough. Renouncing lying for survival purposes can lead someone who is searching for himself to the edge of the precipice. If we were justified in speaking of choice, we would have to weigh up, on the one hand, the advantages and disadvantages respectively of remaining faithful to the most specific aspects of "oneself", while assuming the possible deadly consequences of a rigorous and paradoxical preponderance of the drives of self-preservation ("ego-instincts") and, on the other, of betraying this self in order to survive in the field of relationships, while subjecting oneself to the "diktat" of the libidinal drives. In fact, fortunately perhaps, both paths evolve, as I have stated, concurrently; and, as is the case in many other domains, it is the quantitative factor that has the last word. That being the case, investigating some of the circumstances conducive to the appearance of the phenomenon of the double will help us take the line of argument further.

You will recall that at the beginning of this text I wrote about the approach of death, nightmares, and delusions. What the subject experiences in such moments has the extraordinary power of inducing in him or her a state of total adhesion, without concession. The actions and remarks that the persons or characters exchange are then connoted with what I once called an *indicator of absolute certainty* (de M'Uzan, 1993). These remarks, and the eventual images that go with them, appear in a light of "hyperreality" and the impression one has of touching on something indubitable always prevails over the perception of the sensible world, over the most rational lines of reasoning characteristic of secondary processes. Nothing seems so convincing as the sudden appearance of a monster at the heart of what I have called the *paraphrenic realm*; and this apparition imposes itself decisively, just like a delusional idea, with incomparable clarity.

What can we say, then, about what happens when death is approaching, one of those moments when the phenomenon of the double occurs electively and, more precisely, when the phase of libidinal expansion characteristic of the *work of dying* is over (see Chapter Three).

Two deaths, no doubt, are never similar. On the other hand, one cannot overlook—I hardly dare mention it—the derisory character, in such a moment, of the noise and bustle of life; neither can the vanity of our experiences of loving and hating, and especially of the ambitions deployed during the course of existence, with all that is said in connection with them, be gainsaid. Such reflections have been repeated many times and are almost trivial in the literary sense of the term, but I must repeat them; for, given the situation, the streams of words flowing in every direction are nothing but *senseless verbiage*, just like, of course, the words that I am now proffering. A man, on the point of dying, takes leave of his loved ones: "Go, go now, leave me alone with death," and I would add, with completely certainty, "alone with myself."

It is admittedly easy or provocative—all too easy and provocative—to qualify as *senseless verbiage* the exchanges of all kinds that form human relationships, when one compares them with what is experienced in extreme circumstances, and when it is no longer possible to accept being a stranger to oneself simply to survive. A stranger to oneself, that is to say—it should be clear by now—to the most essential aspect of oneself to which I am referring and not to the self where the unconscious impulses are stirring. How can one fail to think here of Pascalian "entertainment", even if the issues at stake, here and there, are totally different? But there was no "night of fire". So I think it is legitimate to qualify as senseless verbiage what unfolds in relationships when death draws near. But the expression continues to be in use at other moments, for instance, when consciousness simply vacillates fleetingly between waking and sleeping, or in front of certain landscapes that appear to stretch out endlessly, but also during experiences of "artistic seizure" when the subject is confronted with the precise essence of himself.

In anticipation of what is going to follow in this chapter, I want to suggest that it is precisely when a man is faced with losing his ordinary presence in the world before meeting up again with his intimate being that he, who is *unique*, invents a strange and specific language so as to be able to communicate with his double. A new space is then created, an area or realm of truth, a *paraphrenic realm*, where one discovers what is exchanged in all the domains I have just mentioned. Whether they are proffered or "endophasic", the units that make up this language are so heavily charged that it may—I have been giving this thought—have served to inspire Claudel's idea that "*before words*" (my emphasis) (I mean words of communication), there was "a certain intensity, quality, and proportion of tension (that the poet claimed was spiritual)" (Claudel, 1963).

We may suppose, then, that just as the neurotic symptom has its deep origin in this or that archaic configuration of libidinal impulses, the language supporting the relations of the subject with his double has very distant roots in linguistic modalities that are quite foreign to those that subsequently and gradually underpin the natural language of exchanges with others.

Concerning the emergence of language, Winnicott (1971) shows that the child begins by using original and organised sounds to designate the transitional object. It is clear that although these sounds, which can even include words, occur in a field that is not strictly speaking that of communication with a specific person, they none the less remain clearly part of the maternal orbit since, for one thing, they compensate for a deficiency of this order, whether real or only imagined.

How can we fail to subscribe fully to this notion of two languages, one being deployed in the field of relationships, the other in a transitional space? But, as we shall see, this is not what is involved during the subject's dealings with his double. I shall simply suggest at this point that this other language is the heir of the egotic lallation of the very first stages of life, and that its purpose is to boldly assert a presence—just as a felled prey emits an ultimate cry before dying—a way of saying "Me" and again "Me", infinitely.

* * *

"I am the owner of my might, and I am so when I recognize Myself as *unique*. In the *unique one*, the owner himself returns into his creative nothing of which he is born. Every higher essence above Me, be it God or man, weakens the sense of my uniqueness and pales only in the sun of this consciousness. If I found my cause in Myself, the unique one, then my concern rests on its transitory, mortal creator, who consumes himself, and I may say: 'All things are nothing to me'" (Stirner, 1845, p. 490).

It was with this exclamation that Max Stirner, the anarchist philosopher who, it is worth recalling, died in the very year Freud was born, ended *The Ego and His Own* his fundamental work. He was someone for whom the critics of his time, from Feurbach to Marx, did not show much consideration, someone who claimed "at all times and under all circumstances to be my own Self, if I know how to have myself and do not throw myself away on others" (p. 206), someone whose thought we would betray if we were to see nothing in it but the expression of an exacerbated narcissism, in the precise sense of the term, that is, of a vicissitude of the libido. Was Max Stirner narcissistic? Perhaps; but, first and foremost, he was a thinker of the extreme who was driven, even to the point of going adrift, by a secret problem that he was not even aware of himself. "My concern is neither the divine nor the human; not the true, the good, the just, the free, etc., but solely what is mine; and [my concern] is not a general one, but unique, just as I am unique" (p. 3).

In proffering these vehement words in reaction to the *senseless verbiage* that surrounded him, Stirner was clearly not taking himself for a sexual object; neither was he trying to admire his reflection in a mirror or, as is so frequently the case, in the eyes of others. Nor was he in search of instinctual satisfaction in the very place where some sort of erotic excitation might be forthcoming. No, he brazenly stands firm before the world, to be sure, but above all before himself. He questions himself as he is giving birth to himself out of nothing; I will quote him once again: "I am not nothing in the sense of emptiness, but I am the creative nothing out of which I myself as creator create everything" (p. 6)—allow me to remind you here of my quantum metaphor.

It is true that Stirner—and this is how he is generally understood— elaborated a theory of society, a philosophy that more or less only received recognition from the anarchists and Nietzsche. Although Stirner's work was that of a thinker, a utopian thinker, he nevertheless rigorously pursued his dream; and, moreover, he clearly denounced the perverse role of the "inner police" of his conscience, of institutions, and even of the loved object. However, by taking the risk of excluding himself from society, even when the latter was represented by the least conformist of its citizens, Stirner, without realising it, of course, violated a taboo, a taboo protected by a veritable denial, that of *self-begetting*, the underlying motor of his thinking. The psychic activity which animates and sustains the phenomenon of self-begetting allows for the fact that it may be "formalised" secondarily in the form of fantasy, that is to say in the form of a construction with integrative aims. From another point of view, the archaic character of the experience allows us to make the assumption that the fantasy of self-begetting could be included in the primal fantasies, alongside the primal scene, castration, and seduction. This is the thesis Élisabeth Bizouard (1995) puts forward in her book. However, unmasking a denial, even unwittingly, entails the risk of becoming the victim of it oneself.

Consequently, it comes as no surprise that Stirner is tripped up twice by the very problem he reveals: first, by not seeing that the unique and the nothing are linked by relations of twinship; and secondly, notwithstanding the power of the heated accents of his argument, by failing to really gain access to the strange language whose first stones were once laid down by the "infra-subject" and its *paraphrenic twin*, when they freed themselves simultaneously from the first entity of *primordial being*. It is a language that deploys itself in an original realm, a *paraphrenic realm par excellence*, a space that is entirely different from that which defines a relational topography. It should be stressed that, essentially, this language does not derive from a mere distortion of the language of relationships, which is maternal in its innermost nature, but rather, as I have intimated, from egotic lallation, a fluid emission of more or less articulated sounds and devoid of "caesura", which the infant utters *for his own benefit*, before embarking on the acquisition of the keys of communication with objects.

I consider this "language", composed of vocal elements that were common in those far-off times, as an *idiom of identity* that was entirely valid at the time of the interpellation of the double/twin, when it was a question of gradually acquiring a sufficiently assured sense of identity, and which is a mark of authenticity since it belongs to the order of the ego-instincts. Incidentally, I wonder if the psychosomatic practitioners, Claude Smadja (1993) and Gérard Szwec (1993), would agree that certain verbal self-calming techniques echo this first idiom.

Inherent to the nature of the paraphrenic language to come, the *idiom of identity* inevitably clashes with the relational language of survival which is mendacious and, what is more, is often, if not always, marked by the stamp of the part-object. It follows from this clash that what had been a pure expression of the certainty of the I (*Je*), an equivalent of Nothing, tends to become nothing but distant mist which only the paraphrenic and the poet are able to preserve or rediscover. So the *paraphrenic realm* or space has turned into a transactional space where, if I may put it thus, a sort of "evolving verbal concordat" is signed between two languages.

Incidentally, the notion of a double language is a familiar one. But, generally speaking, and contrary to what I have been suggesting so far, it is the maternal, common relational language that is considered to be the first language; and it is the need to preserve a threatened sense of identity that leads the subject to overturn its architecture.

Such is the point of view adopted by Gilles Deleuze in his remarkable preface to the testimony of Louis Wolfson (1970), *Le Schizo et les langues*. In this text, Deleuze clearly demonstrates the similarity between the psychic work of the poet and that of the schizo—I would say the paraphrenic. He reveals the striking analogy that exists between the transformative technique of the schizo and the literary procedure employed by Raymond Roussel within the French language. For both of them the original sentence is transformed by the dismembering and dissolution of the words composing it; it is literally "boned" ("*désossé*") before being replaced with another sentence with a different meaning. Having demonstrated this, however, Deleuze is reluctant to maintain the similarity as such. He points out that with the schizo, the gap of meaning between the original propositions and their conversion is responsible for an irremediable rift, whereas Raymond Roussel fills this gap "with marvellous, proliferating stories that push back the point of departure ever further, covering it over, to the point of hiding it entirely" (Wolfson, 1970, p. 8). Deleuze does not, however, maintain rigorously the distinction that he wanted to make between the language of the poet and that of the schizo, since he acknowledges that, "... through this adventure of words ... this love story, the schizo has certainly created a rift, but his procedure always has a certain symbolic significance" (ibid., p. 22).

In my view, the preservation of this function is only understandable if one recognises that through poetic or paraphrenic language, the effect of a double negotiation looks downstream, in the direction of the "mundane verbiage" that it tortures; it also, and primarily, looks in the direction of the first *idiom of identity*, fully inscribed in the sphere of the so-called ego-instincts. Louis Wolfson, Raymond Roussel, but also Charles Fourier (1836), with his "*Société hongrée d'âges et roquée d'échelons*", the Reverend Father Luigi Maria Sinistrari d'Ameno (see de M'Uzan, 1956), Berbiguier de Terre Neuve du Thym (1990), and many others as well, open up access to the *paraphrenic realm*, a space to which "any man" may sometimes gain access in some of the circumstances I have mentioned, or if he undergoes a "borderline experience".

Another opportunity is offered to us through the encounter with *extreme art*. There we come across the heirs of this lost world, a world that only opens itself up to us if we accept to live for a while with one of the masterly *oeuvres* in which it is represented.

I am referring here to that of Antonin Artaud and, in particular, "The Return of Artaud the Momo" (1947), even though it exacts a heavy price from me to examine it in the cool light of day.

And if, in this spirit, I agree to do so, it is because, in the great work in question, we in fact discover several languages. Gilles Deleuze was not unaware of this and, in a footnote (Wolfson, 1970, p. 17) draws attention to both the munificence of Artaud's oeuvre and a morphological opposition in it between two lexical forms: *les mots déboîtés* (dislocated or fragmented words) and *les mots souffles*—the latter are at once "liquid and cemented blocks that cannot be broken down into smaller units", and are the only ones animated by a principle of totality. I think that Deleuze would like us to search for this principle naturally on the side of the father, of the symbolic father, whereas in my view, you will have guessed, it proceeds from the first dispositions put at the service of emerging identity, in the sense in which I understand it.

With regard to that immense poem, "The Return of Artaud the Momo" (of which I will only be citing a part; for the complete poem see his *Œuvres complètes*, op. cit.), I recorded that several languages can be detected in it; to be precise, there are three. I would say that the first is the language of ordinary communication which, as one would suspect, is highly limited. Here the object is addressed directly, as if he had the possibility of understanding what the poet was communicating in that very instant. The structure of the sentence and the terms employed belong to common language and are governed by thoroughly rational, secondary level processes. The content, on the other hand, which constitutes a singular, positive, and almost unctuous "obverse" side, suggests a catastrophic loss of being, denounces partial aggressive impulses hostile to the construction of the I, and expresses the quest for an identity that was no doubt violated at a very early stage.

> (You take nothing from it, god,
> because it's me.
> You never took anything like that from me.
> I am writing it here for the first time
> I am finding it for the first time.) (1947, p. 14)

It is significant, is it not, that Artaud takes the trouble, or the precaution, of putting only these lines in parentheses?

At the opposite extreme, we come up against the most surprising and, for some, the most "repulsive" language, if I may say so. It is language that is no longer constructed in relation to the encounter between a person who affirms himself sufficiently and the other. It is a language that is constructed, put together, on the basis of the relation uniting the subject and his *paraphrenic twin*, the only interlocutor who is able to understand a discourse comprised of onomatopoeia, fluid sequences without ruptures and which, one day, may culminate in these *mots souffles* of which Deleuze speaks; a language closed in upon itself in order to edify and circumscribe an indubitable and incomparable identity; a veritable fortress, perfect but fragile, of faultless authenticity, that is unreachable for a while, but only for a while.

From this scream, for it is indeed a scream, I cannot avoid citing a brief passage. The reader will understand me, without smiling or moaning, for there is nothing to laugh about:

> o dedi
> a dada orzoura
> o dou zoura
> a dada skizi
>
> o kaya
> o kaya pontoura
> o ponoura
> a pena
> poni (1947, p. 13)

"The Return of Artaud the Momo" ends, a little further on, with a composition of this nature, developed over sixteen lines. But just before, the third language, that of great art, springs forth, with its rough and jagged architecture resulting from a precarious transaction between the subject, his double, and the world, when the verb gains in power and, at the same time, the rhythm of its thrust slows down.

Of this moment I will cite some final fragments containing the words I, ME, and NOTHING written in capital letters, which I take the liberty of reading as a testimony in favour of the ideas that have forced themselves on my mind.

> Of that hoed bone that I am
> In the filth
> of a paradise
> whose first dupe on earth
> was not the father or the mother
> who diddled you in this den
> but
> I
> screwed into my madness
> And what seized hold of me
> That I too rolled my life there
> ME
> NOTHING, *nothing*
> Because I
> I am there
> I am there
> And it is life
> That rolls its obscene palm there
> O.K.
> And afterward?
> Afterward? Afterward?
> The old Artaud
> Is buried
> In the chimney hole
> That he owes to his cold gum
>
> To the day when he was killed!
> And afterward?
> Afterward?
> Afterward! (1947, pp. 18–19)

CHAPTER EIGHT

Death never confesses* (1996)

With gratitude to Gilles Desbordes,
who was not only my patient
but also my collaborator.

"The thought of nothing", Jankélévitch (1977) writes, "is almost a non-thought, the nothingness of the object annihilating the subject. Just as one cannot see an absence, one cannot think of nothing; so that thinking about nothing is not thinking about anything, and is thus not thinking. The pseudo-thought of death is but a variety of somnolence" (p. 39).

Death never confesses .... But what would it have to confess? What secret is it obliged to keep? To tell the truth, I do not know how this formulation suddenly sprang to my mind. Having been asked to speak about the subject once again, however, I started dreaming about it, even though I thought that I had already pursued the matter to its limits in the past (see de M'Uzan, 1974, 1976a, 1981).

*This chapter first appeared as a paper in French in the *Revue française de psychanalyse*, 60(1): 33–47, in 1996.

In principle, thinking and dreaming are two activities that do not go together, and yet …. Letting "things" go none the less, I noticed once again that even when it is directed towards abstract reflection, the activity of thinking often eludes rational control and goes its own way, just as the images in dreams follow on from each other without seeking our opinion. Having stated that, I remain convinced, along with Jean Rostand (1953), that man has no other means of knowing than his reason.

Well, in spite of this profession of faith, ambiguities and contradictions had forced themselves on me once again, especially with regard to the theme I am discussing here. That was why, in a previous contribution, I had no hesitation in sharing the views expressed by three Nobel Prize winners, J. Monod, L. Pauling, and G. Thomson in their manifesto in favour of euthanasia when "life has lost all dignity, beauty and meaning … and when suffering is pointless …". Yet, at the same time, I felt an "error of the ego" was involved which amounted to depriving the dying person of an ultimate and fundamental experience—that is to say, a surprising libidinal expansion and an increased appetite for relationships that urges each one of us to live his or her life to the extreme limits, in conformity with the aspirations of the libido (see de M'Uzan, 1976b).

Since that paper was published, I have had occasion to conduct therapies with two terminally ill patients, both of whom were entirely aware of their condition. They had both already had considerable personal experience of analysis and wanted to do some authentic analytic work once again. Although it may seem surprising under the circumstances, this desire was very similar to that which motivates any one of us to begin an analysis.

The first case concerned a woman who was completed invaded by the metastases of her breast cancer affecting her lungs, her spine, the dome of her skull, her feet, and so on. I shall not be returning to this case report, which has already been published, except to recall two points that are of particular relevance here: the patient was certain that she was, as she put it, "once again involved in a creative process", an activity that was accompanied by a disturbance of ego-boundaries which had allowed, amongst other things, the emergence of a fantasy of the "double" in which it was "the other of herself who was ill … something light, tenuous, a sensation …" (de M'Uzan, 1981, p. 26).

The second case, which I shall dwell on at greater length, was that of a young man whose brain, cerebellum, brain stem, and mediastinum were all affected by the proliferation of metastases, the cause of which was unknown.

The reflections that I am going to share with you stem essentially from what these patients were able to tell me during our work together, thanks to the immense capacities of their mental functioning. It will perhaps be objected that not many people are prepared, at such times, to undertake and pursue the "work" in question. I am not sure that that is true, provided suitable conditions for it can be created. Furthermore, and this is a point worth emphasising, the "power" that both my patients had at their disposal was in no way based on an ignorance of reality. In other words, they were only too tragically aware of the likely outcome of their illness.

Death never confesses ... how should this thought, which came to my mind so strangely, be interpreted? What confession does death refuse to make? First of all, of course, this is merely a manner of speaking, for death can not speak! It must be understood, then, that it is simply a question of that absolutely certain knowledge that for each one of us, life will one day come to an end irremediably. But, as we know, Freud did not fail to point out that doubts about this still persist, even in the most solid of minds, to the point that people sometimes still entertain ideas of personal immortality—I once pointed out that this was the case with Tolstoy—allowing them, on an everyday basis, to behave on an "as if" basis. Consequently, it may be said that if the ego, in its madness, does not succumb to such folly, it is due to the fact that, ever since it has been inhabited by reason, it has entrusted the *"ego of the ego", an agency detached from the Ego through splitting* (for an exploration of the notion of the "ego of the ego", linked to the role of tension between splitting and denial in the destiny of human beings, see de M'Uzan, 1997) with the task of accepting and recognising fully the strictly mortal character of every living organism. The "healthiest" psychical apparatus, that is, one that governs a person who is totally convinced of his irremediable finiteness, thus depends on a so-called psychotic mechanism, a quasi-existential split at the very heart of the ego. I would be inclined to consider the most decisive form of splitting as an operation which isolates, completely and definitively, an "institution" that is extraneous to the systemic instinctual unconscious, where time and death do not exist—a property that confers on psychoanalysis its unique and revolutionary character in the order of thought.

But once its reign is assured, the "ego of the ego" is not simply content to provide protection against a delirious belief in immortality. Throughout life, but especially when death is near and ineluctable, it has very far-reaching consequences, one of which is the close articulation *between the rigorous recognition of the ineluc*table *character of death, on the one hand, and self-preservation on the other*. It was perhaps an intuition of this nature which led Freud (1920g, p. 52), admittedly briefly, to include the "self-preservative instincts" among the death drives. I would suggest, then, that *when the splitting in question has occurred, collusion occurs between self-preservation, even operating in desperation, and the certainty of death*. In other words, the "ego of the ego" plots with self-preservation, *behind the back* of the unconscious, with the aim of reducing its activity as much as possible and of preventing it from winning over new territories in areas where its modalities of being have been rejected for so long already.

Such is the content of the confession that is impossible to make. Why impossible? Because the marginalisation of the voice of the unconscious, at a moment when it is important for it to make itself heard, constitutes a privation of freedom. It involves a mutilation of the subject who is thus deprived of the innovating capacity for work furnished by a perennial unconscious—admittedly, actively involved in neurosis—but which has the project of living indefinitely and, at the very least, until the "end of time", unperturbed. By "living" I mean continuing to grapple with the past so as to reshape it indefinitely, and constantly creating new versions of it which, in the process, bring to light with full force truths that have always been known yet fundamentally ignored.

It was this freedom that gave my patient, whose struggle I have related elsewhere (de M'Uzan, 1981), access to a strange world where, without being "schizo", as she would say, the "I" and the "other" exchange their way of being—an immense theatre that the narrowness of consciousness would like to ignore because it is afraid of getting lost in it, even though it takes for granted that what it will lose is life.

This freedom is probably just an illusion, since it is only conceivable in relation to consciousness; not to mention the fact that, to a large extent, the indefinite rewriting of the past is imposed on the person rather than really being offered to him as a choice, because it proceeds from the most opaque region of his mind from which the decisive orientations of life originate. He is none the less granted a certain margin of freedom; for, as he is always receptive to the call of the figures in waiting at the back of his mind, it is theoretically possible for him to allow himself to be completely carried away by the need to pursue the construction of his mind indefinitely; alternatively, he can "opt" for the only solution offered to a person in whom the "ego of the ego" has prevailed, that is to say, a lucid stoic position, bolstered by austere epicurean rigour. It seems to me that the thesis developed recently by Christian David (1996) to the effect that *mourning for oneself, in advance, is a necessity*, could ideally lend support to the stoic position. Such an attitude is full of dignity, and perhaps wisdom; but on the psychoanalytic level it might well result, as I have suggested elsewhere (de M'Uzan, 1976b), from a narcissistic misunderstanding which often leads to a hypertrophy of the reality-ego.

It may be said that living psychically until the very end, with all the agencies with which our mind is equipped, or, alternatively, attaining an austere state of quietude through the process of mourning one's own self, are solutions that are available to very few people. I am not certain of this, but it has to be admitted that when the patient's entourage (family, friends, healthcare personnel), feeling completely overwhelmed by the situation, begin to withdraw, the patient, who is informed of his condition, often, and perhaps even in most cases, goes through—admittedly at a conscious level only—the phases described by Elisabeth Kübler-Ross (1969), ranging from denial and refusal to a loss of hope, with intermediate stages of anger, bargaining, depression, and glum resignation. The remarks that I am making here follow up on those I have made elsewhere (de M'Uzan, 1974), when I drew attention to that extraordinary phenomenon, which is so readily countercathected by overwhelmed members of the patient's entourage, of a libidinal expansion, a renewed appetite for relationships that leads the dying person to form with his or her "key object" a sort of new being which I have called the "last dyad".

It scarcely needs saying that I had to overcome many reservations before returning to this subject for a fourth time, especially as, I my view, the first vocation of psychoanalysis is to enable us to live rather than to die. If I have decided to do so, it is because, quite by chance, I have once again been confronted in reality with the painful destiny of a young colleague who came to see me to do some fresh analytic work. What was said on that occasion not only confirmed the points of view I had advanced previously, but added new and fundamental elements— the very ones that were the source of the theoretical developments that

I have just set out. Finally, and this is not without importance, various testimonies that I received after the publication of those earlier studies allowed me to see that they had offered the patients' loved ones, as well as psychotherapists, a new understanding of these dramatic situations and a greater capacity to deal with them.

The reproach is often made that clinical "vignettes" only appear in a text or communication for the sole purpose of lending weight to an argument or a theoretical construction that was conceived of independently of the material. I do not share this judgement, far from it, for the utilisation of these famous vignettes has an associative value in the full sense of the term. It reveals the existence of deep connections between the perception of what is contained in a clinical fact and the preconscious psychical activity leading to reflections on it. That being the case, today, instead of inserting fragments of observation into my theoretical exposition, I have preferred to give a fairly detailed account, following its progression over a period of roughly three months, of what happened during the meetings that my patient and I had agreed to organise.

Right from the start, in the preliminary interview, he let me know, without the slightest signs of aggressiveness, which I took as a positive indication, that he was suffering from cerebral and cerebellar metastases that had been discovered following an epileptic seizure, the origin of which was unknown. We both knew that the time we had might be counted, so the work we did was very intense from the outset, in contrast with more run of the mill situations. My future patient talked about minor somatic troubles that had occurred since his mother's death eighteen months earlier. I caught myself thinking eighteen "years"—this was my first parapraxal slip, and I thought that it was highly significant in indicating my wish to be practically the master of time. He thought that these troubles might be the expression of a need to incorporate his mother and to bring her back to life in his inner world.

ME: "Your mother is not your daughter."
         He responded by saying that his daughter, with both his and his wife's agreement, had just left the family home.
HIM: "The house will seem empty."
ME: "That's not a reason to fill it."
HIM: "It's more that I am going to empty it."
         Continuing in the vein of this black humour he was partial to,

he recalled his mother's funeral and how she had wanted her children to carry her coffin.

HIM: "How heavy she was ... she was a very small woman, but heavy. Six months ago, I found I had eczema on one of my fingers, in the very place where my fingers had been holding the handle of the coffin."

The tone was set. Without any hesitation on his part or mine, we agreed to see each other regularly. So he came up from the provinces by car, accompanied by a relative, for two sessions a week during the Christmas holidays, and then every Sunday afternoon.

Without forcing things unduly, I would say that our sessions were marked by three phases of unequal duration. The first, and the longest, extended up until the moment his illness took a sudden turn for the worse; the second continued up until the time when we had to continue our sessions by telephone; and the third was this period when we communicated by telephone.

My patient threw himself body and soul into what we had decided to do! The intensity of his involvement was extreme, and I think I can say that the same was true for me, which goes to explain the accelerated rhythm of our work. It was going to be a sort of condensed analysis—at a very different rhythm, naturally, from his earlier analysis—for, in spite of a few short attempts by both of us to deny reality, we knew what the real situation was.

In this respect, our first session was remarkable. I am thinking about what he said, what I said in response, and about how he made use of what I said. At first, everything happened very fast, and it was even a bit chaotic; but then a thread emerged which, by creating a certain meaning, formed a link between a number of words: embarked, empty, heavy, and mother, with one of us, I do not know which now, mentioning a police inquiry. And he added with reference to the metastases: *"Me voilà salement embarqué"* ("What a terrible mess I'm in").[1] Then, quite naturally, but losing the rhythm of the exchange, he referred, in quite another tone, to the ordeals he was going through in the way of medical examinations (MRI, bronchoscopy, etc.). Then, suddenly getting a grip of himself again, he cried out: "All that is of no interest; that's not what we're here for." And then, more calmly than at the beginning of the session, he took up the words I had said to him during the preliminary interview: "Your mother is not your daughter", and added,

"I am a battlefield between my mother and me." The themes were there: mother and death were inextricably interwoven. In the following sessions it became clear that there was an unconscious project of bringing back to life within himself a mother who was identified with the metastases that were spreading in him with, in particular, in the mediastinum, "a stone or a piece of wood sticking into [his] chest". I thought to myself, "like a statue", rather like the monument that is sometimes erected in the mind of someone in mourning. And the theme became still heavier to the point that his mother, who was the object of the most ambivalent feelings, began to assume several guises, including the very commonplace one of the spider. The shadow side of his mother also found expression when he came to speak about his father's death. My patient was eight years old when his father left the family home, and twelve when the latter died accidentally, though he had continued to see his children regularly up to that point. Speaking about this loss, his mother had exclaimed: "We have found each other again; he has come back to me."

A few sessions later, I took advantage of the half-paranoiac, half-hypochondriacal turn that my patient's remarks took occasionally, for brief moments, to point out to him that what he said he was experiencing corresponded to the active stirrings of a persecuting internal object that was not to be identified with his mother but with a *non-ego* with uncertain boundaries. In fact, when the narcissistic libido is wavering, the ego is still involved, and yet it is already no longer the ego but rather a substance that is difficult to confront, almost impossible to expel. If, by saying this, I had no doubt hoped to further the elaboration of a process of mourning that had been incomplete (is this not always the case?), my interpretation sought to support and extend the psychical apparatus' capacity for theatrical representation, in conformity with its "Jacobinic", synthetising vocation, and its propensity for creating meaning, according to which everything must be integrated, including the pathological, in this instance, the metastases.

Even when the most archaic as well as the most evolved determinants rendered the transference/countertransference reactions terribly complex, a complexity that was further aggravated by the tragic nature of the situation, the occasional ups and downs of the relationship took place against a background of absolute, non-conflictual mutual confidence. It was a non-ambivalent relationship, no doubt nourished by narcissistic elements belonging to both protagonists and comparable to the basic transference described by Catherine Parat (1991, p. 305) "which (in neuroses) allows the stability of the analytic work to be established". This did not, however, prevent the features of the relationship with the "mother/spider" from finding expression at certain moments, albeit very briefly. Neither did it preclude signs of the evolution of the paternal image from asserting themselves.

The hurdles that arose during the work were few and far between, and I am convinced that I was responsible for those that did occur. For example, one day, thinking foolishly about the effort my patient was making to come and see me, and about the time that was at our disposal—and about any number of other things—I offered to prolong the session, which was in many respects an error. He accepted, but soon enough the atmosphere of the session began to change subtly; a vague sense of unease set in and, after about ten minutes, he asked me, in a rather strange tone of voice, if we could stop. He felt "emptied". It occurred to me that the unconscious sources of the interest that I showed for what he was saying, which were materialised in my prolonging the session, might have mobilised an unconscious fantasy in him in which I was identified with the ambiguous mother and was trying to feed off him.

Something similar occurred on another occasion with regard to a dream. This was how he related it: "It was a sort of game, but rather a dangerous one. I was in front of an almost vertical dune consisting of dark grey sand. I had to go through this dune. There was an entry, so there had to be an exit on the other side; but the time available for going through it was limited and regulated by a machine in the form of a cast iron cylinder, also vertical, on which it was written: "*Seine-Inférieure*".[2]

This dream could serve to illustrate the notion of over-determination while, at the same time, highlighting the extraordinary capacities for condensation that my patient regularly demonstrated. Given the situation he was in, I did not comment on the theme of the passage, although one could discuss the anal-sadistic implications of it. The phallic significance of the machine is equally obvious, but what was important for him was that the erotic theme was only discovered at the end of a chain of associations: sand → quicksand → de M'Uzan → Niagara (the 1953 film by Hathaway) → Marilyn Monroe → very little time to get through → Seine-Inférieure → lower body → sex.

Let me say in passing that in reporting this dream in full I wanted to draw attention to the intense dream activity that took place during these months which led, in particular, to a new elaboration of infantile sexuality and to the primal scene. What happened in connection with the "the dream of the dune" led me to note a movement in the countertransference which I had become aware of, although others had eluded me. The day after he had told me the dream, the theme of the "passage", with its rich harmonics, was still powerfully present in my mind, especially as certain associations concerned me directly. All this came back to me during the following session and began to impede my listening, for while he was speaking to me, I began associating for my own benefit: passage → transfer → transfer of substance → organic substance → spider; and all of a sudden I was persuaded that it was a question of his *substance* (that is the only way I can put it) passing into mine. I shared this thought with him. A very understandable reaction of resistance prevented him from understanding at first, but this then receded. It was the first time that a resistance of this kind had manifested itself, but how could it be otherwise when one considers that the substance, the end of my associative chain, which without any shadow of doubt was connected for me with his cancer, had evoked for me at that precise moment the whitish content of the abdomen of a fly!

It goes without saying that transference/countertransference relations do not always turn out to be so unpredictable. This is perhaps a fortunate state of affairs but, all things considered, I prefer such moments to those when the work seems to be getting bogged down— a situation, it has to be said, for which the analyst may be responsible more often than he thinks. As far as I am concerned, during this analytical therapy, I sometimes found it difficult to maintain a level of listening that was appropriate to the material and, above all, to a mode of functioning which, at moments, was frankly archaic. At such times I fell back on a mode of listening employed in classical analytic work, but soon had the impression that something was being lost. On one occasion I found myself thinking: "I'm all at sea; I've got to get stuck in there," an expression that had its place in the context of a sports activity that he had practised …!

He then got irritated: "It's really hard going," he said. Once, he even allowed himself to get a bit discouraged and was ready to give way to fears of what was going to happen. But when I said to him with a certain harshness, "We are not here to moan, but to do something", he quickly adopted the formulation.

In fact, things were hardly ever "hard going". Our work moved along incredibly fast. His whole history—the history of his first years, with the weight of his infantile sexuality—was taken up again, and, as we say, elaborated. Then we discovered that the ever present activity of the maternal imago was masking his relationship with his father, which was much more important than I had at first imagined. We were now dealing, naturally, with a classical Oedipal configuration. But in spite of that we were both aware that something essential was missing. What this was would be revealed during a dramatic session, entirely focused on the recognition, hitherto countercathected, of emotions connected with his father's death.

It was an extremely exhausting session; he had scarcely arrived when he burst into tears. He had had convulsions four times that week … then, very soon after, something strange occurred: he continued sobbing, but suddenly exclaimed: "My father is dead … do you see, my father is dead," literally as if it had just happened. He sobbed all the more. "My father died when I was twelve, and I didn't know." Yet, this was something he had already told me calmly in the first interview. It was overwhelming. Once he had calmed down, he told me at length about the intense depression he had experienced at the time, which had lasted for several years.

After speaking about his father, he quite naturally went on to speak about his son. The way he spoke to me about him or rather what came to his mind at that point, revealed—and I found this quite astonishing—that, in fact, *he* was the son, crying. I pointed this out to him, adding that he was living across three generations. He recognised this and confirmed it without ambiguity. Then I saw him, as it were, split in two, or even in three, and in a sort of void, staring at the ceiling. It was as if he was absent; indeed, he had fallen into one of those states of reverie that he had told me about the week before.

This, then, was how the first phase of our work together ended. However, after a reasonably smooth and orderly evolution which, I can say unreservedly, had led to a re-evaluation of his Oedipal conflicts, with a remarkable freeing up of encysted emotions, something infinitely less clear forced itself briefly upon us. This second phase opened with a session in which I saw him arriving unsteady on his feet. In an ironic tone of voice, he said: "It's the meta (metastasis) in my cerebellum. Apart from that, it's not been a bad week." A long, unusual, and disturbing silence followed. Once again, he began gazing at the ceiling. He had almost gone to the wrong floor, confusing the third floor and the fifth floor, which reminded him that, as a child, he had lived on the third floor of the building until his father died, and "then on the fifth floor with my mother ... and with my brothers and sisters". New Oedipal material now surfaced. However, his silences became more and more frequent and suddenly, in fits and starts, he began gazing upwards and to the right. He was on the point of having an epileptic fit. He was struggling consciously, and warned me that he was afraid he was going to have convulsions. His head now began to jerk in the same direction in which he was gazing. After a short silence—and quite aware of the derisory nature of my injunction—I commanded him firmly to grip his right forearm with his left hand, while repeating several times "three and five" (the two floors in his childhood). He repeated with me out loud "three and five". He struggled like a maniac ... and then the fit suddenly stopped. Almost immediately, he talked about what had just happened, saying that he was very struck by "the connection between representation and neuronal short-circuit", those were his words. And he went on to say that he had the impression that he was on the verge of identifying an image that he sensed was of crucial importance, even though it still eluded him. His daughter's first name came to his mind instead. From that point on the Oedipal material only appeared very fleetingly. What asserted itself above all, in a sort of atomisation, was a series of pregenital representations.

Nevertheless, the situation was deteriorating day by day. I was informed that he would not be able to come to our next session. This was distressing for him, so I proposed to continue our exchanges by telephone; and he was duly relieved. This was the beginning, then, of the third phase of our work together, consisting of just two long sessions of about an hour each.

The first of these sessions turned out to be much less exhausting than I had imagined it would be. This was because the intensity of the level of involvement, on both sides, was in the service of an extreme need to make as much progress as possible with this process of exploration that we were ardently engaged in. Essentially, the material could be described as "sexual", which reminds us once again how imperishable libidinal energy is. First of all—it was scarcely believable, and we were both somewhat alarmed—we saw that the connection between a recent incident and some figures of metaphorical value revealed that, at the bottom of his mind, he had always had the intimate conviction that women were endowed with a penis ... and that, in certain respects, he had spent his whole time looking for it everywhere! This obscure belief, widely shared, is one that the theoretician has no difficulty in recognising, without really knowing it.

Next, with a certain precipitation, and randomly, he remarked on: (1) his resemblance with his mother, whose face he had discovered while looking at himself in a mirror; (2) the breathing of his father who enjoyed sport like him; (3) the connection between sexual activity and breathing; and (4) the "mad" idea concerning the homosexual side of his relationship with his father. He was, of course, familiar with all this, but now it was assuming a new and powerful *valency*. We were both astounded, just as we had been when he was able to acknowledge his father's death in a fully cathected way for the first time.

It is difficult to give you an idea of our last conversation. He was very short of breath, and even holding the telephone receiver was difficult for him. Furthermore, the disordered character of what he had to say had become more pronounced, while retaining its underlying pertinence. If I had to organise his remarks, I would say that the session was oriented from the beginning to the end by the theme of respiration, whose significance we had often observed. Among other things, he recalled how his mother had been breathless and thirsty just before she died. Her? Him? Who? I asked myself. "Orgasm and breathlessness resemble each other; mother and death are mixed up together ... birth, too," he said. I was caught up in all this. He said he could breathe better on his right side.

ME: "On your right side."
HIM: "Towards my parents' bed ... the important thing is to have plenty of fresh water."

Finally, he talked about smells of all kinds including the most disagreeable ones; but also about taste, salty and savoury foods. All the senses were evoked before a final reference was made to castration, my own, as well as that of his former analyst, who had suffered from a degenerative neurological affliction. The sense of touch, which had been forgotten, then found its place when he recalled a childhood scene in which he was standing in a tub, being washed by his mother: "Touching is very powerful ... it was so hot that it was cold; I was alone with my mother, my father had gone away …"—an ultimate evocation of the Oedipal situation. This was the last time he spoke to me.

When the degree of engagement on both sides is so intense, the last words spoken are not the end of the matter.

On the morning of our next appointment, a Sunday, the day we communicated, one of his family circle rang me to say that my patient was no longer able to speak to me. In order to help you understand what was about to happen to me, I will have to recall the details that I was given, even though it costs me to do so. In addition to the cerebral and cerebellar metastases, the brain stem was now affected as well. My patient was plunged into a sub-comatose state from which he emerged only for short instants. His death was imminent; it was a question of days, if not hours.

Now, suddenly, and as if, deep down within me, I had refused to accept reality, I was gripped by *violent feelings of grief*—those are the precise words that come to my mind, and yet I have the feeling that I did not even think of them at the time. The pain accompanied me in the street—I was on the point of going out when I had received the call—and suddenly, flabbergasted, I caught myself humming a poem by Ludwig Uhland (1787–1862) which I had not thought about for decades:

> *Ich hatt' einen Kameraden,*
> *Einen Bess'ren findst du ni't.*
> *Die Trommel schlug zum Streite,*
> *Er ging an meiner Seite*
> *In gleichen Schritt und Tritt.*
>
> *Eine Kugel kam geflogen:*
> *Gilt's mir oder gilt es dir?*
> *Ihn hat es weggerissen,*
> *Er liegt mir vor den Füssen*
> *Als wär's ein Stück von mir.* (1809)

(I had a friend—a better one you will not find—the battle drums were beating—he went at my side, step by step—a bullet flew in our direction—was it for him or for me?—it brought him down—he was lying at my feet—as if he was a part of me.)

"He was lying at my feet, as if he was a part of me." I soon understood that the resurgence of this poem at that precise moment expressed and belonged to the work of mourning that was inevitably going to begin for me.

Two or three days later, my patient's wife told me he had died; the end had been a veritable ordeal. (In fact, his mortal agony proper had lasted seven and a half days, as my patient's wife told me after reading this text. And she added, quite rightly, I think, that my error perhaps indicated a wish to spare her husband the last days which were the most difficult.) He alternated between states of deep coma and waking coma, during which time a real state of disorganisation set in. His wife, who was constantly by his side in these last moments, just as she had been, as he told me, over the last months, talked to him, massaged him, and manipulated him. And when he "was going" in an attack of polypnoea, his wife positioned herself just in front of his face, breathing slowly and calmly until the attack stopped.

A few days later, thinking back over the long weeks that had gone by, I was astonished to see, after the violent feelings of grief that had overcome me on learning of his imminent death, how I had recovered a degree of calmness and even, perhaps, a certain coldness. It could only be a defensive reaction. This was confirmed by the certitude that dawned on me that the literal content of the words I had addressed to his wife had to be interpreted. Protected by repression, I had avoided, unwittingly, giving substance to the obscure desire to "introduce myself" into *her* work of mourning, and had thereby excluded an Oedipal fantasy. Will this fragment of self-analysis suffice to prevent a "psychic sequestration" from forming in me?

A few days after the funeral, my patient's wife sent me a letter in which she told me, in passing, that there was a superb view from the grave of the town and that her husband "would certainly make some black humour of that". She ended by telling me that he had said that "[T]he work with [me] was what was most important."

The reader will perhaps be surprised that I have related at such length the tragic experience of my patient. It is unusual in psychoanalytic writings, but it has helped me illustrate the extreme capacities of human beings in such circumstances. It is not easy, and perhaps even out of place, to return to considerations of a general order, and even to theoretical reflections, after such an exposition, but I have none the less decided to do so briefly. For as can be seen from the first part of this chapter, I have been led to distinguish two orientations in human beings based on the opposition between, on the one hand, a *split* that protects in the mind the certainty of death and, on the other, a *denial* of this same certainty, thanks to the penetration of the voice of the unconscious at *all* levels of the psychical apparatus. The primordial purpose of the first of these orientations is to carry out stoically a process of mourning for oneself; the aim of the second is to take the self-construction of a human being as far as possible. Although this opposition should no doubt only be seen in terms of difference, it could lead us to think in terms of a hierarchy. With regard to the subject I am dealing with, as with many others, this risk is by no means negligible.

As evidence of this, I will cite a fundamental passage from the argument developed by E. M. Cioran (1949) in his *Précis de decomposition*:

> Men can be classed in terms of the most capricious criteria: their humours, their dreams, or their glands. ... But there is something that comes from ourselves, which *is* ourselves, an invisible but internally true reality, a strange and perennial presence that we can conceive of at each instant but which we never dare to acknowledge, and which only has actuality prior to its consummation. This something is death, the true criterion ... the most intimate dimension of all living beings, which separates humanity into two orders that are so irreducible, so far removed from each other, that there is more distance between them than between a vulture and a mole, than between a star and spittle. A gulf of two incommunicable worlds opens up between the man who has a sense of his own death and the one who does not: and yet both die. One is ignorant of his death, while the other is conscious of it; one dies in an instant, the other is constantly dying .... Their common condition sets them poles apart from each other, at two extremes but within one and the same definition; irreconcilable, they suffer the same destiny .... One lives as if he were eternal; the other thinks continually about his eternity and denies it in each thought. (pp. 20–21)

Does this not imply setting up, without the slightest ambiguity, a hierarchy between human beings? Almost a classification, which we naturally reject even when the underlying determining factors of this rejection are more obscure and more equivocal than one would imagine spontaneously. I am obliged, however, to take this risk, and I do so all the more readily since the distinction made by E. M. Cioran is exactly the opposite of mine. For him, the priority consists, providing one has the possibility of doing so, in enjoining the ego to let itself be consumed day after day, throughout life—a process that proceeds from a narcissistic object-choice and expresses a quasi melancholic proposition, since the process of mourning concerns the ego and not the object. But for me, nothing must be allowed to defeat the instinct which "compels every living thing to cling to life" (Freud, 1917e, p. 246); that is to say, to live psychically, to continue to develop itself to the very limit, without this entailing an alteration of the continuity of the object-cathexis.

Once again, it seems that philosophy and psychoanalysis are difficult to reconcile. The thinker holds firmly, as we have just seen, to the pre-eminence of the conscious mind; the *homopsychoanalyticus*, more modestly perhaps, in spite of appearances, acknowledges that he is moved and oriented indefinitely by forces lurking in the depths of his being—forces that escape him by merging with life.

Just as I am on the point of concluding, I am struck by a supreme irony: it occurs to me once again that the thesis that clinical reality has imposed on me finds support, across the centuries, in the life of Socrates. The day before his death, still pursuing the fulfilment of his being, Socrates decides to go on living by finally obeying a recurring dream which says: "Socrates ... make music! Be productive!" He thereby avoids leaving this world without having done "penance for impiety", that is to say, for a Greek, without having fulfilled his destiny (Plato, 1950).

Notes

1. In French "*se laisser embarquer dans une sale histoire*" means "to get mixed up in some nasty business".
2. Maritime department in north-west France.

CHAPTER NINE

The uncanny or "I am not who you think I am"* (2009)

"I am not who you think I am." Here, this formulation is not the reply of a hypocritically prudish young girl to the propositions of an honest man sensitive to her lures. No, it is the *uncanny* that proffers it … provided, that is, the latter is endowed with speech. In any case, one could suppose that the expression lends itself, from the outset, to being inscribed in a universe of words. At the very beginning of his study, Freud devotes many pages to a linguistic approach to the term *"unhe-imlich"*, citing terms which define related emotions: fright, fear, anxiety, horror. Sensitive to his example—but I am exposing myself to introducing nothing more than a worthless parenthesis, even if what follows will show that this is not at all the case—I note that, in the list, a word is missing. It is the word *bizarre*, borrowed from the Italian around 1549. What is missing is often very instructive, is it not? It is perhaps the case here, because Paul Robert's *Dictionnaire de la langue française* states that the word bizarre was first employed as a feminine noun: *"une bizarro"*,

*This text first appeared in French in Danon Boileau & Nayrou (Eds.) (2009) *Inquiétante étrangeté*, pp. 89–98. It was translated into English by Andrew Weller and published in *Reading French Psychoanalysis*, pp. 201–209 (Birksted-Breen, Flanders & Gibeault, 2010). (It is slightly revised for this edition.)

and qualitatively, to designate a *singular* person or thing. Would the feminine, and the question or questions that it raises, have some part to play in the matter?

Freud thinks so, noting that "It often happens that neurotic men declare that they feel there is something uncanny about the female genital organs" (1919h, p. 245). And it was while I was thinking about this remark that I recalled the extreme turmoil experienced one day by a gynaecologist—the profession clearly aggravates the singularity of the emotion. One day, then, while he was having intimate relations with his partner, he was arrested by the thought: "So that's what she's got at the bottom of her belly" (*C'est donc ça qu'elle a au bas du ventre*).

We do not really know here if the *that* is only that. It would be tempting to limit ourselves to the inscription of the matter within the context of a problematic of sexual identity. And yet, even when this position is convincing, one cannot overlook those "experiences" that are *at the very least closely related* to the uncanny, in which anxiety is sometimes absent and where the sexual does not seem to be involved, or at least not regularly. I am thinking, among other things, about the phenomena of depersonalisation. So, would one not be justified in saying that the uncanny forms part of, or is just a moment of, an infinitely larger or different domain than one had imagined? Pushing this proposition to its extreme, it would hardly be a provocation to claim that a situation would be *"unheimlich"* precisely when it is free of all strangeness! Would strangeness be in the process of taking precedence over the uncanny? At any rate, we owe it to ourselves to pursue the quest for a common factor at work in the phenomena in question.

In order to take these considerations further, it is worth recalling, in a very condensed fashion, Freud's basic contention. Having set aside, as a determining factor, the role of intellectual uncertainty alleged by E. Jentsch (1906), as well as the impact of the confrontation with the double inherited from Otto Rank (1914) and regarded as only a predisposing factor, Freud—as we know—argues that the uncanny proceeds from the return of the repressed and castration anxiety: "The fear of castration itself contains no other significance and no deeper secret" (1919h, p. 231). The matter cannot be stated more clearly. It is even with a certain boldness, and almost provocation, that he adds: "I hope the majority of readers will agree with me" (p. 227). Or better still: "I would not recommend any opponent of the psycho-analytic view to select this particular story of the Sand-Man to support his argument that anxiety about the eyes has nothing to do with the castration complex" (p. 231). So we have been warned! But in spite of that, Freud is more ambiguous when he none the less recognises the role of perception at another point in the text. And he even declares that "We must be prepared to admit that there are other elements besides those which we have already laid down as determining the production of uncanny feelings" (p. 247). One cannot underestimate the significance of this correction, whose trace can be found, for example, in the text "A Disturbance of Memory on the Acropolis", written in 1936, thus a long time after the one we are concerned with, where the feeling of uncanniness is referred to notably without any reference to sexuality. Freud recognises that, in front of the Acropolis, he had (or might have had) a momentary feeling that what he saw was not real, and he continues: "Such a feeling is known as a 'feeling of derealization' … just as when the subject feels that a piece of his own self is strange to him" (1936a, pp. 244–245). Following the same train of thought, Freud asserts in the text we are concerned with that when "the subject identifies himself with someone else … he is in doubt as to which his self is, or substitutes the extraneous self for his own. In other words, there is a doubling, dividing and interchanging of the self" (1919h, p. 234). In a footnote, Freud makes an allusion to something similar when he cites two observations by E. Mach in which the subject at first takes the reflection of his image in the mirror for someone else's face (p. 248).

"The 'Uncanny', then, is certainly not simply a work that has been left in a drawer and rescued from oblivion," as Freud claims in a letter to Ferenczi (dated 12 May, 1919). Furthermore, the effort he devotes to studying the phenomenon—one some would consider as almost marginal compared with the other issues that psychoanalysis is faced with—shows that this is not at all the case. Consequently, the uncanny—which, I would add in passing, transcends in any case the specific domain of aesthetics—largely justifies a closer study.

In response to this challenge, and after the points that I have just made, I want to stress again that the term that should be given priority is *strangeness*. Strangeness is an impression that is affirmed each time "natural distinctions" tend to become erased, that is, distinctions between the inside and the outside, the ego and the non-ego, the subject and the object, the familiar and the alien. This is true to the point that the uncanny, which does not tolerate being confined within an overly restrictive notional framework, will become a term that characterises a relationship in which the *disturbing* and the *fascinating* are contrasted. Once again, it is the idea of strangeness that predominates: strangely disturbing, strangely fascinating. Such is the *plus* that must be given to the *new* for these two moments to be visible. This plus is also a minus, for what tends to get lost is the intimate feeling of the ego's specificity. An opportunity arises for introjection, especially as, in the tension between the fascinating and the disturbing, the experience of a correlative vacillation, not necessarily or always accompanied by anxiety, echoes something of the primordial state of being. It is precisely in this connection that I recall Maurice Bouvet's report, in 1960, during the "Congress for French-Speaking Analysts", when, in my intervention, I argued that phenomena of depersonalisation could occur without being accompanied by anxiety, but rather by a sort of exaltation, as can be observed during so-called creative activities or during technical sports exercises that are mastered perfectly.

At this point in my exposition, it seems appropriate to relate certain circumstances encountered in life or in analytic practice which will lend support to what I have just asserted. We will see the important role played in them by perception, a role that Freud at times wanted to reduce, and yet what is experienced is largely induced by phenomena of a sensory order. I remember, then, the peculiar emotion I felt one day upon hearing, at twilight, the unique cry of a blackbird perched on the roof. In an earlier text (de M'Uzan, 1974, p. 26; 1977, p. 155) I studied a situation in which the observation of a relation of strict symmetry with an interlocutor who was facing me across a small table showed that the latter was simply a double, and that consequently it meant that one could be dead without knowing it.

I also recall the dream of a young girl who was hospitalised after making a suicide attempt. It was a recurrent dream. *Walking down a deserted road at night, she hears someone walking behind her. As the footsteps get closer, she starts to run … and at that point wakes up in an acute state of anxiety.* The anxiety was very real. In certain respects this is an ordinary dream in which the determining role of sexuality will easily be recognised. But that is not the end of the matter because the young girl, still intrigued and moved, hoped, each time she had the dream, to turn round one day, in the dream itself, and to discover the identity of her pursuer. Well, one day this happened, but what she then saw, with a mixture of horror and terror, was herself: very old, with dishevelled white hair falling across her face, a sort of reflection of her demented mother. Though there are many interesting points one could comment on here, I would like above all to emphasise the swing from castration anxiety towards an order where sexuality, even narcissistic, is no longer involved. What is involved is something quite different. In another dream reported to me recently by a patient who has been in classical analytic treatment with me now for just a few months, the pursuer was the patient herself. She was pursuing a young woman "who had a reputation for mistreating children". She managed to catch up with the fleeing woman, who suddenly turned round … and my patient, utterly horrified, recognised that it was no other than herself.

Not hesitating to broaden the field in which the uncanny manifests itself, I will mention a curious experience, occurring more or less sporadically, in those moments when the memory of precise events, sometimes among the oldest, is exacerbated to the point of hallucinatory clarity, even though at the same time, and with equal force, there is a powerful impression of never having been anything more than a witness to them. It is an experience completely devoid of anxiety, as if the activity of perception had supplanted every other activity or function.

We know how it is often wise to be careful when reporting a sequence arising from our practice. This is particularly necessary for some of these "vignettes", as we call them, when we have been led to introduce technical variations, or to make, as Michael Parsons (2006) has proposed (in a lecture given at the Paris Psychoanalytic Society), allusive, "open" interpretations that are capable of "undergoing all sorts of surprising transformations in the patient's mind". Uncanny phenomena can occur during a session, whose fruitfulness may be compared with undergoing episodes of depersonalisation. In his time, Maurice Bouvet already took this view, regarding it as a decisive instrument for integrating that which is new.

A female patient, whom I spoke about recently, and who has been in analysis with me for several years, had barely settled down on the couch when she said in a somewhat embarrassed voice:

"I don't know what colour your hair is."
A: "Which hair?" (this may seem a rather surprising question)
P: "Well, the hair you have on your head."
A: "So I have hair on my head."
P: "Oh, I don't know now …"

The episode was free of all anxiety. On the other hand, in this strange, uncanny atmosphere, a certain curiosity, perplexity, and uneasiness were undoubtedly being expressed. But what should be noted above all is that this exchange was the initial phase and motor of a large movement of organic integration of sexuality and identity.

As one proceeds further in the study of the uncanny, one notes a constantly changing perspective in oneself whereby one seeks alternately either to discover what would be in line with Freud's will, a narrow and fundamental specificity of the phenomenon, or to recognise its effects in very diverse domains, as I have argued on several occasions. This leads me to relate the adventure, if I may put it like that, of a young woman during a train journey at night in which uncanniness *connotes perversion*, another domain altogether. Leaving her seat, the young woman went out into the corridor to stretch her legs. It was years ago when trains had compartments and corridors. She stopped, with her forehead pressing against the rain-streaked window. The young woman watched the lights appearing, now and then, through the darkness. A young man, who at first was standing at some distance from her, now approached her. The only unusual thing about him was the large and dark pair of sunglasses he was wearing. Very politely, he asked her what time the train was due to arrive in Paris. She replied, telling him what he wanted to know. However, he persisted, saying that there might be some delay. She suggested he should speak to the ticket inspector. Apologising, the man repeated his request and, to justify doing so, explained that he worked as a make-up artist for radio and television and had to be there at a precise time, which was why he was so anxious. The young woman was now getting a bit impatient when the man suddenly removed his glasses, revealing his heavily made-up eyes and long false eyelashes. In an extreme state of shock, the young woman let out a cry and rushed to the other end of the corridor where another man was standing. She grabbed him by his jacket, saying: "Quick, quick, say something to me quickly." It was as if a sound, speech of any kind, another perception, would wrench her away from the depersonalisation that was overcoming her. She almost no longer knew who she was or where she was.

Whether the experience of uncanniness is expressed in a flamboyant or, alternatively, in a furtive manner, one can infer without excessive boldness that the phenomenon manifests the continuity of those times when indecision characterised a natural state at the far reaches of being—a state, as Freud said, that "strictly speaking is never surmounted". The uncanny commemorates and celebrates a crucial phase in the development of psychic functioning, *a moment when the uncanny finds its primordial basis*, a moment when the indeterminate nature of identity, the daughter of the naturally uncertain character of the frontiers of being, projects into the future an occasional return, a return that is even more insistent than one would imagine it to be, in the form of troubling or disturbing experiences of uncanniness. It is from this situation of a continuum between the inside and the outside, between the self and the non-self, that an evolution occurs towards distinctions, even though they will never acquire a frank and affirmed character. This evolution may be considered as a "psychisation", that is to say, an inscription in the psychosexual register, with the aim of objectalisation. So it is indeed through the intervention of castration anxiety that "the operation of the uncanny", and the mechanics that underlie it, induce the integration, the organic aggregation of the dimensions of identity (*l'identitaire*) and the psychosexual. As an instrument and witness to this psychisation of a primordial state, the uncanny is situated at the intersection of two orders; moreover, it sustains, while translating it, an activity of *negotiation*, a negotiation between what I call, to be precise, the self-preservative, non-instinctual dimension of identity and sexual drive functioning. I must add, as I have often argued, that the term drive should be reserved for object and/or narcissistic sexuality alone.

The dimension of identity belongs to the self-preservative order: it is worth retaining the expression, provided we remember that the term self-preservative defines a programme of development of being— a programme that is essentially genetic, endowed with a duration of application that is limited by the planned extinction of its activity, without the intervention of any kind of drive activity. It is on the basis of this so-called self-preservative programme that maternal seduction (in Jean Laplanche's sense of the term) gives birth to erogenous zones whose activity will demand the psychic activity which is called *drive functioning*. Among others, it is at these moments, or when they return, and almost throughout the whole of life, that the uncanny finds the opportunity of manifesting itself more or less spectacularly. In the negotiation in question, we can see a shift of emphasis from the quantitative towards the qualitative with, to boot, a gain in meaning. In analytic treatments, it is essential to identify the precise stage of this negotiation. Otherwise, the analyst is in danger of thwarting the integration of what is new, which persists alongside experiences of uncanniness. In addition, and perhaps more seriously, the analyst runs the risk of not intervening at the essential moment, but elsewhere.

At this point, I want to return once again to uncanny phenomena in the treatment, as Michael Parsons proposes, and in particular to the sorts of technical initiatives that I referred to earlier when answering my patient with the question, "Which hair?" It was an intervention, it is true, that some would rightly consider destabilising. Well, yes indeed, it is even by virtue of saying things of this kind that *a new path emerges in the psychoanalytic approach to the other*. You may remember that, a long time ago, in 1991, in a paper entitled *"Du derangement au changement"* (From disturbance to change) concerning the management of the most classical psychosexual difficulties, I argued that, prior to any hermeneutic preoccupation, it was useful to provoke an *economic scandal* in the higher psychic systems. That is to say, it is useful to get the psychic energy flowing again where it has become "immobilised" by the regime of binding. Otherwise, no interpretation can be invested, except as an aggravating factor of resistance.

In a similar way, it is advisable to trigger what I shall call a *scandal of identity*—to trigger and even aggravate it, for there is much less to be feared than one imagines. It is a question of intervening in the non-sexual self-preservative field of identity (*vital-identital*),[1] of disturbing (disorganising), undoing as a reference, the famous sense of uniqueness of an integrated organism which is able to recognise others without ambiguity (Greenacre, 1958). It is a state, it is worth noting, which resists all fundamental change. In fact, what is involved is the *recognition that the psychoanalytic treatment has another responsibility* alongside that which proposes to give access to drive mastery while according a maximum of satisfaction compatible with reality. This further responsibility is of cardinal importance when one has in mind the most authentic aspect of the individual, the liberation of his most intimate, primordial self, of permitting or guaranteeing the subject the possibility of acceding to a state of *permanent disquiet*, as I suggested at the last Congress of the European Federation. Psychoanalysis is not what you think it is. I constantly point out, almost to the extent of pleading on its behalf, the importance of linking up with the point where the uncertain—and even more or less secretly durable—and aleatory character of the frontiers between all the orders must be recognised as a fundamental fact of being.

Phenomena of uncanniness are thus not to be seen simply as accidents, even meaningful ones. They must be considered as the trace of an essential activity of the mind. They participate, let us remember, in the constant negotiation operating between two orders (the dimensions of identity and the psychosexual) by revealing a particular and new dimension of psychoanalytic science, that is to say a dimension in which the uncertain and aleatory occupy a nuclear place. And once the hermeneutic dimension tends, even provisionally, even partially, to become marginalised, one finds a legitimate place for psychoanalysis in the domain of hazy frontiers, alongside what has been called the "science of indefinite limits" (de M'Uzan, 2011). I will just give one or two examples. Biology, towards which analysts are sometimes prepared to turn, tells us that the distinction between the *inert* and the *living* is aleatory. Think of quantum physics—Sylvie Faure-Pragier and Georges Pragier (2007) refer to it, as I have also done on several occasions—which suggests that "God might indeed play with the dice". Even mathematics has discovered that there are elements which can belong *more or less* to an ensemble "and that there exists a continuous transition between this ensemble and those elements that do not belong to it" (p. 1).

Let us stop there as if, in the very course of our reflection, a powerful call had summoned us to step back from the universe, where the universe is without certain and defined limits, or rather had invited us to lean on it in order to allow for a demand for *significance* that is better inscribed in the "psychoanalytically familiar", namely, the psychosexual. And this movement brings us back, brings me back, to the beginning of this chapter, to my modest young girl and her charms, to my "bizarro". To my well-behaved young girl who assures the sleeping fetishist of eternity that there is nothing to see … except what she has pinned on her blouse, while letting him know that everything is there and that he can trust her. "I am not who you think I am," she says. But am I not the one now who is proffering these words? What a relief—with the triumph of castration anxiety, perhaps the file opened on the uncanny can now be closed? How tempting it would be to be able to say so. But strangely—yes, strangely, let us keep the term—at this very instant, an invitation appears on the horizon. At this very instant, at any moment, someone will arrive and suggest that his fellow man should stand in front of a mirror and contemplate at length the reflection of a bather in celluloid, the naked bather of former times, pressed closely against the mirror beside his own.

Note

1. The *vital-identital* is a neologism introduced by Michel de M'Uzan. It stands in opposition to Jean Laplanche's term "the sexual". Self-preservation is one of the functions of the *vital-identital*. This term replaces the term *"identitaire"* which can lead to confusion with its usage in other disciplines, notably philosophy.

CHAPTER TEN

Invitation to frequent the shadows*
(2006)

R egarding the question of the psychic transformations brought about by the analytic process, the answers are apparently clear and well known. What is involved is a reorganisation of the relations between the psychical agencies, that is to say, essentially, an extension of the ego's capacities aimed at assuring its mastery over the demands of the drives, a preponderance of secondary processes over primary processes, and an affirmation of the operations of binding, resisting an uncontrolled discharge of excitation. These phenomena, even when they are only achieved in a limited way, are matched by a more or less important "resolution" of the neurotic conflict, and thus a substantial reduction of the symptoms. They are perfectly illustrated by the famous formulation: *"Wo Es war, soll Ich werden"* ("Where id/it is, there ego/I shall be").

Now almost diametrically opposed to these changes, there are others, of a fundamentally different order, which occur during the treatment and may even survive it, possibly constituting an acquisition.

---

*An abridged version of this chapter was presented as a paper at a conference in Athens in 2006 and published in French in the *European Federation of Psychoanalysis Bulletin, 60*: 15–29.

Among these, and this will be the nub of my argument, I have in view an original modality of psychic functioning whose objective—to put it briefly—is no longer to dominate the demands of the drives, or to set up a normalising peace in the subject's "internal equilibrium". On the contrary, the vocation of this very special new form of mental functioning is to disturb the subject, to trouble him profoundly, with the aim of establishing within him that capacity for living which I call a "permanent disquiet", a disposition of the mind which, perhaps, alone makes it possible to invent what has never existed. I have taken advantage of this openness to the primary processes which governs operation, to invert, from time to time, and in a slightly provocative way, that famous proposition by positing: "*Wo Ich ist, soll Es werden*" ("Where ego/I is, there id/it shall be"). It will no doubt be said that this suggestion opens "Pandora's box". True enough, but is it not the case that Freud himself, when he was sailing to the United States and addressing his travelling companions, claimed that he was bringing the plague into the country? It is these singular transformations which will constitute the essence of this chapter. I shall study them where they can be best observed—that is to say, in the more or less classic neurotic structures, where the indication for analysis seems self-evident; but without excluding, however, the field of the so-called "borderline" states, which are perfectly accessible at the price of certain technical variations.

As soon as one endeavours to examine any change in the status of an object or situation, it is necessary, at the outset, to make it clear where one is starting from. In our particular case, before the analytic process gets underway properly speaking, the starting-point is constituted by the neurotic solution found by the patient which, it should be emphasised, is (in spite of sufferings) the effect of a search for equilibrium. This equilibrium is undoubtedly fragile but none the less preserved, relatively speaking, by virtue of the employment of powerful countercathexes whose activity is present throughout the treatment in the form of resistances. This being so, one should not forget that this situation results from real work to which the patient is narcissistically attached. Not to mention the fact that subsequent changes, however beneficial they may be, are in danger of being lived as companions of mourning. Furthermore, the patient begins to have the obscure intuition that he is not who he thinks he is and clings to a demand that is much more ambiguous than one would imagine. Thus, during his first meetings with the analyst, he unconsciously advances two more or less contradictory expectations: according to the first, he hopes to see the "brilliant" character of his neurotic construction confirmed; and according to the second, he hopes to receive help in continuing the edification of his neurosis, which is somewhat incomplete, for he is often at a standstill with this task.

The psychic transformations linked to the development of the analytic process, and the means the analyst has at his disposal for obtaining them, clearly form an ensemble. What is important is the singularity of the matter. It is only for the sake of clarity of exposition that they are distinguished from each other. One notices, in fact, that very often the new modalities of mental functioning only occur when the analyst's interpretative activity has already made a large contribution to them by providing a truly "welcoming presence"—somewhat on the model of the "basic complicity" which, as biologists say, articulates the "viral key" with the "cellular lock". Thus, adopting a strategic perspective, rather like positioning strategies in chess, the analyst, an expert of disorder, even before he engages in the slightest work of interpretation, of "combination", will establish the famous "setting", with the aim of maintaining it strictly until the end of the treatment. This "stressful" initiative, as we say, is capable in itself of engendering an upheaval in the psychic economy, an upheaval that is indispensable because it is a primary factor in the reduction of countercathexes, but also in the liberation of wild representations. Adopting this "policy" implies accepting a relational mode between the analysand and analyst that is based, rather singularly, on a preponderance of the narcissistic cathexes of the libido and, above all, on a tolerance for a certain degree of uncertainty of identity. The word is out.

Significant changes in the functioning of the mind are operative in several "fields" (the fields of identity and drive functioning, and the metapsychological field in the narrow sense). They are of course organically interrelated so that they form a sort of entity endowed with its own destiny but, and I want to emphasise this, an entity whose "leadership" is assured by a significant disturbance or disruption of the ego's frontiers, by the setting up on this site, and in its place, of an *every man's land*. In other words, this boils down to *reserving a privileged place for depersonalisation*, for the phenomena that specify it, and very specifically, for *the impression of change* concerning the perception of both the internal and external world. When the extension of this state does not exceed certain limits, for instance, those posed by the appearance of devastating anxiety, the situation is all the same poles apart from the sort of certificate of mental health described by, among others, Phyllis

Greenacre (1958), characterised by the sense of uniqueness experienced by an integrated organism able to recognise others without ambiguity. That is a highly regrettable, reductive, and, at the very least, grossly distorted condition. How, indeed, could any transformation whatsoever occur in a subject who remains firmly entrenched behind protected and impassable "frontiers", and who would be unable to recognise himself in the other? The internal space of such a subject would in no way allow for the indispensable deployment in himself of a *zone of floating individualisation*, reminiscent of Ferenczi's notion of *introjective ego dilation* or, in Bion's terms, of the existence of a normal degree of projective identification since "there may be something analogous in the personality to the blood capillary system which under extraordinary conditions may dilate" (1977, p. 30).

But what can be observed when the mind has integrated more or less permanently, and as something of positive value, the experience of states of depersonalisation? To put things succinctly, I would suggest a rare or unusual kind of mental functioning which one tends, spontaneously, to associate with the "poet" or the "madman". I shall come back to this point. Before doing so, it is important to have a word about what precedes it and announces it in the session. There is a more or less fleeting but substantial modification of the relation between the metaphorical order, in the service of which the activity of the preconscious operates, and an order that is more respectful of the reality principle. This modification, which occurs from time to time to the advantage of the first of these orders, can of course be maintained beyond the analysis. It expresses an aptitude of the mind that is often only potential.

It is in this context, then, that a rather strange phenomenon emerges during the session which I have called *paradoxical functioning*. I first described it a long time ago in connection with the analyst's countertransference (see Chapter Two), and have dwelt on it since on several occasions, so it will be familiar to most of you. I must, however come back to it—and I apologise for doing so—for, of all the transformations that occur during the analytic process (in fact it is a part of it), it is the most fundamental, the most novel, forming a sort of platform for all the other changes. Here, then, is a cursory description of it, without referring for the time being to the person in whom it occurred.

Suddenly, in the course of the session, strange images, bizarre representations, for instance, a succession of faces slowly dissolving into each other, as in the cinematic process of "fading in, fading out", erupt into consciousness, rather like bubbles of air breaking on the surface of a pond. At other moments, it is hazy bits of abstract ideas, or a reverie, the list is not exhaustive. One notices, moreover, that this transitory phenomenon, rather than arousing anxiety, tends to generate a certain fascination. It seems at the time, though this is only an impression, to be unrelated to what is happening in the session. I would point out that, initially, it was in the analyst, when he "defends" himself less, that I had recognised the phenomenon, while at the same time envisaging, so as not to overlook anything, its countertransferential character, provided that the value of the countertransference as an instrument of *knowledge* is fully recognised. Today what I want to emphasise is that the phenomenon occurs, of course, in parallel and in an imbricated manner, in the analysand. In this interplay, one can see that a common psychical apparatus is being established which is in search of a secret significance. Although it comes quite naturally to mind, *paradoxical functioning* should not be confused with manic activity. And yet I would not refuse *a priori* the comparison because, in one of its "formal" aspects, it is not unrelated to the *excited* character of an exaggerated, caricatural radicalisation of free association, when it takes a "ramified" turn. I would further add that the comparison is all the more conceivable in that one often observes, just when the phenomenon is fading, the insidious setting in of depressive affects—at a time when, it should be noted in passing, interpretations have the best chance of being incorporated and assimilated.

Attacks of depersonalisation—proceeding, then, from the rigorous nature of the setting, still sustained by one of the powers of interpretation—are accompanied by regressive movements, both of which are closely related as are self-preservation and sexuality. This is familiar knowledge, and it is even readily accepted that regression plays a positive part in the analytic process as an instrument of understanding. The fruitfulness of the phenomenon, on the other hand, is less readily recognised. Regression, which is both feared and the object of a severe struggle to thwart it, in fact opens a door for the subject leading to his essential richness, in all its authenticity. This movement may be compared with that which, by inverting the course of excitation, makes it go "backwards" through the censor between the unconscious and the preconscious so as to "revive the forces" in the higher systems.

In the libidinal register of regression, the situation is familiar; in contrast with the rest of his discourse, one observes the analysand "letting through" more representations, hitherto enclaved, of pregenital impulses in the crudest of pictorial forms. These representations form the material which, in due course, will allow the mechanism of sublimation to come into operation. At other times, the movement can come to a standstill, owing to an expansion of fantasy activity or a reverie, even permitting—perhaps a surprising sign of progress for the functional freedom of the mind—"a minor opening towards perversion", as Catherine Parat (1991) puts it so aptly in a text on therapeutic recovery.

Equally significant are phenomena concerning the formal side of regression. This finds expression in the accentuation of the activity of the preconscious, another mark of the enlargement of the capacities of the psyche. This can be observed in a particularly significant way in the analysand's language and dream activity. It is certainly a more pictorial language but still full of slips of the tongue, whose course is marked by the influence of condensation. More plays on words and verbal inspirations appear, and one does not really know where they come from. Even the grammar of the discourse can be affected by it. It is as if, at certain moments, a certain confusion between the I and the you was seeking to establish itself. By a sort of contagious effect, an identical manner of expression appears in the analyst. And then, suddenly, everything returns to normal, secondary level language reasserts itself: once again it is possible to speak about everyday life with its troubles and its joys. One had simply been dreaming.

Let us turn now to dream activity proper. Everyone will have reflected on the modifications that analysis has contributed to it. I scarcely need point out that, generally speaking, it has become quantitatively more important, at least in terms of the number of references that are made to it. This is understandable because the appetite of pregenitality has already increased during waking life. Consequently, the dream necessarily becomes more and more enigmatic. It readily limits itself to an image or a formula in which the distant past, when it is recoverable, is more important than the waking residues reproduced as such. The work of condensation can be clearly sensed here. It is only in these instants, then, that the consciousness of the quasi "consubstantial confusion" of the psychic apparatuses of the analysand and analyst makes it possible to understand why a word proffered by the analyst, even a mere interjection, can have a "mutative" significance, by identifying a meaning as if it lay behind a veil which has suddenly torn. In so doing, what is actual is identified with what is most remote and the dream begins to invade waking life. It is therefore not surprising if, when *paradoxical functioning* sets in and depersonalisation is accentuated, the subject's relations with time are modified. Although the importance of the question is such that it would deserve to be the subject of an entire book, I will only dwell on one or two of the most significant points.

The invasion of consciousness by primary processes and an absence of temporal bearings are characteristics of its place of origin. Here is one example among a hundred that could be given: very often, for the analysand, but also for the analyst, the session which is just ending has in fact just begun; or else, conversely, it never ends! At other times, in a more or less futile effort to control a mode of mental functioning that has become worrying, all the events are evoked in terms of what happened before and after. This is particularly observable in a subject who has an obsessional structure. In any case, the upheaval that is taking place allows what belongs to the distant past to emerge as a present issue of burning importance. The events reported have become at once past and actual, which corresponds to a faculty for developing transferences … and even for preserving this gift beyond the treatment. Such a faculty, infused with life, should not, I think, be deplored, as we too easily have a tendency to do. It is true that in these conditions, the subject, by virtue of an effort that he is more or less unaware of, will continue, as in the sessions, to recover the past in order to reinvent it and recreate it instead of accumulating the contents of it in an ordered way so as to put them in a sort of file. I cannot resist the desire to illustrate one of the determinants of the temporal upheaval brought about by the analytic process. To do so, I shall make use of the famous but hackneyed metaphor of the sandglass. In so doing, I am not thinking so much of the flow of the fine sand contained in the upper receptacle, but above all of the fact that one *turns* the object *upside down*, so that then what is oldest becomes the most recent! Should one forget the metaphor, even though it is a metaphor? Certainly not, if one considers the familiar idea that the act of forgetting, which owes everything to repression, in fact protects memory while sustaining its extension.

The analytic adventure has been costly in time and effort for both protagonists. One would hope, quite naturally, that the transformations that proceed from it are lasting and persist beyond the treatment. What happens when the treatment is over and the sway of the reality principle asserts itself more? The thesis I am defending here leads me to distinguish, as far as the stability of the results is concerned, two equally defendable propositions. In brief, according to the first, the one that is most readily adopted, the desired stability pertains both to the reduction of torment and to an increased capacity to grant oneself moderate drive satisfactions. Such a result undoubtedly deserves respect, even if, concurrently, the familiar, albeit not very ambitious formula comes to mind of the replacement of neurotic suffering by ordinary unhappiness! At any rate, you will have understood that I attach more importance to the second proposition. I do so on the basis of the conviction that the capacities of the psychical apparatus, all of which are partial, go well beyond the limits that we cautiously allow for, on the condition, however, that a policy of uncertainty at the level of identity can be assumed. It will be said that the choice between these two propositions should not be seen in terms of a radical alternative, but that it is the relation between them that must be modulated. This is a rather similar situation to the one that can be found in the domain of art. A letter from Freud to Stefan Zweig (dated 20 July, 1938) helps us to take this discussion a bit further: "From the critical point of view it could still be maintained that the notion of art defies expansion as long as the quantitative proportion of unconscious material and preconscious treatment does not remain within definite limits" (E. Freud, 1960, pp. 448–449). From the standpoint of the propositions I have defended in this chapter, the psychoanalytic process has the fundamental task of pushing back the limits well beyond the margins imposed by *reality-testing*. Without being pessimistic, one can easily imagine that such a mode of mental functioning can only be maintained randomly after analysis. That is why I sometimes fear seeing someone who, during the sessions, acceded to the "rank of poet", thereafter turn into an office clerk ... though there is nothing stopping him from taking an interest in his dreams and his failures, or—and especially if he is an analyst—from returning to the path of the couch again, possibly several times. It is not in waking life that one benefits from one of the strangest powers inherent to the analytic situation—a power to which I attach crucial importance, namely, that of inducing not just the transformation of a state or mode of functioning, but the emergence, almost the birth, in the *every man's land* of identity, of a new "monstrous" entity which I have called a *psychological chimera,* and to which I have given considerable attention, as you know. This object, comparable to an *immaterial being,* if I may put it like that, emanates from the enmeshed activities of the unconscious minds of the analysand and analyst. The chimera, a fabulous/mythical child that exists independently of its creators, pursues a nocturnal existence and, from time to time, becomes activated. It is this that engenders the *paradoxical thoughts* to which I have alluded.

At the beginning of this chapter, I said that I was going, as a matter of priority, to deal with the psychic transformations in question where they are a model of reference, that is to say, where their richness and their scope are most legible. Let us remember that this means, roughly speaking, the so-called neurotic structures. Nevertheless, we should not forget other morbid entities that are accessible to a psychoanalytic approach thanks to the adoption, if needs be, of diverse technical parameters. I am thinking here of "borderline" cases, certain psychotic states, and a number of genuinely psychosomatic affections. I will be referring to this domain in the second part of the chapter which, moreover, will also include the presentation of clinical material and considerations on technique.

* * *

In the first part of this chapter, I presented the psychic transformations, along with their respective evolutions, brought about by the analytic process. I subjected these transformations to critical scrutiny while including them within a particular conception of the phenomena in question. In so doing, I was above all placing the emphasis on the theoretical side of the question. I propose now to tackle the clinical side. It is for the sake of clarity of exposition that I have distinguished, in this order, the two registers. In fact, as we know, they form a whole; and, furthermore, it is even the clinical aspect that should come first, since the necessity of elaborating a theorisation proceeds from it. A reminder may be added regarding a specific difficulty involved in presenting a piece of clinical material. Every analyst has had experience of this. The difficulty lies in the obligation to respect two requirements: that of choosing material that will best serve the purpose of illustration, while respecting confidentiality. As far as I am concerned, I have had to put many things to one side. Thus, alongside some recent, new observations, I have decided also to present certain cases that are more dated but exemplary, and which I have already had occasion to speak about. It is thus the demonstrative value of the observations which, in short, has determined my choice. Finally, I would say that the analyst does not often have the opportunity of recognising the long-term stability of the psychic transformations achieved—that is to say, long after the treatment has been terminated.

The analysand's discourse and the analyst's interpretations or interventions form an ensemble with the positions the analyst adopts on the theory of the technique. They will thus inevitably be intertwined in my presentation of them. Moreover, I am also taking account of classical nosographical distinctions in order to clarify my argument. I insist on doing so, even though these distinctions are open to criticism insofar as they create barriers between morbid entities, whereas the latter only represent a particular moment within a developing process, that is, the sometimes transitory state of a "negotiation" between drive functioning and the problematic of identity. I will deal first with the neurotic states, where the theory of the technique is expressed most easily. The "borderline" states and difficulties related to identity will come next, although we know that the latter find expression in the entire nosographical spectrum. Finally, questions will be raised concerning the irruption of the "psychotic".

The patient, aged about forty, had been in analysis for a little more than two years. Underneath the predominant manifestations, one could easily perceive primitive hysterical anxiety. A new painting had recently been hung on a wall, near the couch. The man remarked on its presence, saying that he preferred the one before which he had found more soothing. Then, suddenly becoming aware of the avoidance involved, he said: "But I am not here to talk about your interiors."

I replied: "That all depends on which!"

A young woman of hystero-phobic structure found she was more and more troubled by the increased "transference closeness", without, however, being clearly conscious of it. Giving, as it were, the floor to the defence, she talked about the distance, the void that she felt she had to maintain around her:

"It is as if I were constantly measuring the space around the couch with a yardstick [*un mètre*]."

A: "A stallion yardstick! [*un mètre étalon!*]"[1]

"A routine analytic comment," it will be said. No doubt, but it should be noted that in both cases (and elsewhere obviously), the predominant activity of countercathexis, already altered by the creation of an upheaval in the psychic economy, had given way in both protagonists to an entirely different form of mental functioning, namely, the metaphorical register, the privilege of preconscious work, so swift in its execution, so efficient in linking up thing-presentations with word-presentations, and so effective in giving the sexual the full place it deserves.

This was how the first of the two patients had become aware, as if in a flash, not only of the curiosity that I aroused in him, but above all of its instinctual drive basis. The woman, for her part, discovered in a decisive way the importance of her erotic sexuality in the transference relationship owing to the concatenation of instinctual drive activity and the defences. And then, and this is by no means negligible, the inscription of the "verbal" in metaphorical concreteness had allowed her to take a certain pleasure in sustaining the internalisation of the content of the interpretation. Such a lesson is not easily forgotten. Working for once in the right direction, the repetition initiated by the patient in these sequences helped to develop in her, over the coming months, the new "manner" of psychic functioning of which I have written.

It may be argued that the content of the interpretations, the particularities of which I presented in the first part of this chapter, can also be formulated in a language governed by secondary processes. This is true, for example, when it is a matter of "fixing" acquisitions or, alternatively, of calming tactically an excessive accentuation of the transference or of regression. In view of this, I cannot help thinking that this mode of interpretative activity is notably for the benefit of the analyst's peace of mind. In fact the analyst cannot easily escape the need to construct solid counter-resistances throughout the treatment. Interpretations that are clear, developed, and rigorously observant of the rules of grammar, never lose their *explicatory character*. And yet, since childhood, we have never listened to explanations that come from "above" as opposed to "within". Such explanations hold the analysand's attention above all intellectually and, moreover, he or she soon turns them into a "defensive bastion" against other interpretations.

Just when one is trying to account for what underlies the respective utterances of the analysand and analyst, one discovers gradually and increasingly as one proceeds a sort of community in the depths of their mental functioning. One might even say a confusion; and this is why the analyst sometimes wonders if the words that have just been uttered were uttered by him or by his patient. Doubt gains ground in both of them.

A woman patient anxiously exclaimed: "But what's happening today? I have the impression that I am not myself."

ME: "You have probably lost me."

HER: "Yes, probably … It's like those souls that change their bodily form or inhabit a different body. But does that mean my mind is no longer in my body?"

These words were uttered as if in a dream, at the heart of a disturbance which is difficult to convey. At other moments, it will only be interjections, or even a mere suspension of breathing. Clearly, such sequences belong to the problematic of identity which I shall deal with more specifically in a moment.

I have already stressed the positive signification, with regard to the analysand's psychic organisation, of the capacity to confront and to go through experiences of depersonalisation in the course of the treatment. Of such an aptitude, which is undoubtedly unusual, it may be said that it provides an opportunity for opening the patient up to a world to which he or she had hitherto only had access vicariously through contemplating works of art. But, for this opportunity to materialise, it is still necessary for the analyst, overcoming his resistances, to be able to maintain with his patient a sufficient degree of "participative communication". Such tuning is indispensable for sustaining interpretative activity, which, it goes without saying, must be included in the question of the transformations achieved by the analytic treatment.

Better still, over the course of years of practice, though sometimes in the very course of one session, the analyst himself undergoes change by virtue of the depth of the exchanges with his patient. His psychic functioning undergoes transformations which he often only becomes aware of secondarily, and which correspond to the changes that are observable in his patient.

This may be why it is not always easy for the analyst to combine "regressing with" and a lucid presentation of his conception of interpretation. This is particularly so when it requires him to tolerate in himself a modification of his status of identity to the point of affirming that a part of himself has momentarily become the patient. In describing the "obligations" that interpretation should observe, I find it is necessary to adopt a discursive language which only corresponds imperfectly to what happens "in the field". The "modalities of being" which govern them are, of course, an integral part of the shared and transitory changes, albeit repetitive, which occur during the sessions. The "obligations" in question, whose articulation is essential but random, are of an *economic* order and of an *immune* order. Of the first, which are concerned with the vicissitude of quantity, enough has already been included here. So I will simply remind you that they aim to provoke an upheaval, an *economic scandal* in the conscious system by using all the means available—that is, maintaining the rigour of the setting, interpreting the countercathexis, making an allusive or incomplete formulation of the interpretation, or making an interpretation which may even be confined to an interjection, as Kutrin A. Kemper (1965) once suggested.

I have chosen a biological metaphor to evoke the "immune obligation". Even when the analytic interpretation is supposed to "enlarge" the subject's self, bringing him, among others, a narcissistic benefit, at first it disturbs him. It disturbs him not only because it brings out of the shadows worrying instinctual drive representations, but also and above all, perhaps, because it is too foreign for the subject, too threatening for his status of identity which has become practically inauthentic—he is not the person he thought he was. It is understandable, consequently, that the interpretation may be rejected; it functions, in fact, in the manner of an anti-gene or, even worse, of a graft of haematopoietic original cells which attack and destroy their host who has become a complete stranger. Fortunately, this is a rare outcome, but equally disastrous transformations can sometimes be observed in clinical psychoanalysis.

Avoiding the other pitfall of sterility, interpretation none the less has better opportunities when its enunciation respects what I call "immune" obligations; that is to say, when it is sufficiently in keeping with what is going on in the analysand's ego. Is it not the case, as is often said, that the best interpretations are those that the patient comes up with himself?

I would be straying too far from my subject if I were to enter into the details of the technical measures which correspond to the "immune" obligations—and those of "identity". Moreover, everyone is perfectly familiar with them. So I will just add that they strive, at the very level of the formulation of the interpretation, of the grammar of verbal expression, to mark explicitly—let me stress this point again—the fragile and random character of the distinctions of identity. For example, the analyst will speak of *him*, as he would of *he* or of *one*; he will take up and use in an identical way the analysand's own terms; the locus of speech will replace the speaker, etc. ... Some will speak of the analyst's *style*, or of some sort of initiative that is somewhat marginal, but whose aim is clear.

In practising his art, the analyst is not supposed to give any advice to his patient. And yet, the patient's reality can provide grounds for concern. One day, alerted by the somatic manifestations of my patient, I considered it justified on "humane" grounds to intervene explicitly on the matter, and so, prolix for once, I said in a dreamy tone:

> "If I was Michel de M'Uzan, I would tell my patient that an appointment with his doctor was justified; but I am not Michel de M'Uzan, so I said nothing."

The presence here of the trace of the transferential object can be clearly recognised.

Here, then, among many possible others, needless to say, are a few random clinical sequences which exemplify the unknown richness to which mental functioning can, strangely enough, gain access in the form of a new capacity to cross frontiers and to hear in the night other whispers of life:

> A woman patient said: "We are but one, owing to an effect of transparency. Each of us can be seen in the other; when each one is in the other, that makes but one."
>
> Another patient was irritated at being unable to consider me either as a friend or as an enemy. Then, in a dreamy state, she said: "… You are an extension of me; no, you are part of me. You only exist through me—and in me."

One patient, who was invaded by anxiety at the mere mention of a repugnant and repetitive experience, told me about the hallucinatory vision of a rabbit's head, placed on a tray, in the process of dissolving. It was a part of herself which did not belong to her, even though it was herself: "An unknown zone which is me and which will prevail over the other part … and I will be nothing more than that …"

It might be said without hesitation that such material is characteristic of the so-called borderline states. All, or almost all, of the ingredients are united here which can be found in a DSM4. But in saying that, one has said nothing; or, more precisely, one has forgotten that the words uttered are messages. Far from being solely the expression of an "infirmity", these words express the advances of a mind that is in the process of exploring, with anxiety—but how could it be otherwise—the dark regions of the mind.

Ever since my article on "Countertransference and the paradoxical system" (de M'Uzan 1976a, cf. Chapter Two) I have been deeply interested in the mental activity of "borderline" subjects. Already at that time, I was discovering in its very characteristics what leads one to pose, without reservation, at least in my eyes, an indication of analysis; and, I would add, even more easily than with the neurotic entangled in his inevitable and innocent cheating. The "borderline" patient, for his part, gets involved in the adventure with extreme gravity, for the stakes are vital. He reveals what is "imprisoned" and dormant in each one of us. He travels quite a long way down this path and confronts on everyone else's behalf, and as well as he can, the torments of an encounter with insanity. It is out of this frequentation that the *chimera* and *paradoxical thoughts* of which I have written will emerge.

The limits of time and space imposed on the presentation of case material have led me to select only one of the cases which enabled me to recognise the state of *paradoxical functioning* and the *chimera* that engenders it.

The history is that of a young woman, a librarian, whose treatment, which had been in progress for quite a long time, had been affected by some addictive episodes and by the occurrence of slightly strange reveries. Her halting way of speaking, tortuous in its development, lent an unusual character to what she was saying. There was nothing, though, that was really disquieting, especially as the countercathexis was nourished by important cultural references. Soon after the beginning of the session in question, the patient reminded me—she was still struck by the fact—that she had left her last session saying to me, unusually, "*Au-revoir, Monsieur*". In association to these words she related an episode from her early childhood, which until then had been more or less forgotten: one day, escaping from the family home, she was walking along when she found herself (as she describes it today) in the police station. She found herself standing on a table, with men around her—policemen—who were questioning her. And it was at this very moment that I experienced a slight sense of depersonalisation, without anxiety, but which surprised me—in short, the state I have already described, and against the background of which *paradoxical thoughts* emerged into consciousness. An unusual thought came to my mind: "I would happily gobble you up, you handsome sailor." I said nothing of this to the patient, and nothing either of an association which came to me soon after in connection with Billy Budd, the hero of Herman Melville's short story, which I felt intuitively was related to the "*Monsieur*" at the beginning of the session. The patient, however, continued the narrative, the reconstruction of her childhood memory. Still at the police station, and feeling very ashamed, she saw her uncle enter. I associated to one of her dreams; I asked her to continue her narrative in which there was mention of a paving stone covered with a black fabric which made her think of a tombstone, and then of a table her father had offered her. She did not like the object and wanted to choose another one, a real dining table (*table à manger*). She then referred to some local dishes from her own country which she had found really distasteful; "… and yet," she insisted, "*j'étais de bonne composition.*" Following on immediately and without evaluating the logic of the sequences, I replied: "In saying '*de bonne composition*', you mean 'good to eat' (*bon à manger*)!" (see Chapter Two, Note 1). Taken aback, a little worried, and then dreamily, she replied: "Yes, it's true! I am thinking again now of that Uncle Pierre who used to frighten me so much. He used to say to me: 'I'm a lion; I'm going to eat you.' I was fascinated, excited, and terrified." In this episode, the emergence of a disturbed sense of identity in me had led me to have the unusual thought: "I will gobble you up", and then, without any apparent justification, I had asked her to resume her account of an old dream. There was nothing clearly determined in my action; just the barely conscious willingness to follow, while according them credit, the *paradoxical thoughts* dictated by the *chimera*. At the end of this phase in the treatment, a repression with its roots in the drives and oral eroticism was lifted, in such a way that it would colour the Oedipal conflicts of the patient, in her past, and also in the actuality of her transference.

I will now turn, in conclusion, to psychosis or, as I prefer to say, "the irruption of the psychotic in the individual". You may be astonished to see me discussing a domain with which the analyst, generally speaking, has nothing to do, at least in his practice. And if, thinking perhaps of the free intervals in the course of a manic-depressive psychosis, the analyst decides to embark on this adventure, drawing on various technical variations, what will be the nature of the psychic transformations he or she can hope to witness? I decided none the less to touch on the question, because I had a case in which several elements were combined in an exemplary way, constituting the source, as we shall see, of extremely profound reflections. First, and we will find plenty of reasons here for remaining modest, I have in mind a case undertaken at the beginning of my career, at a time when only my faith in psychoanalysis could make up for my lack of experience. I will then comment on the efficacy of a technical measure used, as it were, by reflex, without really thinking about it—a measure that was perhaps rather stupid if one considers the dramatic character of the context. Finally, this case offered the possibility not only of observing immense transformations, but also of following their stability a long time after the end of the treatment proper. In recounting the episode, I will only present what is strictly related to the theme of the changes brought about by the analytic process.

A very long time ago, then, a married woman, aged about forty, with two children, was referred to me by the service of gastroenterology where she was being followed for chronic colitis. As she lived in the provinces, we agreed—it is essential to point this out—to adapt the timetable of her sessions to this situation. So it was that my patient came to see me every other week, for three or even five sessions, sitting, at her request, on the edge of the couch. Over the last three years, approximately, since the beginning of the treatment, I had been able to observe, though without taking sufficient account of it, the gravity of her mental state. Had she not presented fleeting hallucinatory episodes? Had she not let me know, on one occasion, that she was in constant communication with me between the sessions, that I was permanently listening to her, etc. ...? Well, "one both knows and does not know"; I did not want, and absolutely refused, to recognise how dangerous the situation was. (The exposition of what governs this sort of denial belongs to another occasion.) And yet the signs were not lacking. So, and it is very important to make this clear, my patient regularly listened in fascination to an excellent radio programme: it was a sort of dialogue, written by Roland Dubillard, in which two characters, Grégoire and Amédée, exchanged humorous and heretical remarks. For her, I was one of the protagonists, and I had chosen this means to address secret messages to her. *The programme was broadcast "live".* How can one be so "scatterbrained" as I was? So, one day, without paying attention, I informed her of the time of the next session, which was precisely at the time of the programme. Even by twisting reality in all directions, I could not be simultaneously in the studio and in my consulting room. The unfailing interference of reality was cataclysmic.

My patient arrived at the arranged time. Looking pale, with her hair dishevelled and her eyes full of hate, she sat down on the edge of the couch. She subjected me to a torrent of insults: I was an abominable individual, the perfect bastard, I had destroyed her, it was irremediable … etc., etc. Above all, she did not want to give up listening to her programme. As she had brought a little transistor with her, she turned it on, at full volume. The programme continued. She hurled abuse at me with intense fury. Finally, there were threats. Then, suddenly calm again, indeed far too calm, she plunged her hand into her bag and announced that she was going to "shoot" me at the end of the programme (or the session, I don't know any more). "You only have twenty minutes to live …"; "fifteen minutes only." I feared that a physical confrontation would become unavoidable, while I was searching for the "right interpretation", among those which owe their absolute efficacy to psychoanalytic theory! To no avail, evidently. And it was then that suddenly and without really being conscious of the meaning of what was going through my mind, I retorted coldly: "By listening to the programme instead of making use of your session, you are losing money." It is hardly possible to imagine a more trivial statement than that, and yet its effect was staggering. Having become silent, the patient seemed to be paralysed for a moment, but then collapsed in a heap, reduced to a sort of bundle. After a while, she finally sat up again, sobbing, with tears streaming down her face. For the rest of the session she cried. A decisive step, there and then, and for the future of the treatment, had been taken.

Without losing any of the capacities she had acquired with such difficulty for travelling on the fringes of the solid delimitation of beings and things, my patient did not go through any more worrying episodes. And, since we are concerned here with the long-term stability of the transformations obtained during the treatment itself, I want to add that the young woman managed to separate from a husband who was undoubtedly paranoiac, and to take up again—it had become a necessity—her former profession as a French teacher in a *lycée*; and, finally, giving new life to a largely inhibited vocation, she embarked on a literary career which was even to be crowned with a prestigious prize. After the end of the treatment, my patient came to visit me every two or three years, or even more, to speak about "one thing and another", and let me understand that shame had given way to a certain sense of guilt, but guilt that was very tolerable.

It is obvious that such a case history would justify and require a lengthy commentary. How can one account, in just a few words, for the efficacy of my interpretation which irreducibly brought to bear the weight of a reality caught in the concreteness of its vulgarity? One has to make a choice. Here, I will confine myself to the role of an effect of reduplication since, prior to my intervention, I had already showed, unambiguously, that I was neither Grégoire nor Amédée. An ultimate belief in the eventual ubiquity of people was not within the reach of the young woman either. Likewise, delusion, the ultimate solution was inaccessible to her. And then, returning more than once to what had happened, I understood that one of the mainsprings of the "mutative" character of my interpretation—what am I saying there?—lay in the revelation of a similarity between madness and excess of reality!

Perhaps I will succeed in giving an idea of this relationship by citing an anecdote, reported by the physician Etienne Klein (2005, p. 83), concerning the illustrious Nobel Prize winner for physics, Paul Dirac. Paul Dirac seems to have been a man who was given to being extremely terse; so it was difficult to get a word out of him. One day, Paul Dirac and Wolfgang Pauli, another Nobel Prize winner in physics, found themselves travelling together on a train. For more than an hour, Dirac had remained silent. Pauli, looking for some way or other to strike up a conversation, saw in the distance a flock of sheep that had recently been shorn. He said to Dirac: "It looks as if those sheep have been shorn recently." Dirac cast a glance in their direction and answered: "At least on this side." How can one be more scientific than that?!

Note

1. In French *un mètre étalon* is a "yardstick or standard metre", but *étalon* also means "stallion", thereby introducing an allusion to the erotic transference.

PART IV

BACK TO OBJECT-RELATIONS

CHAPTER ELEVEN

Object-relations: between whom, between what; for whom, for what?* (2008)

Looking dazed and unsteady on her feet, she walked into the room and said in a flat voice, "I am a piece of myself." Her eyes flitted around the room without settling on anything, and her expression was blank as if the features of her face had been erased.

Another analysand murmured, perhaps for his own benefit, "One day I will be able to feel the skin on my body."

After a long silence, a young woman, who was lying rigidly on the couch, "was dreaming" out loud: "There are no trees … at home it's empty … the voices have fallen silent, as for the images it's even worse … denuded space … one has to roll up into a ball and wait until the wind dies down." I was then astonished by a strange thought that crossed my mind, though I kept it to myself: "And what if I were in your throat?"

It was almost the end of the session and the patient was panic-stricken by the idea that I could allow her to leave in spite of her state

---

*First published as "L'objet, la réalité: la règle et le tact" in the 2008 APF Bulletin, pp. 27–43.

of dereliction and in spite of the fact that she was no longer able to recognise herself. I heard myself saying to her, in a low voice: "Your contours are in my pocket."

We know that at such moments the images and thoughts that emerge in the analyst's mind are an integral part of what is going on in the other person; sometimes they elude the analyst unless, without knowing why, he is not allowing himself to express them.

Like anyone who is referring to their own experience, I could give endless examples of such remarks. Although they are made during what sometimes seems to be quite an ordinary exchange, these remarks in fact circumscribe a universe in which the clear delimitation between beings—between beings and things—vacillates, and where everything becomes uncertain. Indeed, the very process of contemplating this deprives reason of its powers of discrimination. It is a universe in which the most varied emotions are deployed, ranging from unbearable terror to unimaginable coldness—a universe in which uncontrollable agitation and rigid immobility are juxtaposed.

"Serious personality disorders", "borderline states", so-called "narcissistic" neuroses, certain "somatoses", too, and especially entities where one has the feeling that there are "existential difficulties"— there is no shortage of ways for defining the disorder in question, which is immediately perceived as different from the condition of the "common neurotic". In spite of that, we continue to speak of the subject and the object and of the encounter between them, not without experiencing, it must be conceded, a certain sense of malaise that is only partially lifted by the reference to the "transitional". Is it possible, then, to maintain the full specifying status of the notion of the object-relations, which claims to be globalising, when we are considering and trying to understand what is going on between human beings or parts of them?

What becomes of the object-relationship when the status of the protagonists' identity, particularly that of the other, the patient, is uncertain or vague, as is the case with the nosographical entities in question, where we are genuinely dealing with the "zero degree" of the matter? Not to mention the fact that this order is far from homogeneous.

There is no shortage of analysts who have interested themselves in this singular world. I can obviously only mention a few of them here; but their contributions show that studies on this subject have existed for a long time.

You will bear with me, I hope, if I begin by citing the writings of Maurice Bouvet (1960) on object-relations in particular, and on depersonalisation. A long time ago now, they were a real eye-opener for me.

I am also thinking of Winnicott, of course, and of his transitional objects, which are without question relevant to the present discussion. It is greatly to be feared that these transitional objects may well have been lacking in the lives of some subjects.

As early as 1974, Didier Anzieu quite rightly stressed the fact that the body, as a *pre-sexual and vital* global fact of human reality, was precisely what we disregarded or denied. As we know, this led to the notion of the skin-ego, allowing the child to represent himself on the basis of the experience of his body surface.

Pierre Fédida (1978) in an article on entities which, from a classical standpoint are not indicated for analysis, and where the problem of absence is fundamental, posits the *objeu*, which is perhaps akin to the transitional object. This led him to take an interest in the world of boundaries or frontiers. A remarkable illustration of this can be found in the case of one of his patients who had feared going crazy ever since she had started "looking for an inside, everywhere outside".

The work of René Spitz deserves consideration. With regard to the development of object-relations, he describes three successive stages and, in particular, a pre-object stage during which the newborn baby is held to live in a state of non-differentiation with its environment. This state precedes a state in which the other, before becoming other, is only a "gestalt". In "detailing" the development of object-relations, these views none the less run the risk of imposing an over-rigorous notion of regularity.

Rich studies on the subject have thus been carried out by analysts whose theoretical or doctrinal positions did not necessarily overlap. Incidentally, we quite often discover that the research devoted to the subject expressed the end of a process of reflection that had undoubtedly begun a long time before. My intention here is therefore not simply to set out my conclusions, but the personal *adventure* which has led me to them. By way of circumscribing this adventure, I shall be focusing on the relations between object-relations and the problematics of identity. This adventure, comprising different stages and a secret determinism which was often only recognised retrospectively, developed over the course of many years. Inevitably one cannot help wondering about how much freedom one actually has at one's disposal. So each stage was loaded with theoretical exigencies that had to be taken into account in subsequent developments. Furthermore, it was necessary of course to abandon notions that had been adopted spontaneously, almost without thinking about it.

In order to make the latest developments more intelligible, it may be helpful if I relate a singular experience I had back in 1974, right at the beginning of this adventure—one, you may recall, that I wrote about at the time. In what were otherwise quite ordinary circumstances, a relative of mine was sitting on the other side of a small table, opposite me, when an unusual thought unexpectedly crossed my mind: "What if I were dead … and still didn't realise it." It was clear that the reality of the proposition would be confirmed if, on noticing the rigorous symmetry of his movements with mine, the person opposite me turned out to be nothing more than a specular image! Anyone who sees his double in front of him must die. The disturbance that this incident engendered in me led me to write a text entitled *"S.j.e.m."* ("If I were dead") (de M'Uzan, 1974) which appeared in issue 9 of the *Nouvelle Revue de Psychanalyse*, bearing the evocative title *"Le dehors et le dedans"* ("The outside and the inside"), at the same time as Didier Anzieu's article, *"Le moi-peau"* ("The skin ego")!

Many people have had similar experiences to the one I had then. I think they are often at the origin, shall we say, of theoretical constructions which, to my mind, paradoxically draw a certain guarantee of authenticity from them. This reminds me of something Pierre Marty once said: "The edifice of psychosomatics is based on one's stomach and one's dead."

If it is conceivable to dream of being dead and alive at the same time, if we accept the idea that the ego is never completely separate from the non-ego, and if, further, we acknowledge that primary identification has the capacity of intervening beyond a point that we can imagine or accept, then the notion of object-relations may be criticised for being aleatory. I will often have occasion to return to this point. The same is true of the famous certificate of health concerning identity characterised by the sense of uniqueness experienced by an integrated organism that is capable of recognising others without ambiguity …. I shall say no more! It thus seemed expedient to replace the word "identity" with the notion of a *spectrum of identity* corresponding to the *loci* and quantities cathected by narcissistic libido, from an internal pole to an external one which coincides with the representation of the other.

Experiences of this kind naturally lead, as in a filiation, to the observation of modifications in the mental functioning of the analysand and analyst during the course of a session. This led me to recognise a new entity, almost a new "being", arising from the encounter between the unconscious mental activities of the protagonists, to which I have given the name *psychological chimera* in order to account for both its fabulous and monstrous character.

Finally, the heavily insistent nature of this issue led me to think that a specific language necessarily corresponded to the world in question. I have called this the *idiom of identity*, a language comprised of sounds and elements that are initially non-verbal, and whose trace can be found in the activity of the *chimera*. Even though I am using the term language, it is not my intention at all to enter into the field of the linguist. Nevertheless, I think it is acceptable to employ the term to designate the *idiom of identity*; for, even if one places it at some distance from an endophasic production, it is not totally foreign to it. Protolanguage, then? Perhaps! In spite of everything! Even if it is preceded by a pure cry but followed by vociferation, the initial stages of the infant's expectations of what the object will be and of its relationship with him, this language is first and foremost the heir of the incomprehensible sounds of the infant who first utters it for himself even before he belongs to some sort of *transitional subject*. Later on this language will assume a paraphrenic character, sometimes with extreme poetic accents, as in the work of Antonin Artaud, a point I shall come back to later. I want to stress that this language does not so much ensure communication with others as it does the manifestation of a *primordial being*. A primordial being whose activity is incessant and which, in order that the subject may survive—and even before we can legitimately speak of *inside and outside*—had, by virtue of a fabulous operation, invented a *double*. Before distinguishing oneself from the non-ego, it is necessary, is it not, to have first differentiated oneself from oneself?

From the very beginning, and no doubt over the course of the years, the derivatives of the *idiom of identity*, in their successive forms, are endowed with an essential function of negotiation. Negotiation, that is, between on the one hand operational interpellations, completely infiltrated by the sexual *drives*, and, on the other, exigencies specific to a non-libidinal and purely identity-based order of need that is alien to the sexual. Such a proposition will undoubtedly give rise to much discussion. It is in this order, then, that the violent expectations and necessities of the body will find expression electively, being illustrated brilliantly by what I call the *passage into onomatopoeia*. Gilles Deleuze evokes something similar in connection with the poem by Antonin Artaud entitled "The Return of Artaud the Momo". With his close relations, Artaud always pleaded the cause of the body! Passage into onomatopoeia: "... o kaya ponoura/o ponoura/o pona poni." Antonin Artaud often accompanied these onomatopoeia "economically" with noisy puffing sounds and explosive cries, while banging with his hammer on a block of wood at his home in Ivry. It was definitely a language which, without ever being forgotten, celebrated the first moments of human relationships; but, first and foremost, it asserted bluntly the words "I, ME, NOTHING", in capitals in the poem—the reverse of which would perhaps have been mutism.

The negotiation in question is expressed, then, among others, at the level of language—languages, we should say, as they are observed in treatments, with their respective prevalences and entanglements. So on the one hand we discover the traces of the *idiom of identity* and, on the other, during a discourse that is much too explicative and rational, the insistent eruptions of forms of expression akin to those found in dreams, revealing the powerful intervention of preconscious activities. There is a certain degree of pertinence in evaluating this rapport insofar as the form it takes often intervenes decisively in a person's destiny. I will give an illustration of this in a moment. Such an evaluation, moreover, governs certain strategic choices of the analyst. Depending on the particular case and situation, the analyst is led not only to provoke an indispensable economic disturbance, resulting in a temporal regression, but also to provoke a "scandal of identity", a disintegration of boundaries, a certain degree of depersonalisation—a necessary condition if the new is to have a chance of emerging and of being accepted, that is to say, transformed into "ego". Bizarre interventions, the emission of syllables, illogical constructions, or apparently absurd utterances are all part of the dispositions capable of provoking this scandal of identity. Such interventions are reminiscent of the "allusive interpretations" of Kutrin A. Kemper (1965), albeit introduced in a different spirit, consisting of isolated words, incomplete sentences, interjections, etc. There is therefore no reason to fear, quite to the contrary, "the transitory disintegrating effect of interpretations" referred to by Andrew Peto (1959); nor, indeed, their destructuring effect on the object-relationship, whose equilibrium is restored largely by virtue of the instruments employed to ensure that optimal distance is maintained between the protagonists.

To illustrate the consequences of a faulty evaluation of the rapport between sexual drive activity and the problematic of identity, in the sense in which I understand it, that is, as non-libidinal, I will now, as announced not far above, present two particularly striking cases. One day, a long time ago, two colleagues, who were master clinicians but who, alas, are no longer with us, sought my opinion, knowing full well the interest I had in psychosomatics. Within a relatively short space of time each of them shared with me, in a questioning spirit, the same painful experience. The two cases in question were classical psychoanalytic treatments for which the diagnosis of obsessional neurosis was clinically convincing. However, both patients, one just after the end of treatment, and the other, right in the middle of it, had suddenly developed extremely serious ulcero-haemorrhagic rectocolitis. All the analytic work had been directed at what was only the neurotic fringe of the morbid state, while the economic factors were operating elsewhere. The analysis had "bypassed" the essential issue. No one is immune to such a misadventure.

It is difficult, I think, to appreciate correctly the degree of pertinence of referring to clinical practice to support a theoretical construction which depends on logical exigencies. As far as I am concerned, I cannot do without such references, especially as I have often started out from a fact I have observed or experienced.

However much weight is accorded to clinical material, there always comes a moment in the course of our reflections when we need to identify the theoretical or doctrinal references to which we have referred and on which we have leaned. Thus, in identifying the specificity of an order of identity which is neither sexual and drive-related nor narcissistic, I am upholding the lasting validity of what is called the first instinctual dualism. Let it be clear, however, that I am already amputating the notion of *self-preservation* of its designation as *drive*. In my opinion, the term drive must be reserved "metapsychologically" for the sexual domain, whether at the object or narcissistic level. Not to mention the fact that the term is improper for naming that which orients the organic foundations of the human being, namely, *an essentially genetic programme*—I have referred to this before—which has the task of organising, with its various stages, not only the development and protection of the person, but also his preordained finiteness. This implies, let me say in passing, rejecting the notion of a special drive, the so-called death drive. For me, pre-Oedipal maternal seduction, as conceived by Jean Laplanche (1987) in his *New Foundations for Psychoanalysis*, with which I am wholly in agreement, intervenes in this programme. I would simply add that while I fully adopt the notion of enigmatic signifiers, impregnated by unconscious sexual values, which the human infant has the task of decoding, my particular emphasis is on the fact that, concurrently, this seduction engenders the "germination" of erogenous zones within this *essentially genetic programme* to which I have referred—erogenous zones whose specific activity will impose on the psychical apparatus an original task, namely, the creation, the *invention* of *sexual drive activity*. Let us remember that one of Freud's definitions of the drive is "the demand made upon the mind for work in consequence of its connection with the body" (1915, p. 122).

At this point in my argument, I realise that reflections, lived experiences, and theoretical references had, in spite of certain singularities, acquired a finite order that was sufficiently in keeping with the demands of reason, even while positing, as I have just done, the notion of a genetic programme. And this situation gave rise to a certain sense of agitated perplexity which, if the truth is to be told, I had experienced at other moments of this adventure and even well before it began. But this time, the "smell" of the thing was insistent and different. So it was necessary to take account of the fact. The impact of the indecisive nature of identity, this curious system of frontiers, on the ordering of the subject's relations with the figures that represent his objects can deteriorate, at particular moments, to the point of powerfully affecting not only the analysand but the analyst as well. This much we know. This phenomenon leads to more or less important and more or less fleeting changes in the sense the analyst has of himself, in his mental functioning, and mobilises in him unexpected thoughts and sometimes surprising technical initiatives, while at the same time evoking the memory of experiences that are rooted in the very distant past, albeit of decisive influence when it comes to shedding light on his fascinations. Thus when one is setting out one's ideas on a particular subject, it is helpful if one refers to what lay, in part at least, at their origin. Just as, in the lines above, I pointed up the importance of a confrontation with the specular image, here I am referring to childhood episodes that are related to depersonalisation. It is arguable, I think, that relations with people and things, and also with himself, had become very unsure for a certain child, when, defying the laws of gravity, he felt himself drawn to jump into the space or void of a stairwell. The same was true, was it not, when this same child, who was so calm, saw this space breaking up around him, as if for ever? A powerful determinism, of distant origins, may thus be said to preside, perhaps to a large extent, over the intellectual options retained subsequently, over the choice of themes such as the one "chosen" here—that is to say the dismemberment of the relational order. This constraint has to be added to that traced by unconscious impulses: should it be regarded as a wound or a source of richness?

But there is something else! As one advances, plunged into a process of reflection and writing, sometimes, all of a sudden—one might think they were ways of avoiding the issue—a series of images, trains of thought, constructions, lines of reasoning, emerge at great speed. After being tempted to reject them, one realises that, albeit bizarre, they are indeed relevant to the subject in question, and that, in the present case, they concern, let me repeat, the relations of the self with objects and with itself. There is invention here, the invention of a story. It could be that of an encounter, an encounter with someone who, saying absurd and frightening things, hears himself replying: *"Mais chassez vite cela!"* ("Dismiss all that from your head immediately!"). Only to find, on the contrary, that his mind has been taken over entirely. How ambiguous the French word *"chasser"* is, for it means both to *expel* and to *hunt*. On the face of it, one would choose expel, that is, the act of evacuating something from one place in the direction of another. However, owing to the fact that the "ill-fated words" have been proffered, are they not already outside? And so the friendly advice is useless. Unless, that is, we know too much about the nature of this outside. In any case, we cannot restrict ourselves to the surrounding atmosphere; we must not talk "wildly". But then the "ill-fated words" to be expelled might have another addressee than the one who gave the advice. It could be the subject hearing himself speak, hearing his own complaint which may contain a piece of future advice; but he is already ready to abandon it, without trying another. But no sooner have the ill-fated words been heard by the interlocutor who gave the good advice than they are returned to the sender, which cancels out his egotistical attempt, thereby adding an absurdity. And so, gradually, in this to and fro, the bizarreness of the situation becomes clearer; for, infinitely, and like in a play of mirrors facing each other, the one who hears is the one who speaks, while the other expresses himself from afar. Or rather, if one of them only speaks for himself, the other, the dispenser of "friendly" advice only exists in an uncertain manner, unless he resembles the subject to a great extent; in short, unless he is invented. The object thus only exists if he is the subject himself!

Such sequences are capable of provoking or accentuating in any one of us a state of internal instability or a dangerous state of excitement which, like interlocking Russian dolls, governs the need to expel from the mind, with the aim of re-establishing a certain stability, some of its contents along with unspeakable thoughts. No doubt there is a growing temptation to argue that in the abysses of the mind there is only one space and that the "subject", untiringly, speaks to no other than himself. The problem is perhaps unbearable and so, in order to deal with it, we imagine the existence of frontiers or boundaries, even if they are vague. Unless we make the assumption that *the thought or thoughts to be dismissed are not even present in the mind of the person who has expressed them before they have been expressed.* One of the most singular capacities of the psychical apparatus would thus be to emit thoughts that are not present in it, but which exist only by virtue of their enunciation. To recover our footing again, let us consider a quantum metaphor: we know that the atomic nucleus, containing only protons and neurons, is capable of emitting electrons even though they do not exist in it. Consequently, the notion of object-relations, which has already been put to the test in connection with the question of the modification of relations between individuals through the mechanisms of identification and projection, might only concern an exiguous territory which, in addition, is in no way vital in the strict sense of the term.

The eruption of apparently absurd scenarios, sustained by an implacable logic, as in the experience of having to reject something that has been said, leads to the emerging feeling that something must still happen which is undoubtedly opposed by powerful resistances. It is as if the mind refused to envisage the intervention of unusual modalities in the construction of identity and the specification of the object. The intellect protests, then, and by neutralising the emotions, by evacuating the "psychological soup", it seeks to maintain the *"belles différences"*—those that Freud reproached Groddeck for ignoring. But the attempt fails when the body is condemned to affirm itself alone. Too alone, it runs the risk of destroying itself on the spot, unless mendacity, conveyed by an ambiguous message, succeeds in postponing the planned extinction of the subject.

These thoughts never cease to return and to force themselves on me, stimulating a "spiral" of meditations—the word is very ambitious— meditations whose outcome is uncertain. Right at the beginning of this text, I cited some remarks made by analysands in which the ambiguity of their relationship with their body could be considered as forming an integral part of the picture observed in "borderline states", with their narcissistic implications. This remains pertinent. Now, in the discourses that I am going to report, I want to stress the *dimension of identity*, as I conceive of it, without omitting anything that is related to sexual drive activity, while stressing the impact of my understanding of the problematics of identity and of human relationships on interpretative activity. As I wrote a few lines above, it is no longer simply a question of supporting, or even inducing, a formal and even temporal regression to facilitate the emergence of repressed instinctual material, but of aggravating the indispensable disturbance of the sense of identity which makes it possible to accede to what is new. A certain comicality is inherent to the material in question. This is inevitable and, I would add, significant, as is the case each time that the so-called natural "being there" (*Dasein*) of beings or things is flouted. It has to be faced. You will forgive me, I hope, for not refraining from referring to such moments which are often so decisive in analysis. They occur, depending on the case, and on the nature and degree of progress in the work, at various levels of the analysand's mental functioning, yet very close to the field that is most familiar to us, for here I am respecting an order, namely, the neurotic horizon, which is delimited by pleasure and castration anxiety. Intuitively, however, one senses—without admitting it fully to oneself—that it is worth encouraging the regression that is underway.

Somewhat embarrassed and hesitant, the patient evoked the end of the last session. She was not pleased with herself. She had the impression she had wanted to hold my attention. She also feared that she had not been recognised. I intervened immediately, saying: "I would not have appreciated your '*brouet*' [brew or gruel]!" She laughed briefly, then seemed confused, thought she understood, and felt bizarre. It is clear that the spontaneous, unpremeditated, and intuitive use of the old-fashioned and rarely used word "*brouet*" caused the compromise established between a voracious oral instinct and a hitherto tenacious defence to vacillate more than an explicative or rational interpretation would have done. Furthermore, owing to the element of surprise it provoked, the word *"brouet"* was endowed with a certain seductive power, it has to be conceded; at the same time, though, it had the virtue of initiating a displacement of a topographical order. The debate was going to take place completely at a preconscious level and under the jurisdiction of its principles. What was it necessary to know, what was it necessary to understand? We began to be elsewhere. The relationship between us was taking on another form.

I will now report the essential exchanges from another case, even stranger than the first, which were also expressed over the course of two sessions.

The patient's analysis—it is worth pointing out—had been in progress for several years already. It was the very beginning of a session. The analysand said with an air of embarrassment: "I don't think I any longer know what colour your hair is ..." (this surprised her).

ME: Staying close to her perplexity and seizing on the important role of perceptual activity so as to introduce the body into the question of identity, I replied: "Which hair?"
HER: "The hair on your head."
ME: "So I have some hair on my head."
HER: "What? Well, I don't know now ... but you're not bald, are you?" she asked.
ME: "What do you think?"

Castration and depersonalisation are intermingled here, and we may wonder if it is not in the prevalence of the rapport between them that the introjective capacities find an essential path for their accomplishment. In the present case, my interventions, which were certainly quite transparent but apparently unreasonable, prevented defensive countercathexes from blocking the situation, while maintaining a necessary "economic instability". This was borne out in the following session when the patient came back spontaneously to the episode. She corrected herself, saying she was no longer uncertain, but added none the less that "We cannot concern ourselves *simply* with hair." As we say, she both knew and did not know where the word "simply" was leading her. She became confused once again, but it was no longer to do with the fidelity of her perceptions. It is understandable that she repeated that she no longer knew whether I had any hair, adding that she did not know what to say any more. For my part, I asked her what I was supposed to understand by this. My second intervention, "So I have some hair on my head" redirected the exchange in a progressive direction towards "castration anxiety". This does not always happen—for instance, when need affirms its demands insistently under the eventual and misleading cover of masochistic provocations which, in fact, are put to the service of tracing the frontiers of identity.

My patient got irritated, asking: "Why do I mistreat my body. Why do I inflict so many small *effacements* on my self? Is it to reassure myself?" The word *effacement* was out of place here, but aptly described what was going on. Nevertheless, a bit troubled, I only went part of the way: "So that I camp where you are?" But it was only in the evening that the right formulation came to my mind: "You want me to come to the place where you are hesitating to be." From experience, I am convinced that this way of intervening, of interpreting, at certain moments, corresponds, by an extension of its scope, to the earliest initiatives of language in infancy.

It would have been possible to leave things there and to disregard the fact that the end of the "adventure" had not been reached. This was so in spite of the fact that certain formulae, very much related to the subject, had erupted into consciousness, which opened out onto surprising propositions, albeit logical—too logical perhaps, which were reminiscent of the first phases of existence, of immersion in the world of objects. And it was not by chance that a Tamul proverb came to my mind, which I had once quoted as an epigraph to an article: "Once you are on a tiger's back, it is difficult to get off."

Before continuing, it is perhaps worth recalling, in passing, the solipsistic risk to which the notion of object-relation is *paradoxically* exposed. This is particularly the case when erosion at the frontiers of the inside and the outside is accentuated, for distinctions between representations then become blurred to the point of affecting fantasy activity itself. I keep coming back to this point, but how can one avoid doing so when there is a danger that confrontations between protagonists may occur separately, within each person's mind, and in a state of mutual ignorance. Only the analytic situation, at the heart of the strange apparatus of thinking formed by the analyst and analysand together, has the potential, we hope, of allowing the contours of differentiation between the protagonists to emerge.

As if pursuing these considerations was subject to a sort of gravitational effect, the questions I am raising concerning object-relations lead us, as I have already advised, to focus our attention on the earliest phases of the construction of the subject, even before the notion of cathexis fully acquires its organising function. You may recall that I drew attention to the essential importance of the invention/creation of a double as a necessary prerequisite for the discovery of the object and for establishing relations with it. The operation in question is necessarily governed by a specific and archaic mechanism with obvious distinctive virtues. I am referring to *splitting*. I will come back to this, but would simply like to point out here that this so-called destructive mechanism has a bad reputation which is due to its functional degradation. "Primordial splitting" is the metaphorical echo, if you like, of the first cellular divisions which break up a perfect unity with a view to participating in the accomplishment of a programme of life—that is to say, of death that is programmed and deferred. During this time, and even before there is any question of recognising the "outside" world, a world that includes the subject himself who strives to integrate bits of it, the opposition is not between cathexis and decathexis but between splitting and cathexis.

The highly theoretical character of a construction sometimes gives rise to a certain perplexity, but there again …. This is one of the reasons that leads me, before going any further, to return to clinical experience and to report a few sequences taken from one of the sessions on which my elaboration is partly based. It was a session—of which there were many others like it during the course of this analysis—of a young woman whose severe suffering, related to problems of identity, and which found expression among other ways through states of depersonalisation, was matched by her rare intelligence. It was an extremely trying session, consisting of a long and almost uninterrupted discourse, which in itself was unusual. What she was saying was sometimes almost inaudible and sounded like a sort of long and somewhat breathless respiration underpinning the expression of extreme affects. It is difficult to convey the atmosphere faithfully.

During the session before the one I have selected, what we call an attack on linking had manifested itself powerfully, along with an attack on psychoanalysis, on myself, of course, and on all the work that had been done so far. The following day things continued in the same vein. The attack first took the form of an almost incomprehensible, muffled verbal expression. Then, she raised her voice, complaining in a masochistic mode—another clinical form of aggression—about the way she was destroying herself, destroying everything. And then she suddenly changed tack: "Attacking and destroying are the only means I have left if I want to continue to exist, to exist for myself." I did not catch everything she said. Then she returned fleetingly to the relational level, saying, "I am afraid of the sessions, but I can't do without them ... you are drawing me away from my inner being ... You should put me inside you in order to reconstitute me." A brief moment of silence ensued before the proposition was inverted: "Inside me, you would be a part of me ... there would no longer be any difference between us ...." Overcoming the moment of silence as well as the confusion, as in dreaming, she let slip: "Do we have to make links with that?" And then a note of strangeness returned: "Are these elements that need to be given meaning ...? Why do I feel it is necessary, whatever it costs, to go through a certain order of meaning to find my boundaries?" It was at this precise moment, a nodal moment, that a manifest relationship between egotistical splitting and distinctive affect, ready to look in another direction, expressed itself. "The present moment," she said, "one of unsticking ... the unsticking I am afraid of ... there is something to share ... or to be mixed together ... the torments are ahead ... once again I must do things with my hands, my eyes, my body ... my body which is now like a stone, permeated or hermetic." Later in the session, having formulated the wish to be turned upside down without being destroyed, she maintained that she "lived in solitude, face to face with herself, full of hatred", and that this prevented her from being with me.

Thus, in certain treatments, or at certain moments of any treatment, we discover the distant echo and the secret celebration of the time when splitting occurred necessarily and decisively. I am referring to a "primordial splitting" which, as I wrote earlier, may have biological roots. It is primordial because it is first, essential, and foundational. The "mechanism" animating it is certainly operative in classical splitting in its diverse senses, but is in no way designed to ensure, at the heart of an ego that is still far from constituted, the coexistence of different and contradictory dispositions in relation to reality. As *the mechanism of a mechanism, it is in the service of a singular activity of construction rather than a defensive effort*. This splitting is at work throughout existence; but its status is precarious as soon as it is no longer wholly occupied with necessity, and thus with survival, for then it begins to gain in quality, and this quality is called *hate*, its heir.

While I had no hesitation in proposing the notion of "an essentially genetic programme" ensuring the development, preservation, and finiteness of the individual, I am more reserved—and I find this striking— when referring to an articulation between biology and metapsychology. I almost refrained from doing so, even temporarily, although the matter is almost self-evident. In any case, that is what we are given to understand by the psychoanalyst Jacques Ascher and the haemotologist Jean-Pierre Jouet, with whom I have had lengthy discussions concerning the graft of haemopoietic stem cells. I am thinking of their book entitled *La Greffe* (Ascher & Jouet, 2004). In their respective domains, there is an identical readiness to resort to metaphorical language: "biological chimera", induced by the allograft, *psychological chimera*, according to the expression I have chosen. But that is not all, and this point is of special concern to us today, for we are faced with the fact that issues of identity are intertwined with the strangest and the most tragic forms of human relationships. It is very understandable, too understandable, that the host subject rejects the graft as radically other, perfectly strange, and unassimilable. But sometimes—and this is the most inconceivable and intolerable aspect of the problem—identities are exchanged. The intolerance no longer concerns the identity *of the other in oneself, but one's own identity, via the other in oneself*. And the graft attacks the subject who has become the perfect stranger, the other. It attacks him and kills him. But it does not kill him in just any old way; it kills him by flaying him alive, that is to say—and it is not insignificant—at the level of the skin, the boundary between the inside and the outside, which disintegrates, as if abraded. Excluded from himself, it is as if the subject has become the victim of the most ferocious hatred. The word hatred forces itself upon me; it was precisely this word that had come to me spontaneously as the qualitative heir of splitting; and it was this word that led me all the same to reserve a place for biology in the matter at hand.

But the suggestion that hatred plays a role in the construction of the human subject should disconcert us profoundly, even when we have known for a long time that the other is discovered in hate. But there is more. Here we need to take a step backwards. Before hatred, which was not yet hatred, there was lurking, powerfully, a fundamental *self-hatred*, the self-hatred that works with a view to establishing the subject himself ... and, if everything goes well, to announcing what, one day, will be sufficiently different from oneself. The first drama is there, for hatred has the task of operating right in the middle of what is still barely a space and is also capable of disintegrating in an instant. The body screams from the very fact of existing; the process of constructing ourselves requires, as it were, the "blow of an axe". Well, we should not forget to tremble when, paraphrasing a well-known saying, we are on the point of proclaiming: "O, my objects, there are no objects!"[1]

Note

1. This is a colourful paraphrase of Montaigne's saying (borrowed from Aristotle): "*O mes amis, il n'y a nul ami!*" ("O my friends, there is no friend!") (1965, p. 190).

CHAPTER TWELVE

Reconsiderations and new developments in psychoanalysis* (2011)

A ttempting to reconsider the coherence of the Freudian psycho-analytic corpus is no easy task. It is fair to say, I think, that this prodigious theoretical edifice has more than proved its worth; after more than a century its foundations still hold firm, whereas, during this same period, many other scientific notions have collapsed. To take the risk of embarking on this adventure, it is necessary to have been seized by an insistent sense of rigorous necessity. This necessity had been evacuated for many years, even though it was founded on concurrent arguments belonging to several registers: theoretical and clinical, but also technical in the conduct of treatments.

That being so, how can one fail to be sensitive to arguments which, quite rightly, maintain that in fields like psychoanalysis, art, and science, vacillations of a linear logic, contradictions, and even areas of incoherence, are not merely an integral part of the discipline but serve to ensure its depth and fidelity to the movement of life. Well, in spite of that, the perplexity aroused by the imprecision or even the incompatibility

---

*This text was first published in French in *Nouveau développements en psychanalyse: autour de l'oeuvre de Michel de M'Uzan* (see Baruch, 2011).

affecting the relations between notions, between the fundamental concepts, requires us to continue to subject them to critical and rigorous examination. This is a considerable task in itself and one that I can only evoke here in support of my argument, that is, the exposition of the essential elements of a theoretical or doctrinal edifice that is rigorously Freudian, but freed from certain approximations and areas of incoherence just mentioned, to which I will return briefly. It is still necessary, however, in order to be able to embark on this adventure with a sufficient sense of legitimacy, to find the right "manner" of doing so. I am thinking, in particular, of the *constructive critique* proposed by Jean Laplanche which aims to "make Freud's work creak in the extreme", "putting it to work".

I have just pointed out that the motives underlying the proposition of new developments in psychoanalysis belonged to three registers: theoretical, clinical, and technical.

In the theoretical register, I will confine myself to three subjects: the critique of the notion of the drive, including the death drive; the abandonment of the theory of seduction by Freud in 1897; and, with the second topography, the second theory of the instincts, for it is necessary to be very rigorous in our use of the term drive. Metapsychologically speaking, the term drive only has its place in the psychosexual order, with its source, its thrust, its aim, and its object. Strictly speaking, therefore, and I want to stress this point, there is no self-preservative *drive*, but a principle of functioning in the service of the accomplishment of what is essentially a genetic programme in which the emergence of drive functioning is *"anticipated"*. I will come back to this point later.

Furthermore, and correlatively, the notion of the death drive must be abandoned. In the first place because, strictly speaking, the term drive does not correspond at all to metapsychological desiderata; and, more fundamentally, because natural death is not the result of the intervention of a specific force, but the outcome of a *programme of life* which is designed to last for a predetermined length of time until its extinction. In this connection, I would like to remind you of Freud's own attitude: in the first paragraph of the sixth chapter of *Beyond the Pleasure Principle* (1920g), he initially situates death on the side of self-preservation before detaching it in order to set it in opposition to it; and then, finally, in this same chapter, he claims that he is not even sure himself whether or not he believes in this proposition!

Two initiatives taken by Freud add still further to this perplexity owing to their powerful impact on the theoretical edifice. The first, which Jean Laplanche (1987, 2007) has denounced, qualifying it as a "cataclysm" for psychoanalysis, concerns the abandonment of the theory of seduction in 1897. It will be recalled that, as he was unable to continue to uphold the role of the father as a paedophile seducer, Freud came to regard seduction as a pure fantasy. I concur entirely with Laplanche's point of view here.

The second initiative, whose consequences in my view are equally weighty, concerns the introduction of the second topography and the second theory of the instincts. Not that the contributions of this initiative should be rejected; what is to be deplored, though, is that they affected what was essential in the analytic world, namely the *systemic unconscious* (first topography), with all its characteristics. Whatever may be said about it, the revolutionary and scandalous character of the systemic unconscious was affected—perhaps in order to erase the third narcissistic injury inflicted on humanity after Copernicus and Darwin. The unconscious tended to become a mere *quality* that could be found in the ego and in the superego alike! Ernest Jones, Freud's biographer, said that if Freud had died in 1915, we would have had a complete picture of psychoanalysis in its classical form. Let us be quite clear—and I want to insist on this point lest there be any misunderstanding—if I remain firm regarding the rejection of the notion of the death drive, I am not proposing in any way to "shelve", as it were, what is called the second topography and the theoretical contributions that followed after 1920, but rather to subject them to what I would call "thought hygiene". When a theoretical construction has proved its worth—which was the case of psychoanalysis in 1915, subsequent discoveries and contributions cannot simply be added to it, and even less substituted for it; the "new" must strive to respect the conditions permitting its aggregation, its organic integration into the "old". With the turning point of 1920, this was not always the case. It is scarcely necessary to point out that the subject would require a lengthy treatment which clearly does not have its place here; for I have restricted myself to considering only what is strictly necessary for the purpose of ensuring the legitimacy and comprehension of the rest of my argument.

Among the reasons that continue to sustain the initiative to embark on new developments in psychoanalysis, in addition to those just mentioned, are, as I explained at the outset, those that pertain to the register of clinical practice and, even more so, to technique. I will move on to this now—at least it will have the advantage of being less austere (!) even if, logically speaking, it is here that the exposition of the new developments in psychoanalysis ought to have had its place. In order to give things a more convincing demonstrative "basis", I will present a few sequences of clinical material, while taking account of, shall we say, the nosographical spectrum in all its diversity. The matter is of unquestionable importance; for, as I have regularly had occasion to observe, the analyst, when intervening verbally, formulates his interventions, his interpretations, using an identical form of language—that is to say, explicative, ordered, "secondarised" language which is more or less respectful of grammar. By contrast, the utterances of analysands form a large spectrum ranging from the cry to the most obsessionally organised commentaries. And this is without taking into account that the analyst takes on—perhaps more often nowadays—pathologies of a psychotic, identity-related, or psychosomatic nature, whose modalities of expression differ with each analysand.

In the exposition of the cases that follow, we will see the extent to which the very notion of "technical flexibility" is insufficient to describe what can be expected from the analyst. We will be able to appreciate the importance, when the analyst speaks, makes interventions, or gives interpretations, of the identity he adopts in response to his analysand's discourse: in the first case the role of transference-object is explicitly assumed; in the second case, the transferential value of the analyst is clear but implicit, and his remarks allow the analysand to discover it; in the third case, the analyst's utterances are oriented by the fluctuating and indecisive character of the subject's frontiers of identity. In the last case reported, the analyst's remarks are totally alien to the psychosexual field.

If I accord considerable value to this clinical material (and I am only citing part of it here), it is because it shows the range of the nosographical spectrum proposed to the analyst today; but it is also and primarily because, in conjunction with the necessities of theoretical reflection articulating the sexual and the dimension of identity, it lends support to the foundations of the new developments I am concerned with.

The first of the cases selected concerns a female analysand who, in the course of recent sessions, had constantly been making remarks aimed at devaluing herself radically, even if in the service of resistance: she was less than nothing; she knew nothing. The situation was spectacular and continued during the following hour. At the height of her self-depreciative peroration, I said to her: "I don't require so much." She made no reply, but seemed none the less to have been stopped in her tracks. In the following session, returning to the episode, she claimed that she did not understand what I had meant, what the meaning of my words was! And it took her some time before she finally grasped that I had been speaking as a *transference-object* to whom she was giving an account of herself. O resistance, when you have us in your grip!

Let us consider now the remarks of a cultivated female patient whose richness of mentalisation was remarkable. It was in connection with a dream. It was not a nightmare, she said, and yet, retrospectively, she felt rather ashamed of it. In an unknown place, a village, in a little square, she found herself standing in front of a clock, not a church clock, she added. She had a little box in her hand. She knew that there were some tools in this little box. A man she hardly knew approached her. He was also holding a box, but it was a big box in which she knew there were tools. The patient asked the man what he was going to do. "Wind up the clock," he replied. And she began to feel ashamed for not having understood this immediately. The tool in the box, the man's large box, the meaning was so clear that all I needed to say was "box and tool" for her to understand the sexual metaphor, as if in a moment of illumination. This gave rise to a sudden lifting of repression. I did not even have to assume the paternity of my intervention. The words I had uttered came from "elsewhere", like an impersonal commentary. It was still essential, though, that no verb, no inflexion entered into it.

The case I am going to refer to now belongs to quite a different universe. The patient, a young woman, had been in "couch-armchair" analysis for several years. Some extremely worrying episodes had required several hospitalisations in a psychiatric setting, during which time contact was maintained by telephone. She was afflicted by cataclysmic disturbances of her sense of identity and, in particular, by frightening experiences of depersonalisation. At such moments she was unable to speak. Sitting on the edge of the couch, she would turn her head back and forth, left and right, in a total state of turmoil, as if she was devastated. That day, however, she none the less managed to articulate in a hoarse voice that it was "just the beginning" and that she was going to "slip". Losing her contours, she was, in the strict sense, depersonalised. And then, at the heart of this debacle, I was very pleased to hear her speak about her absolute uselessness and her unworthiness, for the arrival of words showed that the narcissistic dyke had not given way completely. The situation still remained delicate, however. And it was only in the following hour that it became certain that hospitalisation was no longer necessary. Yet it was a session where everything seemed to disintegrate. She began to devalue everything: the objects on the table, everything that was present in the room. Finally, there was a frenetic outburst of hatred, hatred of herself, of others, of me, of course, with a powerful wish to tear me to pieces and, more reassuringly, to devour me. Being aware of the volatilisation of the frontiers between beings and between things, I replied offhand: "You want to tear me to pieces, inside myself, where I will cut you up into bits." Though taken aback at first, she finally said "Yes", to which I replied: "It's a question of appe-tite!" The contours of her ego were still very loose, but there was now a shift away from a severe sense of uncertainty regarding her identity towards a level of drive functioning that was very archaic, but none the less inscribed within the psychosexual domain.

For the third observation illustrating some of my positions, I will not draw on my own session material but on material reported in an exchange between colleagues, which I shall call the imperious installa-tion of a "flagstone of identity." An experienced female colleague told me about an incident that some may find rather banal. The session had finished; but just as she was leaving, the patient suddenly turned round and kissed my colleague. Quite overcome, she apologised, saying that she had not been able to stop herself. At first a little troubled, the analyst remained silent and immobile for a brief moment and then, drawing on her experience, invited her patient to come back into her office. This was perfectly reasonable and, in my view, preferable to resorting to a com-monplace statement such as, "We can speak about this in the next ses-sion." So they went back into the office, stopped, and stood facing each other. Trying to reassure her patient, the analyst told her that anyone can be overcome by emotion. This basically constituted a sort of exon-eration from guilt, the reverse of which is a narcissistic injury, "You're not capable of committing a sin", which aggravates the regression. It would have been more appropriate, or more prudent, I think, to leave the affective and erotic dimension momentarily "on the sidelines", as it were, and to enlist the help of perception—perception which corre-sponds in the first place to a fundamental phase in the installation of psychic functioning (see Scarfone, 2008b). So I suggested that rather than tranquillising her patient, she could have said, "We both found ourselves standing in front of the door", hoping thereby to participate in the construction of this "flagstone of identity" I have referred to.

In addition to the critical examination of the theoretical corpus, the clinical material that I have just retraced supports—I will come back to this point further on—the new developments that seem to me to be essential. Let me recall briefly the foundations, already presented, of the initiative, namely, the rejection of the notion of the death drive as well as the notion of drive for self-preservation. The consequences of this go well beyond a simple question of vocabulary when I substitute the term *vital-identital* for the expression self-preservation, since the latter is only *one* of the functions of "organic being", to use the expression proposed by Freud in *Inhibitions, Symptoms and Anxiety* (1926d). As this point is essential, I reassured myself in passing that the translation was correct by returning to the *Gesammelte Werke* (XIV, pp. 119–120). Freud (1991) indeed writes: *"Bei ausserer Gefahr unternimmt das organische Wesen einen Fluchtversuch …."* ("In the case of external danger the organism has recourse to attempts at flight"). Let us note the neuter *das* in *"das organische Wesen"*, "organic being". It is thus the *vital-identital* that enters into relation with the psychosexual domain or, better, "the sexual" (*le sexual*) of Jean Laplanche (2007). This *sexual* includes both the object and narcissistic poles, of course.

The *vital-identital* and the potential "sexual" in waiting express in the reality of life, that is, in the development of being with its finitude, the activity of a programme, largely genetic in essence, triggered by the encounter between male and female gametes in a sufficiently hazardous manner to preserve a role for history. The execution of this programme, with its stages and its determined duration depends, it cannot be denied, first on the engagement of energy which is initially "without quality" and produced, as we know, essentially by intracellular formations, the mitochondria.

Thus the history of the development of being is also one of the destiny of energy, of force, of which the economic point of view is the metapsychological "echo". But in order to be tenable these views must receive further "theoretical underpinning". Let me recall the two "accidents", already mentioned, which affected the analytic science, namely, the abandonment of the theory of seduction and the second theory of the instincts.

The crucial underpinning is supplied by the theory of seduction as elaborated by Jean Laplanche. I will recapitulate on the essential points.

For Jean Laplanche, the seduction of the *infans* (i.e., the speechless newborn) during the ministrations of care by the adult consists of messages that are "contaminated" by the latter's unconscious. Through the "hermeneutical activity" of deciphering these messages, the *infans* thus begins to constitute his unconscious. While accepting, with reserve, this conception, I have been concerned primarily with the emergence of drive functioning, sexual drive functioning, *leaning on* the *vital-identital*, which corresponds, in fact, to the Freudian theory of anaclisis. For me, seduction, especially maternal seduction, leads to the emergence, the liberation, the "burgeoning" *on top of* this *vital-identital* (the self-preservative field, if you will) of the erogenous zones, whose activity requires the activation of a specific work by the psychical apparatus, work that is called *drive*. The drive is thus an "invention" of the psychical apparatus, which was considered by Freud as a "fiction".

There is justification, therefore, for speaking of a certain parallelism between the evolution of "organic being", the *vital-identital*, in the direction of the "psychosexual subject", and the evolution of the status of an energy that is initially "without quality", in the service of the integrated functioning of the organism, towards libidinal drive activity. Clearly, it is not a question of substituting one order or status for another, but rather of degrees of imbrication, with, depending on the moments or epochs, the more or less affirmed but significant prevalence of one register over another—I have spoken of "negotiation"—capable of defining structures more or less clearly.

I would like to refer in passing to a remark formulated by Alain Gibeault during one of our exchanges at the ASM13 (a mental health association in the 13th arrondissement of Paris). For him libidinal drive activity *could be present* from the outset and, at the same time, the "narcissistic" would have its place *in* the *vital-identital*. I would respond to this conception by saying that the emergence of the drive, of sexual drive functioning, is *anticipated* in the genetic programme from the beginning, just as puberty is before it is expressed in reality, but that the *temporal gap*, even minimal, in the phenomenon is indispensable. The formulation according to which "the object is cathected before being perceived" (Serge Lebovici, 1961) is certainly an attractive one. The *infans* of the earliest phases of life would, however, have to be endowed with sufficiently defined frontiers for it to be possible in its case to speak of an object. The breast, unlike his big toe, is part of the newborn baby. For me the function precedes identification.

To return to my argument, I must point out that in reporting clinical sequences and in signalling the large nosographical spectrum deployed, ranging from the "factual and mechanical" (*opératoire*) level to the metaphorical level, I have stressed the need for the analyst to adapt his interventions, in both their form and content, to the status of his analysand's identity. This is where one of the difficulties lies: it goes without saying that we are not dealing here with entities that are clearly distinct from each other. It has to recognised that in any case there is always a transitional *every man's land* in which "organic being", its representation, endures in the subject. There is imbrication. The same is true of "energy without quality" and libidinal energy, as I have suggested. And if I attribute prime importance to metaphorical language, it is because it has an impact at the level of the preconscious, where changes can occur. But what happens when the balance leans too far towards the *vital-identital*? How do we account for the status of being in this situation? When we intervene, if we do, how do we manage to be in tune with the speech proffered by the other? Some time ago, Gilbert Diatkine, somewhat maliciously, asked me if non-sexual, "actual" energy was accessible to interpretation in any other way than by being transformed into libidinal energy. The question is very pertinent, even though it suggests a "secondarised" uniqueness of the analyst's identity. Now in these cases the analyst must be able to let this identity "of good company" be altered, and to adopt strange modalities of psychic functioning which extend even beyond what is induced by libidinal regression. This is what happens, among other things, when *the shadow of narcissistic failure falls on the subject*.

By contrast, it is easy to be "in tune" with the neurotic discourse as it is expressed in the following sequence. After the session had begun in a somewhat "factual and mechanical" mode, the analysand asked herself: "What am I going to be able to say?" Wishing to reanimate the situation by speaking in her place and by correcting her remark, I said, "I have nothing to say to you," which shifted the observation in the direction of exchange with an object. The analysand continued, without really being aware of the seductive implication of what she was going to say. She began by talking about a woman friend of hers who had spoken highly to her of the qualities of a miracle face cream—a slight giggle showed that she had sensed obscurely the possibility of an intention—and she added: "*Il n'est pas toujours nécessaire de plaire aux gens*" ("It's not always necessary to please people"). And I retorted, "My name is not *Jean*", thereby underlining the transferential determinism involved. Here we are at the heart of the natural vocation of psychoanalysis. But as I have often repeated, the psychoanalyst does not hesitate, or no longer hesitates, to venture into other territories, that is to say, whether he is fully aware of it or not, where the "economic" is governed more by the principles that order the *vital-identital* than by those that govern the "sexual".

But, as the reader will have noticed in what has been said so far—and I will be come back to this point—in the field of clinical practice we are "called to order"; for, we are not faced with two distinct fields (the *vital-identital* (self-preservative) and the sexual), but with two fields that are related to each other and imbricated. The *vital-identital* is no doubt better represented at the *cerebral* level, while the sexual finds its privileged place in the *psychical apparatus*.

The project that I am defending here, and there is nothing scandalous about it, serves to correct certain inaccuracies, shall we say, in the theoretical edifice, as we have seen, and to restore the balance in the relations between the two registers mentioned. The hermeneutic vocation of psychoanalysis—instead of promoting the development of a process—has undoubtedly, among other things, accentuated the disequilibrium of this rapport in favour of the sexual. This can lead to serious errors in the management of treatments. The aim of redressing the balance, then, is to restore the rightful place of the *vital-identital*, the most spectacular expression of which occurs during the first stages of the development of the human child and *never ceases* to manifest itself throughout life, and even more so during its decline which begins very early on.

It could be argued that the psychoanalyst is extremely well-armed for venturing into the exploration of new territories with their idioms. That is no doubt the case, and it was not without reason that Freud himself often turned to literature for support for his propositions. Did he not say that the artist (though this is not quite exact) achieves his objectives almost directly, effortlessly, whereas the psychoanalyst only progresses by dint of hard work?

It is thus natural, when we have seen just how important—much more so than is generally recognised—is the role played by the non-drive related *status of identity* in the first stages of life, with its powerful imprint throughout life, to see what writers, some of whom are particularly sensitive to the issue, have said about it. We are perfectly entitled to listen to what the poet intimates when the notions of inside and outside have no meaning, when the idea of frontiers do not obtain, and to see what happens when an "energy without quality" is accumulated and unleashed in organic being. We should not forget that such a situation is always ready to be reactivated, in its own way. Paul Claudel (1963) states that: "Before the word there exists a certain intensity, quality and proportion of tension" (which the poet claims is spiritual). Julien Gracq (remarks recorded by Michka Assayas and Noël Herpe at Saint-Florent-le-Veil, 16 December, 1995), comparing novels and films, remarked: "A film is obliged to show; the novel must never show, it is itself vision. One can neither draw nor invent the scene of a novel; I myself, when I write, do not see my characters. That's not how things happen. I insist, it's the sound of the words, of the sentence that evokes presences, even if they are a bit nebulous." I would add that such presences are uncertain, initially unnamed, and endowed with indistinct limits. I can imagine, and I do not hesitate to say it again, the sharp criticisms that may be mobilised by points of view which concern a time when the elementary economy is dominant, when the relatively firm distinctions between subject and object are still to come, and when the emergence of the libidinal suffers, as I have said, from a slight time-lag, even if tiny. Moreover, very few people have attempted to depict what the human being experiences in the earliest phases of life. Among those who have, I would mention a Russian author brought to my attention by Murielle Gagnebin. The author, Andrei Biely (1915) evokes in an extraordinary manner in the first pages of his *Kotik Letaev*, "the ineffable appearance of the life of the newborn baby". I shall take the liberty of citing a long passage from it:

> There was no division into "I and not-I." I was obviously delighted to read that. "There was no space and time ..."—you will probably say that I am a bit too .... Instead of this, there was a condition of the tension of sensations; as if it was all expanding: it was spreading out, it was smothering ... I am alone in the unembraceable. Nothing is inside, all is outside ... This is what the little child would have said if he had been able to speak, if he had been able to understand; and speak he could not; and understand he could not. In that far-distant time there was no "I" ... There was a puny body; and consciousness, embracing it, experienced itself in impenetrable unembraceability; none the less, penetrated by consciousness, the

body puffed up with growth, as if it were a Grecian sponge drawing water into itself; consciousness was outside the body; and in the place of the body was sensed an immense canyon: of consciousness in our meaning, where there were still no thoughts, where they were still appearing ... My childly body is a delirium of "*Mothers*" ... You are not you because next to you an *old woman*—half-adheres to you: spherical and searing; that's her *swelling*; and you, no: you are all right, not bad, nothing to complain about ... The first conscious moment of mine is—a dot. It penetrates the meaninglessness; and expanding, it becomes a sphere, but the sphere disintegrates: meaninglessness, penetrating it, tears it apart .... The skin became for me like a vault: such is the way we perceive space; my first impression of it is that it is a corridor ... The rooms are parts of my body, they have been cast off by me, they hang over me, in order to fall apart on me afterwards. Sensations separated from skin ... here is my image of entrance into life; a corridor, a vault, gloom, serpents are chasing me. (pp. 9–17ff)

Biely's effort is impressive, but he none the less uses secondary language to express the status of primary organic being. We can appreciate the scale of the work which attempts to study the actual "language" that existed when it was the *vital-identital* that spoke the loudest. It was almost ten years ago now that I first dwelt on this topic (see Chapter Six), while at the same time recalling the contribution of Gilles Deleuze to the question (see the preface to Wolfson, 1970). But it would be a display of excessive caution to fail to try, at least, to propose a direction of research. Let me say in passing that over the course of the years I have been led to correct, to clarify, some of my designations. This is understandable, though, as what I am suggesting today expresses a line of reflection that began a very long time ago with obstinacy and which demands terminological innovations, as we have seen.

To return to my argument, we can see that, with Biely, we are dealing with a sort of testimony concerning the experience of the *infans*—which is less paradisiacal than we would like to believe. But what can be said about the "language" of that time, or rather at certain of its moments, when, as I am constantly repeating, "organic being" was devoid of sufficient frontiers, when the inside and the outside only had meaning for the observer, and when the "Jacobinic" vocation of the programme of life was only concerned with governing the relations between energies without quality and so-called libidinal energies?

It is often the stumbling blocks to this task that allow one to get an idea of what is involved here. I cannot avoid recalling, even very briefly— for I have already done so amply, certain moments of the poetic language of Antonin Artaud (1947), which I call discourse in onomatopoeia, for example in *Artaud le Mômo*:

> o dedi
> a dada orzoura
> o dou zoura
> a dada skizi, etc. ...

This discourse follows on from the cry, surging forth at the dawn of the one who will establish himself between a still imperfectly delineated being and the other of life. It is an *idiom of identity* which certainly has relational exchanges in view, and which alternates with the egotic lallations of a newborn baby who only addresses himself to a still largely undefined self.

Regarding the cases I have presented, you will recall that I insisted on the need for the analyst, when he intervenes, to be "in tune" with the form taken by the analysand's discourse. This form reveals the state of "negotiation" between the *vital-identital* and the sexual. It is none the less clear that the psychoanalyst cannot—though this is not strictly true!— use language that corresponds strictly to words which are still strongly impregnated by the primary *idiom of identity*. He has to find something else. Some analysts have been aware of this more or less obscurely. I am thinking, for instance, of Kutrin A. Kemper (1965), although he would perhaps not be in complete agreement with the way I understand his reflection, and whose work I have cited in "La bouche de l'inconscient" (de M'Uzan, 1978b). His "allusive interpretation" consists of incomplete sentences, isolated words, illogical constructions, simple vowels, or even sounds. This technique tends to provoke in a timely manner a permanent reorganisation of cathetic energy, or a real disruption of the economic status quo, which is sometimes indispensable. Certain ideas of A. Peto (1963), positing the role of a fragmentising function of the ego in the process of sublimation, can also be understood in this sense.

We are touching here on a universe whose pathological aspect can be discovered in those situations when it is *behaviour* that becomes language, as I have suggested in my article, "Slaves of Quantity" (de M'Uzan, 1984); Gérard Szwec (1993), for his part, speaks of "voluntary galley slaves".

Having set out the reasons for imposing important modifications pertaining to essential points of the psychoanalytic edifice, including their consequences for interpretative activity, I could have left matters there. However, as we have seen, the notions of indeterminacy, uncertainty, and vagueness came back constantly and forcefully each time the relations between apparently distinct orders were under consideration. The idea of the dissolution of frontiers, of imbrication, made itself felt insistently, even though an essential aspect of being was at stake. The matter could not be overlooked; on the contrary, it had to be taken very seriously. A new field of developments—and this will be my conclusion—is thus opening up for psychoanalysis which coincides, I believe, with certain preoccupations of Georges Pragier and Sylvie Faure-Pragier (2007). In this connection I have referred to psychoanalysis as the "science of indefinite limits" (de M'Uzan, 2011) which, along with other disciplines, will keep biology, for example—a domain in which the frontier between the inert and the living is unstable and uncertain—in good company. But then we will have to accept that beyond its therapeutic project, psychoanalysis, as I had the occasion to suggest one day (de M'Uzan, 2006; cf. Chapter Four in this book), is a source of "permanent disquiet".

REFERENCES

Abraham, N. & Torok, M. (1972). Introjecter, incorporer. Destins du cannabalisme. *Nouvelle Revue de Psychanalyse, 6*: 111–122. In: S. Lebovici & D. Widlöcher (Eds.), *Psychoanalysis in France*. New York: International Universities Press, 1980.

André, J. (2008). Le dernier râle d'Éros. In: *La chimère des inconscients. Débat avec Michel de M'Uzan*. Paris: Presses Universitaires de France.

Anzieu, D. (1974). Le moi peau. *Nouvelle Revue de Psychanalyse, 3*: 195–208.

Artaud, A. (1947). *Artaud le Mômo*. Paris: Bordas. Reprinted in *Œuvres complètes*, vol. XII, Paris: Gallimard, 1974. [Artaud the Mômo. In: B. Bador (Trans.), *Watchfiends and Rackscreams, Works from the Final Period*. New York: Exact Change Press, 1995.]

Ascher, J. & Jouet, J.-P. (2004). *La Greffe: entre biologie et psychanalyse*. Paris: Presses Universitaires de France.

Baruch, C. (Ed.) (2011). *Nouveau développements en psychanalyse: autour de l'œuvre de Michel de M'Uzan*. Paris: EDK.

Bégoin, J. (1984). Présentation: quelques repères sur l'évaluation du concept d'identification. *Revue française de psychanalyse, 48*(2): 483–491.

Berbiguier de Terre Neuve du Thym (1990). *Les Farfadets*. Paris: Jérome Million.

Biely, A. (1915). *Kotik Letaev*. G. J. Janecek (Trans.). Ann Arbor, MI: Ardis, 1971.

Bion, W. R. (1967). The imaginary twin. In: *Second Thoughts*. London: Heinemann.

Bion, W. R. (1977). *Two Papers: the Grid and the Caesura*. London: Karnac, 1989.

Birksted-Breen, D., Flanders, S. & Gibeault, A. (Eds.) (2010). *Reading French Psychoanalysis*. London: Routledge & the Institute of Psychoanalysis.

Bizouard, E. (1995). *Le cinquième fantasme, auto-engendrement et impulsion créatrice*. Paris: Presses Universitaires de France.

Bouvet, M. (1960). Dépersonnalisation et relations d'objet. In: *Œuvres psychanalytiques 1, La relation d'objet. Névrose obsessionnelle, dépersonnalisation* (pp. 295–435). Paris: Payot, 1968.

Cioran, E. M. (1949). *Précis de décomposition*. Paris: Gallimard, Les Essais, XXXV.

Claudel, P. (1963). *Réflexions sur la poésie*. Paris: Gallimard, Coll. Idées.

Cohen, A. (1954). *Book of My Mother*. B. Cohen (Trans.). Archipelago, 1997.

David, C. (1983). Souffrance, plaisir et pensée. In: *Confluents psychanalytiques*. Paris: Les Belles Lettres.

David, C. (1996). Faire le deuil de soi-même. *Revue française de psychanalyse, 60*(1): 15–32.

Dennett, D. (1991). *Consciousness Explained*. Boston: Little, Brown.

Eissler, K. (1955). *The Psychiatrist and the Dying Patient*. New York: International Universities Press.

Fain, M. (1969). Ebauche d'une recherche concernant l'existence d'activités mentales pouvant être considérées comme prototypiques du processus psychanalytique. *Revue française de psychanalyse, 33*(5–6): 929–962.

Faure-Pragier, S. & Pragier, G. (2007). *Repenser la psychanalyse avec les sciences*. Paris: Presses Universitaires de France.

Fédida, P. (1978). L'objeu, jeu et enfance: l'espace psychothérapeutique. In: *L'absence* (pp. 97–195). Paris: Gallimard.

Fenichel, O. (1945). *A Psychoanalytic Theory of Neurosis*. New York: W. W. Norton.

Ferenczi, S. (1912). On the definition of introjection. In: M. Balint (Ed.), E. Mosbacher et al. (Trans.), *Final Contributions to the Problems and Methods of Psychoanalysis*. London: Hogarth and the Institute of Psychoanalysis, 1955.

Ferenczi, S. (1920). The further development of an active therapy in psychoanalysis. In: *Further Contributions to the Theory and Technique of Psycho-Analysis*. London: Hogarth, 1952.

Fliess, R. (1942). The metapsychology of the analyst. *Psychoanalytic Quarterly, 11*: 211–227.

Fourier, C. (1836). *La Fausse industrie morcelée, répugnante, mensongère, et l'antidote l'industrie naturelle, combinée, attrayante, véridique donnant quadruple produit.* Paris: Bossange Père, p. 812. Cited in de M'Uzan (1956), *Anthologie du délire.* Paris: Éditions du Rocher, p. 283.

Freud, E. (Ed.) (1960). *Letters of Sigmund Freud.* T. & J. Stern (Trans.). New York: Basic.

Freud, S. (1900a). *The Interpretation of Dreams. S. E., 4 & 5.* London: Hogarth.

Freud, S. (1911b). Formulations on the two principles of mental functioning. *S. E., 12.* London: Hogarth, pp. 218–226.

Freud, S. (1914 g). Remembering, repeating, and working-through. *S. E., 12.* London: Hogarth, pp. 147–156.

Freud, S. (1915c). Instincts and their vicissitudes. *S. E., 14.* London: Hogarth, pp. 117–140.

Freud, S. (1916–1917). *Introductory Lectures on Psychoanalysis. S. E., 16.* London: Hogarth, pp. 243–463.

Freud, S. (1917e). *Mourning and Melancholia. S. E., 14.* London: Hogarth, pp. 243–258.

Freud, S. (1919h). The "uncanny". *S. E., 17.* London: Hogarth, pp. 217–252.

Freud, S. (1920g). *Beyond the Pleasure Principle. S. E., 18.* London: Hogarth, pp. 7–64.

Freud, S. (1922a). Dreams and telepathy. *S. E., 18.* London: Hogarth, pp. 197–220.

Freud, S. (1926d). *Inhibitions, Symptoms and Anxiety. S. E., 20.* London: Hogarth, pp. 87–172.

Freud, S. (1936a). A disturbance of memory on the Acropolis. *S. E., 22.* London: Hogarth, pp. 239–250.

Freud, S. (1937c). Analysis terminable and interminable. *S. E., 23.* London: Hogarth, pp. 216–253.

Freud, S. (1937d). Constructions in analysis. *S. E., 23.* London: Hogarth, pp. 255–269.

Freud, S. (1991). *Gesammelte Werke (G. W.).* Frankfurt am Main, Germany: Fischer.

Freud, S. & Ferenczi, S. (1996). *The Correspondence of Sigmund Freud and Sandor Ferenczi, Vol. 2, 1914–1919.* P. Hoffer (Trans.). Cambridge, MA: Belknap Press.

Fuchs, S. H. (1937). On introjection. *International Journal of Psychoanalysis, 18*: 269–290.

Gagnebin, M. (1996). *Michel de M'Uzan.* Paris: Presses Universitaires de France.

Gagnebin, M. & Milly, J. (Eds.) (2012). *Michel de M'Uzan ou le saisissement créateur.* Paris: Champ Vallon, Coll. L'or d'Atalante.

Gitelson, M. (1952). The emotional position of the analyst in the psychoanalytic situation. In: *Psychoanalysis: Science and Fiction.* New York: International Universities Press, 1973.

Glover, E. (1955). *The Technique of Psychoanalysis.* New York: International Universities Press.

Green, A. (1966–67). Primary narcissism: structure or state? In: A. Weller (Trans.), *Life Narcissism, Death Narcissism.* London: Free Association Books (FAB), 2001.

Green, A. (1971). Projection: from projective identification to project. In: *On Private Madness* (pp. 84–103). London: Hogarth, 1986 [reprinted Karnac, 1997].

Green, A. (1983). *Life Narcissism, Death Narcissism.* A. Weller (Trans.). London: Free Association Books (FAB), 2001.

Greenacre, P. (1958). Early physical determinants in the development of the sense of identity. In: *Emotional Growth* (pp. 113–127). New York: International Universities Press, 1971.

Greenacre, P. (1958). *Emotional Growth, Vols. 1 & 2.* New York: International Universities Press, 1971.

Greenson, R. (1960). Empathy and its vicissitudes. *International Journal of Psychoanalysis, 41*: 418–424.

Greenson, R. (1967). *The Technique and Practice of Psychoanalysis.* London: Hogarth.

Groddeck, G. (1969). *La maladie, l'art et le symbole.* Paris: Gallimard.

Hartmann, H. (1958). *Ego Psychology and the Problem of Adaptation.* New York: International Universities Press.

Heidegger, M. (1927). *Being and Time.* J. Macquarrie & E. S. Robinson (Trans.). London: SCM Press, 1962.

Heimann, P. (1950). On counter-transference. *International Journal of Psychoanalysis, 31*: 81–84.

Heimann, P. (1977). Further observations on the analyst's cognitive process. *Journal of the American Psychoanalytic Association, 25*(2): 313–333.

Hollande, C. & Soulé, M. (1970). Pour introduire un colloque sur la compulsion de répétition. *Revue française de psychanalyse, 34*(3): 373–406.

Jankélévitch, V. (1977). *La mort.* Paris: Flammarion.

Jentsch, E. (1906). Zur Psychologie des Unheimlichen. *Psychiatrisch-Neurologische Wochenscrift, 8.* [English translation: On the Psychology of the Uncanny, R. Sellars (Trans.). *Angelaki, 2*(1): 7–16, 1995.]

Jones, E. (1911). On dying together. In: *Essays in Applied Psychoanalysis.* London: Hogarth, 1951.

Jones, E. (1997). *La théorie et pratique de la psychanalyse.* Paris: Payot.

Kafka, F. (1991). *Blue Octavo Notebooks*. Cambridge, MA: Exact Exchange.

Kemper, K. A. (1965). L'interprétation par allusion: ses rapports avec les relations et les perceptions préverbales. *Revue française de psychanalyse, 29*(1): 89–104.

Klein, E. (2005). *Il était sept fois la révolution*. Paris: Flammarion.

Kübler-Ross, E. (1969). *On Death and Dying*. London: Tavistock.

Laplanche, J. (1987). *New Foundations for Psychoanalysis*. D. Macey (Trans.). Oxford: Basil Blackwell, 1989.

Laplanche, J. (2007). *Freud and the Sexual*: Essays 2000–2006. J. Fletcher, J. House, N. Ray (Trans.). International Psychoanalytic Books, 2011.

Lebovici, S. (1961). La relation objectale chez l'enfant. *Psychiatrie de l'enfant, 3*(1): 147–226.

Lebovici, S. & Widlöcher, D. (Eds.) (1980). *Psychoanalysis in France*. New York: International Universities Press.

London, J. (1904). *The Sea-Wolf*. New York: Bantam, 1963.

Lubin, A. (1946). Porteurs de lances. In: *Le passager clandestin* (pp. 55–56). Paris: Gallimard, 2005.

M'Uzan, M. de (1956). *Anthologie du délire*. Paris: Éditions du Rocher.

M'Uzan, M. de (1965). Intervention on the report by R. Loewenstein (La psychologie psychanalytique de Hartmann, Kris et Loewenstein). *Revue française de psychanalyse, 30*: 5–6, 1966.

M'Uzan, M. de (1966). Transferts et névrose de transfert. *Revue française de psychanalyse, 32*(2): 235–245, 1968. Also in *De l'art à la mort* (pp. 67–74). Paris: Gallimard, 1977.

M'Uzan, M. de (1967). *Acting out* "direct" et *acting out* "indirect". In: *Revue française de psychanalyse, 32*(5–6): 995–1000, 1968. Also in *De l'art à la mort* (pp. 75–82). Paris: Gallimard, 1977.

M'Uzan, M. de (1969). Le même et l'identique. *Revue française de psychanalyse, 34*(3): 441–451.

M'Uzan, M. de (1970). Le même et l'identique. In: *De l'art à la mort* (pp. 83–97). Paris: Gallimard, 1977.

M'Uzan, M. de (1972). Un cas de masochisme pervers. In: *La sexualité perverse* (pp. 13–47). Paris: Payot. Also in *De l'art à la mort*, Paris: Gallimard, 1977.

M'Uzan, M. de (1973). A case of masochistic perversion and an outline of a theory. *International Journal of Psychoanalysis, 54*: 455–467.

M'Uzan, M. de (1974). "S.j.e.m.". Le dehors et le dedans. *Nouvelle Revue de Psychanalyse, 9*: 23–32. [If I were dead. *International Review of Psychoanalysis, 5*: 485–490, 1978.] Also in *De l'art à la mort*, Paris: Gallimard, 1977.

M'Uzan, M. de (1976a). Contre-transfert et système paradoxal (paper read at the Paris Psychoanalytical Society, 18 May, 1976). *Revue française de psychanalyse, 40*(2): 575–590. Also in *De l'art à la mort*. Paris: Gallimard, 1977.

M'Uzan, M. de (1976b). Le travail du trépas. In: *De l'art à la mort*. Paris: Gallimard, 1977.

M'Uzan, M. de (1977). *De l'art à la mort*. Paris: Gallimard.

M'Uzan, M. de (1978a). If I were dead. *International Review of Psycho-Analysis*, 5: 485–490.

M'Uzan, M. de (1978b). La bouche de l'inconscient. *Nouvelle Revue de Psychanalyse*, 17: 89–98. Also in *La bouche de l'inconscient*. Paris: Gallimard, 1994.

M'Uzan, M. de (1981). Dernières paroles. *Nouvelle Revue de Psychanalyse*, 23: 117–130. Also in *La Bouche de l'inconscient*. Paris: Gallimard, 1994.

M'Uzan, M. de (1983). La personne de moi-même. *Nouvelle Revue de Psychanalyse*, 28: 193–208.

M'Uzan, M. de (1984). Slaves of quantity. R. B. Simpson (Trans.). *Psychoanalytic Quarterly*, 72: 711–725, 2003.

M'Uzan, M. de (1988). Stratégie et tactique à propos des interprétations freudiennes et kleiniennes. *Revue française de psychanalyse*, 52(3): 657–664.

M'Uzan, M. de (1989). Pendant la séance. *Nouvelle Revue de Psychanalyse*, 40: 147–163.

M'Uzan, M. de (1991). Du dérangement au changement. *Revue française de psychanalyse*, 60(2): 325–337. Reprinted in *La bouche de l'inconscient* (pp. 115–128). Paris: Gallimard, 1994.

M'Uzan, M. de (1993). L'indice de certitude. *Nouvelle Revue de Psychanalyse*, 48: 181–190.

M'Uzan, M. de (1994). *La bouche de l'inconscient*. Paris: Gallimard.

M'Uzan, M. de (1996). La mort n'avoue jamais. *Revue française de psychanalyse*, 60(1): 33–47.

M'Uzan, M. de (1997). Les yeux de Chimène. *Revue française de psychanalyse*, 61(4): 1113–1119. Reprinted in *Aux confins de l'identité*. Paris: Gallimard, 2005.

M'Uzan, M. de (1999). Le jumeau paraphrénique ou aux confins de l'identité. *Revue française de psychanalyse*, 63(4): 1135–1151.

M'Uzan, M. de (2001). À l'horizon: le facteur actuel. In: *Aux confins de l'identité*. Paris: Gallimard, 2005.

M'Uzan, M. de (2003). Slaves of quantity. *Psychoanalytic Quarterly*, 72: 711–725.

M'Uzan, M. de (2005). *Aux confins de l'identité*. Paris: Gallimard.

M'Uzan, M. de (2006). Invite à la fréquentation des ombres. *European Federation of Psychoanalysis Bulletin*, 60: 15–29.

M'Uzan, M. de (2008). La relation d'objet: entre qui, entre quoi? pour qui, pour quoi? In: L'objet, la réalité: la règle et le tact, *APF Bulletin*, (pp. 27–43).

M'Uzan, M. de (2009). L'inquiétante étrangeté ou « je ne suis pas celle que vous croyez ». In: L. Danon Boileau & F. Nayrou (Eds.), *Inquiétante étrangeté*. Paris: Presses Universitaires de France.

M'Uzan, M. de (2011). Reconsidérations et nouveaux développements en psychanalyse. In: C. Baruch (Ed.), *Nouveau développements en psychanalyse: autour de l'oeuvre de Michel de M'Uzan*. Paris: EDK.

Marty, P. (1958). La relation objectale allergique. *Revue française de psychanalyse, 22*(1): 5–35.

Marty, P. & M'Uzan, M. de (1963). La pensée opératoire. *Revue française de psychanalyse, 37*: 345–356. [Republished in 1994 in *Revue française psychosomatique, 6*: 197–207.]

Meltzer, D. (1984). Les concepts d' « identification projective » (Klein) et de « contenant » « contenu » en relation avec la situation analytique. *Revue française de psychanalyse, 48*(2): 541–551.

Montaigne, M. de (1965). *Les essais*, 1, 13. P. Villey (Ed.). Lausanne, Switzerland: La Guilde du Livre. [Also in: *On Friendship* (1.28). London: Penguin, 2004.]

Nemiah, J. C. & Sifneos, P. E. (1970). Psychosomatic illness: a problem in communication. *Psychotherapy & Psychosomatics, 18*(1–6): 154–160.

Neyraut, M. (1974). *Le transfert*. Paris: Presses Universitaires de France.

Norton, J. (1963). Treatment of a dying patient. *Psychoanalytic Study of the Child, 18*: 541–560.

Ogden, T. (1994). The analytic third: working with intersubjective clinical facts. *International Journal of Psychoanalysis, 75*(1): 3–19.

Parat, C. (1991). À propos de la thérapeutique analytique. *Revue française de psychanalyse, 55*(2): 303–324. Also in *L'affect partagé*. Paris: Presses Universitaires de France.

Parsons, M. (2006). Le contre-transfert de l'analyste sur le processus psychanalytique. *Revue française de psychanalyse, 70*(2): 385–404.

Peto, A. (1959). De l'effet désintégrant transitoire des interprétations. *Revue française de psychanalyse, 25*(4–6): 791–799.

Plato (1950). Prélude au dernier entretien, 60 (e). In: *Œuvres complètes, Phédon, ou de l'âme*. Gallimard, Bibliothèque de la Pléiade.

Rank. O. (1914). *The Double: A Psychoanalytic Study*. H. Tucker Jr. (Trans.). Chapel Hill, NC: University of North Carolina Press, 1971.

Rank, O. (1924). *Le traumatisme de la naissance*. Paris: Payot, 1968.

Rank, O. (1932). *Don Juan. Une étude sur le double*. Paris: Denoël & Steele.

Reich, A. (1951). On counter-transference. *International Journal of Psychoanalysis, 32*: 25–31.

Reich, W. (1927). *The Function of the Orgasm: Sex-Economic Factors of Biological Energy*. T. Wolfe (Trans.). London: Panther, 1968.

Reich, W. (1933). *Character Analysis*. New York: Orgone Institute Press, 1945.

Reik, T. (1936). *Surprise and the Psychoanalyst*. London: Kegal Paul, Trench & Trubner.

Rostand, J. (1953). *Ce que je crois*. Paris: Grasset.

Scarfone, D. (2008a). Les multiples tirages de soi: répétition et identité dans l'œuvre de Michel de M'Uzan. In: *La chimère des inconscients*. Paris: Presses Universitaires de France.

Scarfone, D. (2008b). L'examen de réalité: une histoire d'amour. In: L'objet, la réalité: la règle et le tact. *APF Bulletin* (pp. 101–118). Paris: Presses Universitaires de France.

Smadja, C. (1993). A propos des procédés auto-calmants du moi. *Revue française de psychosomatique, 4*: 9–26.

Spitz, R. A. (1958). *The First Year of Life. A Psychoanalytic Study of Normal and Deviant Development in Object Relations*. New York: International Universities Press, 1965.

Stirner, M. (1845). *The Ego and His Own*. S. Byington (Trans.). New York: Tucker, 1907. [Also published as *L'Unique et sa propriété*, P. Gallissaire & A. Sauge (Trans.). Paris: Editions L'Âge d'Homme, Bibliothèque l'Âge d'Homme; and as *Der Einzige und sein Eigentum*. Leipzig: Otto Wigand, 1845.]

Strachey, J. (1934). The nature of the therapeutic action of psycho-analysis. *International Journal of Psychoanalysis, 15*: 127–159.

Szwec, G. (1993). Les procédés auto-calmants par la recherche répétitive de l'excitation (les galériens volontaires). In: *Revue française de psychosomatique, 4*: 27–67.

Tausk, V. (1933). On the origin of the influencing machine in schizophrenia. *Psychoanalytic Quarterly, 2*: 519–556.

Torok, M. (1968). Maladie du deuil et fantasme du cadavre exquis. *Revue française de psychanalyse, 32*(4): 715–733.

Uhland, L. (1809). *Der gute Kamerad*.

Viderman, S. (1970). *Construction de l'espace analytique*. Paris: Denoël.

Winnicott, D. W. (1971). *Playing and Reality*. London: Tavistock.

Wolfson, L. (1970). *Le Schizo et les langues* (Preface G. Deleuze). Paris: Gallimard.